Books & Characters
French & English

By

Lytton Strachey

Books & Characters
French & English
by Lytton Strachey

Copyright © 2023

All Rights reserved.

No part of this publication may be reproduced, stored in a retrieval system, or transmitted in any form or by any means, electronic, mechanical, photocopying or Otherwise, without the written permission of the publisher.
The author/editor asserts the moral right to be identified as the author/editor of this work.

ISBN: 978-93-60465-74-2

Published by

DOUBLE 9 BOOKS

2/13-B, Ansari Road
Daryaganj, New Delhi – 110002
info@double9books.com
www.double9books.com
Tel. 011-40042856

This book is under public domain

ABOUT THE AUTHOR

English author and reviewer Giles Lytton Strachey was born on March 1, 1880, and died on January 21, 1932. He created a new type of biography that combines psychological understanding and sympathy with sarcasm and wit. He was one of the founders of the Bloomsbury Group and wrote Eminent Victorians. The James Tait Black Memorial Prize was given to his book Queen Victoria (1921). On March 1, 1880, Strachey was born at Stowey House in Clapham Common, London. He was the fifth son and eleventh child of Lieutenant General Sir Richard Strachey, an officer in the British colonial armed forces, and his second wife, Jane Grant, who became a leading supporter of women's right to vote. The name "Giles Lytton" came from a Gyles Strachey from the early 1600s and the first Earl of Lytton, who was friends with Richard Strachey when he was Viceroy of India in the late 1870s. Another person who was Lytton Strachey's uncle was the Earl of Lytton. There were thirteen children born to the Stracheys. Ten of them lived to adults, including Lytton's sister Dorothy Strachey and his youngest brother, the psychoanalyst James Strachey.

CONTENTS

RACINE 7

SIR THOMAS BROWNE 23

SHAKESPEARE'S FINAL PERIOD 32

THE LIVES OF THE POETS[1] 45

MADAME DU DEFFAND[2] 49

VOLTAIRE AND ENGLAND[3] 66

A DIALOGUE 83

VOLTAIRE'S TRAGEDIES 86

VOLTAIRE AND FREDERICK THE GREAT 97

THE ROUSSEAU AFFAIR 116

THE POETRY OF BLAKE[8] 124

THE LAST ELIZABETHAN 134

HENRI BEYLE 153

LADY HESTER STANHOPE 168

MR. CREEVEY 174

INDEX 180

RACINE

When Ingres painted his vast 'Apotheosis of Homer,' he represented, grouped round the central throne, all the great poets of the ancient and modern worlds, with a single exception—Shakespeare. After some persuasion, he relented so far as to introduce into his picture a *part* of that offensive personage; and English visitors at the Louvre can now see, to their disgust or their amusement, the truncated image of rather less than half of the author of *King Lear* just appearing at the extreme edge of the enormous canvas. French taste, let us hope, has changed since the days of Ingres; Shakespeare would doubtless now be advanced—though perhaps chiefly from a sense of duty—to the very steps of the central throne. But if an English painter were to choose a similar subject, how would he treat the master who stands acknowledged as the most characteristic representative of the literature of France? Would Racine find a place in the picture at all? Or, if he did, would more of him be visible than the last curl of his full-bottomed wig, whisking away into the outer darkness?

There is something inexplicable about the intensity of national tastes and the violence of national differences. If, as in the good old days, I could boldly believe a Frenchman to be an inferior creature, while he, as simply, wrote me down a savage, there would be an easy end of the matter. But alas! *nous avons changé tout cela*. Now we are each of us obliged to recognise that the other has a full share of intelligence, ability, and taste; that the accident of our having been born on different sides of the Channel is no ground for supposing either that I am a brute or that he is a ninny. But, in that case, how does it happen that while on one side of that 'span of waters' Racine is despised and Shakespeare is worshipped, on the other, Shakespeare is tolerated and Racine is adored? The perplexing question was recently emphasised and illustrated in a singular way. Mr. John Bailey, in a volume of essays entitled 'The Claims of French Poetry,' discussed the qualities of Racine at some length, placed him, not without contumely, among the second rank of writers, and drew the conclusion that, though indeed the merits of French poetry are many and great, it is not among the pages of Racine that they are to be found. Within a few months of the appearance of Mr. Bailey's book, the distinguished French writer and brilliant critic, M. Lemaître, published a series of lectures on Racine, in which the highest note of unqualified panegyric sounded uninterruptedly from beginning to end. The contrast is remarkable, and the conflicting criticisms seem to represent, on the whole, the views of the cultivated classes in the two countries. And it is worthy of note that neither of these critics pays any heed, either explicitly or by implication, to the opinions of the other. They are totally at variance, but they argue along lines so different and so remote that they never come into collision. Mr. Bailey, with the utmost sang-froid, sweeps on one side the whole of the literary tradition of France. It is as if a French critic were to assert that Shakespeare, the Elizabethans, and the romantic poets of the nineteenth century were all negligible, and that England's really valuable contribution to the poetry of the world was to be found among the writings of Dryden and Pope. M. Lemaître, on the other hand, seems sublimely unconscious that any such views as Mr. Bailey's could possibly exist. Nothing shows more clearly Racine's supreme dominion over his countrymen than the fact that M. Lemaître never questions it for a moment, and tacitly assumes on every page of his book that his only duty is to illustrate and amplify a greatness already recognised by all. Indeed, after reading M. Lemaître's book, one begins to understand more clearly why it is that English critics find it difficult to appreciate to the full the literature of France. It is no paradox to say that that country is as insular as our own. When we find so eminent a critic as M. Lemaître observing that Racine 'a vraiment "achevé" et porté à son point suprême de perfection *la tragédie,* cette étonnante forme d'art, et qui est bien de chez nous: car on la trouve peu chez les Anglais,' is it surprising that we should hastily jump to the conclusion that the canons and the principles of a criticism of this kind will not repay, and perhaps do not deserve, any careful consideration? Certainly they are not calculated to spare the susceptibilities of Englishmen. And, after all, this is only natural; a French critic addresses a French audience; like a Rabbi in a synagogue, he has no need to argue and no wish to convert. Perhaps, too, whether he willed or no, he could do very little to the purpose; for the difficulties which beset an Englishman in his endeavours to appreciate a writer such as Racine are precisely of the kind which a Frenchman is least able either to dispel or even to understand. The object of this essay is, first, to face these difficulties, with the aid of Mr. Bailey's paper, which sums up in an able and interesting way the average English view of the matter; and, in the second place, to communicate to the English reader a sense of the true significance and the immense value of Racine's work. Whether the attempt succeed or fail, some important general questions of literary doctrine will have been discussed; and, in addition, at least an effort will have been made to vindicate a great reputation. For, to a lover of Racine, the fact that English critics of Mr. Bailey's calibre can write of him as they do, brings a feeling not only of entire disagreement, but of almost personal distress. Strange as

RACINE

When Ingres painted his vast 'Apotheosis of Homer,' he represented, grouped round the central throne, all the great poets of the ancient and modern worlds, with a single exception—Shakespeare. After some persuasion, he relented so far as to introduce into his picture a *part* of that offensive personage; and English visitors at the Louvre can now see, to their disgust or their amusement, the truncated image of rather less than half of the author of *King Lear* just appearing at the extreme edge of the enormous canvas. French taste, let us hope, has changed since the days of Ingres; Shakespeare would doubtless now be advanced—though perhaps chiefly from a sense of duty—to the very steps of the central throne. But if an English painter were to choose a similar subject, how would he treat the master who stands acknowledged as the most characteristic representative of the literature of France? Would Racine find a place in the picture at all? Or, if he did, would more of him be visible than the last curl of his full-bottomed wig, whisking away into the outer darkness?

There is something inexplicable about the intensity of national tastes and the violence of national differences. If, as in the good old days, I could boldly believe a Frenchman to be an inferior creature, while he, as simply, wrote me down a savage, there would be an easy end of the matter. But alas! *nous avons changé tout cela*. Now we are each of us obliged to recognise that the other has a full share of intelligence, ability, and taste; that the accident of our having been born on different sides of the Channel is no ground for supposing either that I am a brute or that he is a ninny. But, in that case, how does it happen that while on one side of that 'span of waters' Racine is despised and Shakespeare is worshipped, on the other, Shakespeare is tolerated and Racine is adored? The perplexing question was recently emphasised and illustrated in a singular way. Mr. John Bailey, in a volume of essays entitled 'The Claims of French Poetry,' discussed the qualities of Racine at some length, placed him, not without contumely, among the second rank of writers, and drew the conclusion that, though indeed the merits of French poetry are many and great, it is not among the pages of Racine that they are to be found. Within a few months of the appearance of Mr. Bailey's book, the distinguished French writer and brilliant critic, M. Lemaître, published a series of lectures on Racine, in which the highest note of unqualified panegyric sounded uninterruptedly from beginning to end. The contrast is remarkable, and the conflicting criticisms seem to represent, on the whole, the views of the cultivated classes in the two countries. And it is worthy of note that neither of these critics pays any heed, either explicitly or by implication, to the opinions of the other. They are totally at variance, but they argue along lines so different and so remote that they never come into collision. Mr. Bailey, with the utmost sang-froid, sweeps on one side the whole of the literary tradition of France. It is as if a French critic were to assert that Shakespeare, the Elizabethans, and the romantic poets of the nineteenth century were all negligible, and that England's really valuable contribution to the poetry of the world was to be found among the writings of Dryden and Pope. M. Lemaître, on the other hand, seems sublimely unconscious that any such views as Mr. Bailey's could possibly exist. Nothing shows more clearly Racine's supreme dominion over his countrymen than the fact that M. Lemaître never questions it for a moment, and tacitly assumes on every page of his book that his only duty is to illustrate and amplify a greatness already recognised by all. Indeed, after reading M. Lemaître's book, one begins to understand more clearly why it is that English critics find it difficult to appreciate to the full the literature of France. It is no paradox to say that that country is as insular as our own. When we find so eminent a critic as M. Lemaître observing that Racine 'a vraiment "achevé" et porté à son point suprême de perfection *la tragédie*, cette étonnante forme d'art, et qui est bien de chez nous: car on la trouve peu chez les Anglais,' is it surprising that we should hastily jump to the conclusion that the canons and the principles of a criticism of this kind will not repay, and perhaps do not deserve, any careful consideration? Certainly they are not calculated to spare the susceptibilities of Englishmen. And, after all, this is only natural; a French critic addresses a French audience; like a Rabbi in a synagogue, he has no need to argue and no wish to convert. Perhaps, too, whether he willed or no, he could do very little to the purpose; for the difficulties which beset an Englishman in his endeavours to appreciate a writer such as Racine are precisely of the kind which a Frenchman is least able either to dispel or even to understand. The object of this essay is, first, to face these difficulties, with the aid of Mr. Bailey's paper, which sums up in an able and interesting way the average English view of the matter; and, in the second place, to communicate to the English reader a sense of the true significance and the immense value of Racine's work. Whether the attempt succeed or fail, some important general questions of literary doctrine will have been discussed; and, in addition, at least an effort will have been made to vindicate a great reputation. For, to a lover of Racine, the fact that English critics of Mr. Bailey's calibre can write of him as they do, brings a feeling not only of entire disagreement, but of almost personal distress. Strange as it may seem to those who have been accustomed to think of that great artist merely as a type of the frigid pomposity of an antiquated age, his music, to ears that are attuned to hear it, comes fraught with a poignancy of loveliness whose peculiar quality is shared by no other poetry in the world. To have grown familiar with the voice of Racine, to have realised once and for all its intensity, its beauty, and its depth, is to have learnt a new happiness, to have discovered something exquisite and splendid, to have enlarged the glorious boundaries of art. For such benefits as these who would not be grateful? Who would not seek to make them known to others, that they too may enjoy, and render thanks?

M. Lemaître, starting out, like a native of the mountains, from a point which can only be reached by English explorers after a long journey and a severe climb, devotes by far the greater part of his book to a series of brilliant psychological studies of Racine's characters. He leaves on one side almost altogether the questions connected both with Racine's dramatic construction, and with his style; and these are the very questions by which English readers are most perplexed, and which they are most anxious to discuss. His style in particular—using the word in its widest sense—forms the subject of the principal part of Mr. Bailey's essay; it is upon this count that the real force of Mr. Bailey's impeachment depends; and, indeed, it is obvious that no poet can be admired or understood by those who quarrel with the whole fabric of his writing and condemn the very principles of his art. Before, however, discussing this, the true crux of the question, it may be well to consider briefly another matter which deserves attention, because the English reader is apt to find in it a stumbling-block at the very outset of his inquiry. Coming to Racine with Shakespeare and the rest of the Elizabethans warm in his memory, it is only to be expected that he should be struck with a chilling sense of emptiness and unreality. After the colour, the moving multiplicity, the imaginative luxury of our early tragedies, which seem to have been moulded out of the very stuff of life and to have been built up with the varied and generous structure of Nature herself, the Frenchman's dramas, with their rigid uniformity of setting, their endless duologues, their immense harangues, their spectral confidants, their strict exclusion of all visible action, give one at first the same sort of impression as a pretentious pseudo-classical summer-house appearing suddenly at the end of a vista, after one has been rambling through an open forest. 'La scène est à Buthrote, ville d'Epire, dans une salle du palais de Pyrrhus'— could anything be more discouraging than such an announcement? Here is nothing for the imagination to feed on, nothing to raise expectation, no wondrous vision of 'blasted heaths,' or the 'seaboard of Bohemia'; here is only a hypothetical drawing-room conjured out of the void for five acts, simply in order that the persons of the drama may have a place to meet in and make their speeches. The 'three unities' and the rest of the 'rules' are a burden which the English reader finds himself quite unaccustomed to carry; he grows impatient of them; and, if he is a critic, he points out the futility and the unreasonableness of those antiquated conventions. Even Mr. Bailey, who, curiously enough, believes that Racine 'stumbled, as it were, half by accident into great advantages' by using them, speaks of the 'discredit' into which 'the once famous unities' have now fallen, and declares that 'the unities of time and place are of no importance in themselves.' So far as critics are concerned this may be true; but critics are apt to forget that plays can exist somewhere else than in books, and a very small acquaintance with contemporary drama is enough to show that, upon the stage at any rate, the unities, so far from having fallen into discredit, are now in effect triumphant. For what is the principle which underlies and justifies the unities of time and place? Surely it is not, as Mr. Bailey would have us believe, that of the 'unity of action or interest,' for it is clear that every good drama, whatever its plan of construction, must possess a single dominating interest, and that it may happen—as in *Antony and Cleopatra*, for instance—that the very essence of this interest lies in the accumulation of an immense variety of local activities and the representation of long epochs of time. The true justification for the unities of time and place is to be found in the conception of drama as the history of a spiritual crisis—the vision, thrown up, as it were, by a bull's-eye lantern, of the final catastrophic phases of a long series of events. Very different were the views of the Elizabethan tragedians, who aimed at representing not only the catastrophe, but the whole development of circumstances of which it was the effect; they traced, with elaborate and abounding detail, the rise, the growth, the decline, and the ruin of great causes and great persons; and the result was a series of masterpieces unparalleled in the literature of the world. But, for good or evil, these methods have become obsolete, and to-day our drama seems to be developing along totally different lines. It is playing the part, more and more consistently, of the bull's-eye lantern; it is concerned with the crisis, and nothing but the crisis; and, in proportion as its field is narrowed and its vision intensified, the unities of time and place come more and more completely into play. Thus, from the point of view of form, it is true to say that it has been the drama of Racine rather than that of Shakespeare that has survived. Plays of the type of *Macbeth* have been superseded by plays of the type of *Britannicus*. *Britannicus*, no less than *Macbeth*, is the tragedy of a criminal; but it shows us, instead of the gradual history of the temptation and the fall, followed by the fatal march of consequences, nothing but the precise psychological moment in which the first irrevocable step is taken, and the criminal is made. The method of *Macbeth* has been, as it were, absorbed by that of the modern novel; the method of *Britannicus* still rules the stage. But Racine carried out his ideals more rigorously and more boldly than any of his successors. He fixed the whole of his attention upon the spiritual crisis; to him that alone was of importance; and the conventional classicism so disheartening to the English reader—the 'unities,' the harangues, the confidences, the absence of local colour, and the concealment of the action—was no more than the machinery for enhancing the effect of the inner tragedy, and for doing away with every side issue and every chance of distraction. His dramas must be read as one looks at an airy, delicate statue, supported by artificial props, whose only importance lies in the fact that without them the statue itself would break in pieces and fall to the ground. Approached in this light, even the 'salle du palais de Pyrrhus' begins to have a meaning. We come to realise that, if it is nothing else, it is at least the meeting-ground of great passions, the invisible framework for one of those noble conflicts which 'make one little room an everywhere.' It will show us no views, no spectacles, it will give us no sense of atmosphere or of imaginative romance; but it will allow us to be present at the climax of a tragedy, to follow the closing struggle of high destinies, and to witness the final agony of human hearts.

It is remarkable that Mr. Bailey, while seeming to approve of the classicism of Racine's dramatic form, nevertheless finds fault with him for his lack of a quality with which, by its very nature, the classical form is incompatible. Racine's vision, he complains, does not 'take in the whole of life'; we do not find in his plays 'the whole pell-mell of human existence'; and this is true, because the particular effects which Racine wished to produce necessarily involved this limitation of the range of his interests. His object was to depict the tragic interaction of a small group of persons at the culminating height of its intensity; and it is as irrational to complain of his failure to introduce into his compositions 'the whole pell-mell of human existence' as it would be to find fault with a Mozart quartet for not containing the orchestration of Wagner. But it is a little difficult to make certain of the precise nature of Mr. Bailey's criticism. When he speaks of Racine's vision not including 'the whole of life,' when he declares that Racine cannot be reckoned as one of the 'world-poets,' he seems to be taking somewhat different ground and discussing a more general question. All truly great poets, he asserts, have 'a wide view of humanity,' 'a large view of life'—a profound sense, in short, of the relations between man and the universe; and, since Racine is without this quality, his claim to true poetic greatness must be denied. But, even upon the supposition that this view of Racine's philosophical outlook is the true one—and, in its most important sense, I believe that it is not—does Mr. Bailey's conclusion really follow? Is it possible to test a poet's greatness by the largeness of his 'view of life'? How wide, one would like to know, was Milton's 'view of humanity'? And, though Wordsworth's sense of the position of man in the universe was far more profound than Dante's, who will venture to assert that he was the greater poet? The truth is that we have struck here upon a principle which lies at the root, not only of Mr. Bailey's criticism of Racine, but of an entire critical method—the method which attempts to define the essential elements of poetry in general, and then proceeds to ask of any particular poem whether it possesses these elements, and to judge it accordingly. How often this method has been employed, and how often it has proved disastrously fallacious! For, after all, art is not a superior kind of chemistry, amenable to the rules of scientific induction. Its component parts cannot be classified and tested, and there is a spark within it which defies foreknowledge. When Matthew Arnold declared that the value of a new poem might be gauged by comparing it with the greatest passages in the acknowledged masterpieces of literature, he was falling into this very error; for who could tell that the poem in question was not itself a masterpiece, living by the light of an unknown beauty, and a law unto itself? It is the business of the poet to break rules and to baffle expectation; and all the masterpieces in the world cannot make a precedent. Thus Mr. Bailey's attempts to discover, by quotations from Shakespeare, Sophocles, and Goethe, the qualities without which no poet can be great, and his condemnation of Racine because he is without them, is a fallacy in criticism. There is only one way to judge a poet, as Wordsworth, with that paradoxical sobriety so characteristic of him, has pointed out—and that is, by loving him. But Mr. Bailey, with regard to Racine at any rate, has not followed the advice of Wordsworth. Let us look a little more closely into the nature of his attack.

'L'épithète rare,' said the De Goncourts,'voilà la marque de l'écrivain.' Mr. Bailey quotes the sentence with approval, observing that if, with Sainte-Beuve, we extend the phrase to 'le mot rare,' we have at once one of those invaluable touch-stones with which we may test the merit of poetry. And doubtless most English readers would be inclined to agree with Mr. Bailey, for it so happens that our own literature is one in which rarity of style, pushed often to the verge of extravagance, reigns supreme. Owing mainly, no doubt, to the double origin of our language, with its strange and violent contrasts between the highly-coloured crudity of the Saxon words and the ambiguous splendour of the Latin vocabulary; owing partly, perhaps, to a national taste for the intensely imaginative, and partly, too, to the vast and penetrating influence of those grand masters of bizarrerie—the Hebrew Prophets—our poetry, our prose, and our whole conception of the art of writing have fallen under the dominion of the emphatic, the extraordinary, and the bold. No one in his senses would regret this, for it has given our literature all its most characteristic glories, and, of course, in Shakespeare, with whom expression is stretched to the bursting point, the national style finds at once its consummate example and its final justification. But the result is that we have grown so unused to other kinds of poetical beauty, that we have now come to believe, with Mr. Bailey, that poetry apart from 'le mot rare' is an impossibility. The beauties of restraint, of clarity, of refinement, and of precision we pass by unheeding; we can see nothing there but coldness and uniformity; and we go back with eagerness to the fling and the bravado that we love so well. It is as if we had become so accustomed to looking at boxers, wrestlers, and gladiators that the sight of an exquisite minuet produced no effect on us; the ordered dance strikes us as a monotony, for we are blind to the subtle delicacies of the dancers, which are fraught with such significance to the practised eye. But let us be patient, and let us look again.

> Ariane ma soeur, de quel amour blessée,
> Vous mourûtes aux bords où vous fûtes laissée.

Here, certainly, are no 'mots rares'; here is nothing to catch the mind or dazzle the understanding; here is only the most ordinary vocabulary, plainly set forth. But is there not an enchantment? Is there not a vision? Is there not a flow of lovely sound whose beauty grows upon the ear, and dwells exquisitely within the memory? Racine's triumph is precisely this—that he brings about, by what are apparently the simplest means, effects which other poets must strain every nerve to produce. The narrowness of his vocabulary is in fact nothing but a proof of his amazing art. In the following passage, for instance, what a sense of dignity and melancholy and power is conveyed by the commonest words!

> Enfin j'ouvre les yeux, et je me fais justice:
> C'est faire à vos beautés un triste sacrifice
> Que de vous présenter, madame, avec ma foi,
> Tout l'âge et le malheur que je traîne avec moi.
> Jusqu'ici la fortune et la victoire mêmes
> Cachaient mes cheveux blancs sous trente diadèmes.
> Mais ce temps-là n'est plus: je régnais; et je fuis:
> Mes ans se sont accrus; mes honneurs sont detruits.

Is that wonderful 'trente' an 'épithète rare'? Never, surely, before or since, was a simple numeral put to such a use—to conjure up so triumphantly such mysterious grandeurs! But these are subtleties which pass unnoticed by those who have been accustomed to the violent appeals of the great romantic poets. As Sainte-Beuve says, in a fine comparison between Racine and Shakespeare, to come to the one after the other is like passing to a portrait by Ingres from a decoration by Rubens. At first, 'comme on a l'oeil rempli de l'éclatante vérité pittoresque du grand maître flamand, on ne voit dans l'artiste français qu'un ton assez uniforme, une teinte diffuse de pâle et douce lumière. Mais qu'on approche de plus près et qu'on observe avec soin: mille nuances fines vont éclore sous le regard; mille intentions savantes vont sortir de ce tissu profond et serré; on ne peut plus en détacher ses yeux.'

Similarly when Mr. Bailey, turning from the vocabulary to more general questions of style, declares that there is no 'element of fine surprise' in Racine, no trace of the 'daring metaphors and similes of Pindar and the Greek choruses—the reply is that he would find what he wants if he only knew where to look for it. 'Who will forget,' he says, 'the comparison of the Atreidae to the eagles wheeling over their empty nest, of war to the money-changer whose gold dust is that of human bodies, of Helen to the lion's whelps?... Everyone knows these. Who will match them among the formal elegances of Racine?' And it is true that when Racine wished to create a great effect he did not adopt the romantic method; he did not chase his ideas through the four quarters of the universe to catch them at last upon the verge of the inane; and anyone who hopes to come upon 'fine surprises' of this kind in his pages will be disappointed. His daring is of a different kind; it is not the daring of adventure but of intensity; his fine surprises are seized out of the very heart of his subject, and seized in a single stroke. Thus many of his most astonishing phrases burn with an inward concentration of energy, which, difficult at first to realise to the full, comes in the end to impress itself ineffaceably upon the mind.

C'était pendant l'horreur d'une profonde nuit.

The sentence is like a cavern whose mouth a careless traveller might pass by, but which opens out, to the true explorer, into vista after vista of strange recesses rich with inexhaustible gold. But, sometimes, the phrase, compact as dynamite, explodes upon one with an immediate and terrific force—

C'est Vénus toute entière à sa proie attachée!

A few 'formal elegances' of this kind are surely worth having.

But what is it that makes the English reader fail to recognise the beauty and the power of such passages as these? Besides Racine's lack of extravagance and bravura, besides his dislike of exaggerated emphasis and far-fetched or fantastic imagery, there is another characteristic of his style to which we are perhaps even more antipathetic—its suppression of detail. The great majority of poets—and especially of English poets—produce

their most potent effects by the accumulation of details—details which in themselves fascinate us either by their beauty or their curiosity or their supreme appropriateness. But with details Racine will have nothing to do; he builds up his poetry out of words which are not only absolutely simple but extremely general, so that our minds, failing to find in it the peculiar delights to which we have been accustomed, fall into the error of rejecting it altogether as devoid of significance. And the error is a grave one, for in truth nothing is more marvellous than the magic with which Racine can conjure up out of a few expressions of the vaguest import a sense of complete and intimate reality. When Shakespeare wishes to describe a silent night he does so with a single stroke of detail—'not a mouse stirring'! And Virgil adds touch upon touch of exquisite minutiae:

> Cum tacet omnis ager, pecudes, pictaeque volucres,
> Quaeque lacus late liquidos, quaeque aspera dumis
> Rura tenent, etc.

Racine's way is different, but is it less masterly?

> Mais tout dort, et l'armée, et les vents, et Neptune.

What a flat and feeble set of expressions! is the Englishman's first thought—with the conventional 'Neptune,' and the vague 'armée,' and the commonplace 'vents.' And he forgets to notice the total impression which these words produce—the atmosphere of darkness and emptiness and vastness and ominous hush.

It is particularly in regard to Racine's treatment of nature that this generalised style creates misunderstandings. 'Is he so much as aware,' exclaims Mr. Bailey, 'that the sun rises and sets in a glory of colour, that the wind plays deliciously on human cheeks, that the human ear will never have enough of the music of the sea? He might have written every page of his work without so much as looking out of the window of his study.' The accusation gains support from the fact that Racine rarely describes the processes of nature by means of pictorial detail; that, we know, was not his plan. But he is constantly, with his subtle art, suggesting them. In this line, for instance, he calls up, without a word of definite description, the vision of a sudden and brilliant sunrise:

> Déjà le jour plus grand nous frappe et nous éclaire.

And how varied and beautiful are his impressions of the sea! He can give us the desolation of a calm:

> La rame inutile
> Fatigua vainement une mer immobile;

or the agitated movements of a great fleet of galleys:

> Voyez tout l'Hellespont blanchissant sous nos rames;

or he can fill his verses with the disorder and the fury of a storm:

> Quoi! pour noyer les Grecs et leurs mille vaisseaux,
> Mer, tu n'ouvriras pas des abymes nouveaux!
> Quoi! lorsque les chassant du port qui les recèle,
> L'Aulide aura vomi leur flotte criminelle,
> Les vents, les mêmes vents, si longtemps accusés,
> Ne te couvriront pas de ses vaisseaux brisés!

And then, in a single line, he can evoke the radiant spectacle of a triumphant flotilla riding the dancing waves:

> Prêts à vous recevoir mes vaisseaux vous attendent;
> Et du pied de l'autel vous y pouvez monter,
> Souveraine des mers qui vous doivent porter.

The art of subtle suggestion could hardly go further than in this line, where the alliterating v's, the mute e's, and the placing of the long syllables combine so wonderfully to produce the required effect.

But it is not only suggestions of nature that readers like Mr. Bailey are unable to find in Racine—they miss in him no less suggestions of the mysterious and the infinite. No doubt this is partly due to our English habit of associating these qualities with expressions which are complex and unfamiliar. When we come across the mysterious accent of fatality and remote terror in a single perfectly simple phrase—

> La fille de Minos et de Pasiphaé

we are apt not to hear that it is there. But there is another reason—the craving, which has seized upon our poetry and our criticism ever since the triumph of Wordsworth and Coleridge at the beginning of the last century, for metaphysical stimulants. It would be easy to prolong the discussion of this matter far beyond the boundaries of 'sublunary debate,' but it is sufficient to point out that Mr. Bailey's criticism of Racine affords an excellent example of the fatal effects of this obsession. His pages are full of references to 'infinity' and 'the unseen' and 'eternity' and 'a mystery brooding over a mystery' and 'the key to the secret of life'; and it is only natural that he should find in these watchwords one of those tests of poetic greatness of which he is so fond. The fallaciousness of such views as these becomes obvious when we remember the plain fact that there is not a trace of this kind of mystery or of these 'feelings after the key to the secret of life,' in *Paradise Lost*, and that *Paradise Lost* is one of the greatest poems in the world. But Milton is sacrosanct in England; no theory, however mistaken, can shake that stupendous name, and the damage which may be wrought by a vicious system of criticism only becomes evident in its treatment of writers like Racine, whom it can attack with impunity and apparent success. There is no 'mystery' in Racine—that is to say, there are no metaphysical speculations in him, no suggestions of the transcendental, no hints as to the ultimate nature of reality and the constitution of the world; and so away with him, a creature of mere rhetoric and ingenuities, to the outer limbo! But if, instead of asking what a writer is without, we try to discover simply what he is, will not our results be more worthy of our trouble? And in fact, if we once put out of our heads our longings for the mystery of metaphysical suggestion, the more we examine Racine, the more clearly we shall discern in him another kind of mystery, whose presence may eventually console us for the loss of the first—the mystery of the mind of man. This indeed is the framework of his poetry, and to speak of it adequately would demand a wider scope than that of an essay; for how much might be written of that strange and moving background, dark with the profundity of passion and glowing with the beauty of the sublime, wherefrom the great personages of his tragedies—Hermione and Mithridate, Roxane and Agrippine, Athalie and Phèdre—seem to emerge for a moment towards us, whereon they breathe and suffer, and among whose depths they vanish for ever from our sight! Look where we will, we shall find among his pages the traces of an inward mystery and the obscure infinities of the heart.

> Nous avons su toujours nous aimer et nous taire.

The line is a summary of the romance and the anguish of two lives. That is all affection; and this all desire—

> J'aimais jusqu'à ses pleurs que je faisais couler.

Or let us listen to the voice of Phèdre, when she learns that Hippolyte and Aricie love one another:

> Les a-t-on vus souvent se parler, se chercher?
> Dans le fond des forêts alloient-ils se cacher?
> Hélas! ils se voyaient avec pleine licence;
> Le ciel de leurs soupirs approuvait l'innocence;
> Ils suivaient sans remords leur penchant amoureux;
> Tous les jours se levaient clairs et sereins pour eux.

This last line—written, let us remember, by a frigidly ingenious rhetorician, who had never looked out of his study-window—does it not seem to mingle, in a trance of absolute simplicity, the peerless beauty of a Claude with the misery and ruin of a great soul?

It is, perhaps, as a psychologist that Racine has achieved his most remarkable triumphs; and the fact that so subtle and penetrating a critic as M. Lemaître has chosen to devote the greater part of a volume to the discussion of his characters shows clearly enough that Racine's portrayal of human nature has lost nothing of its freshness and vitality with the passage of time. On the contrary, his admirers are now tending more and more to lay stress upon the brilliance of his portraits, the combined vigour and intimacy of his painting, his amazing knowledge, and his unerring fidelity to truth. M. Lemaître, in fact, goes so far as to describe Racine as a supreme realist, while other writers have found in him the essence of the modern spirit. These are vague phrases, no doubt, but they imply a very definite point of view; and it is curious to compare with it our English conception of Racine as a stiff and pompous kind of dancing-master, utterly out of date and infinitely cold. And there is a similar disagreement over his style. Mr. Bailey is never tired of asserting that Racine's style is rhetorical, artificial, and monotonous; while M. Lemaître speaks of it as 'nu et familier,' and Sainte-Beuve says 'il rase la prose, mais avec des ailes,' The explanation of these contradictions is to be found in the fact that the two critics are considering different parts of the poet's work. When Racine is most himself, when he is seizing upon a state of mind and depicting it with all its twistings and vibrations, he writes with a directness which is indeed naked, and his sentences, refined to the utmost point of significance, flash out like swords, stroke upon stroke, swift, certain, irresistible. This is how Agrippine, in the fury of her tottering ambition, bursts out to Burrhus, the tutor of her son:

> Prétendez-vous longtemps me cacher l'empereur?
> Ne le verrai-je plus qu'à titre d'importune?
> Ai-je donc élevé si haut votre fortune
> Pour mettre une barrière entre mon fils et moi?
> Ne l'osez-vous laisser un moment sur sa foi?
> Entre Sénèque et vous disputez-vous la gloire
> A qui m'effacera plus tôt de sa mémoire?
> Vous l'ai-je confié pour en faire un ingrat,
> Pour être, sous son nom, les maîtres de l'état?
> Certes, plus je médite, et moins je me figure
> Que vous m'osiez compter pour votre créature;
> Vous, dont j'ai pu laisser vieillir l'ambition
> Dans les honneurs obscurs de quelque légion;
> Et moi, qui sur le trône ai suivi mes ancêtres,

> Moi, fille, femme, soeur, et mère de vos maîtres!

When we come upon a passage like this we know, so to speak, that the hunt is up and the whole field tearing after the quarry. But Racine, on other occasions, has another way of writing. He can be roundabout, artificial, and vague; he can involve a simple statement in a mist of high-sounding words and elaborate inversions.

> Jamais l'aimable soeur des cruels Pallantides
> Trempa-t-elle aux complots de ses frères perfides.

That is Racine's way of saying that Aricie did not join in her brothers' conspiracy. He will describe an incriminating letter as 'De sa trahison ce gage trop sincère.' It is obvious that this kind of expression has within it the germs of the 'noble' style of the eighteenth-century tragedians, one of whom, finding himself obliged to mention a dog, got out of the difficulty by referring to—'De la fidélité le respectable appui.' This is the side of Racine's writing that puzzles and disgusts Mr. Bailey. But there is a meaning in it, after all. Every art is based upon a selection, and the art of Racine selected the things of the spirit for the material of its work. The things of sense—physical objects and details, and all the necessary but insignificant facts that go to make up the machinery of existence—these must be kept out of the picture at all hazards. To have called a spade a spade would have ruined the whole effect; spades must never be mentioned, or, at the worst, they must be dimly referred to as agricultural implements, so that the entire attention may be fixed upon the central and dominating features of the composition—the spiritual states of the characters—which, laid bare with uncompromising force and supreme precision, may thus indelibly imprint themselves upon the mind. To condemn Racine on the score of his ambiguities and his pomposities is to complain of the hastily dashed-in column and curtain in the background of a portrait, and not to mention the face. Sometimes indeed his art seems to rise superior to its own conditions, endowing even the dross and refuse of what it works in with a wonderful significance. Thus when the Sultana, Roxane, discovers her lover's treachery, her mind flies immediately to thoughts of revenge and death, and she exclaims—

> Ah! je respire enfin, et ma joie est extreme
> Que le traître une fois se soit trahi lui-même.
> Libre des soins cruels où j'allais m'engager,
> Ma tranquille fureur n'a plus qu'à se venger.
> Qu'il meure. Vengeons-nous. Courez. Qu'on le saisisse!
> Que la main des muets s'arme pour son supplice;
> Qu'ils viennent préparer ces noeuds infortunés

Par qui de ses pareils les jours sont terminés.

To have called a bowstring a bowstring was out of the question; and Racine, with triumphant art, has managed to introduce the periphrasis in such a way that it exactly expresses the state of mind of the Sultana. She begins with revenge and rage, until she reaches the extremity of virulent resolution; and then her mind begins to waver, and she finally orders the execution of the man she loves, in a contorted agony of speech.

But, as a rule, Racine's characters speak out most clearly when they are most moved, so that their words, at the height of passion, have an intensity of directness unknown in actual life. In such moments, the phrases that leap to their lips quiver and glow with the compressed significance of character and situation; the 'Qui te l'a dit?' of Hermione, the 'Sortez' of Roxane, the 'Je vais à Rome' of Mithridate, the 'Dieu des Juifs, tu l'emportes!' of Athalie—who can forget these things, these wondrous microcosms of tragedy? Very different is the Shakespearean method. There, as passion rises, expression becomes more and more poetical and vague. Image flows into image, thought into thought, until at last the state of mind is revealed, inform and molten, driving darkly through a vast storm of words. Such revelations, no doubt, come closer to reality than the poignant epigrams of Racine. In life, men's minds are not sharpened, they are diffused, by emotion; and the utterance which best represents them is fluctuating and agglomerated rather than compact and defined. But Racine's aim was less to reflect the actual current of the human spirit than to seize upon its inmost being and to give expression to that. One might be tempted to say that his art represents the sublimed essence of reality, save that, after all, reality has no degrees. Who can affirm that the wild ambiguities of our hearts and the gross impediments of our physical existence are less real than the most pointed of our feelings and 'thoughts beyond the reaches of our souls'?

It would be nearer the truth to rank Racine among the idealists. The world of his creation is not a copy of our own; it is a heightened and rarefied extension of it; moving, in triumph and in beauty, through 'an ampler ether, a diviner air.' It is a world where the hesitations and the pettinesses and the squalors of this earth have been fired out; a world where ugliness is a forgotten name, and lust itself has grown ethereal; where anguish has become a grace and death a glory, and love the beginning and the end of all. It is, too, the world of a poet, so that we reach it, not through melody nor through vision, but through the poet's sweet articulation—through verse. Upon English ears the rhymed couplets of Racine sound strangely; and how many besides Mr. Bailey have dubbed his alexandrines 'monotonous'! But to his lovers, to those who have found their way into the secret places of his art, his lines are impregnated with a peculiar beauty, and the last perfection of style. Over them, the most insignificant of his verses can throw a deep enchantment, like the faintest wavings of a magician's wand. 'A-t-on vu de ma part le roi de Comagène?'—How is it that words of such slight import should hold such thrilling music? Oh! they are Racine's words. And, as to his rhymes, they seem perhaps, to the true worshipper, the final crown of his art. Mr. Bailey tells us that the couplet is only fit for satire. Has he forgotten *Lamia*? And he asks, 'How is it that we read Pope's *Satires* and Dryden's, and Johnson's with enthusiasm still, while we never touch *Irene*, and rarely the *Conquest of Granada*?' Perhaps the answer is that if we cannot get rid of our *a priori* theories, even the fiery art of Dryden's drama may remain dead to us, and that, if we touched *Irene* even once, we should find it was in blank verse. But Dryden himself has spoken memorably upon rhyme. Discussing the imputed unnaturalness of the rhymed 'repartee' he says: 'Suppose we acknowledge it: how comes this confederacy to be more displeasing to you than in a dance which is well contrived? You see there the united design of many persons to make up one figure; ... the confederacy is plain amongst them, for chance could never produce anything so beautiful; and yet there is nothing in it that shocks your sight ... 'Tis an art which appears; but it appears only like the shadowings of painture, which, being to cause the rounding of it, cannot be absent; but while that is considered, they are lost: so while we attend to the other beauties of the matter, the care and labour of the rhyme is carried from us, or at least drowned in its own sweetness, as bees are sometimes buried in their honey.' In this exquisite passage Dryden seems to have come near, though not quite to have hit, the central argument for rhyme—its power of creating a beautiful atmosphere, in which what is expressed may be caught away from the associations of common life and harmoniously enshrined. For Racine, with his prepossessions of sublimity and perfection, some such barrier between his universe and reality was involved in the very nature of his art. His rhyme is like the still clear water of a lake, through which we can see, mysteriously separated from us and changed and beautified, the forms of his imagination, 'quivering within the wave's intenser day.' And truly not seldom are they 'so sweet, the sense faints picturing them'!

> Oui, prince, je languis, je brûle pour Thésée ...
> Il avait votre port, vos yeux, votre langage,
> Cette noble pudeur colorait son visage,
> Lorsque de notre Crète il traversa les flots,
> Digne sujet des voeux des filles de Minos.
> Que faisiez-vous alors? Pourquoi, sans Hippolyte,
> Des héros de la Grèce assembla-t-il l'élite?

> Pourquoi, trop jeune encor, ne pûtes-vous alors
> Entrer dans le vaisseau qui le mit sur nos bords?
> Par vous aurait péri le monstre de la Crète,
> Malgré tous les détours de sa vaste retraite:
> Pour en développer l'embarras incertain
> Ma soeur du fil fatal eût armé votre main.
> Mais non: dans ce dessein je l'aurais devancée;
> L'amour m'en eût d'abord inspiré la pensée;
> C'est moi, prince, c'est moi dont l'utile secours
> Vous eût du labyrinthe enseigné les détours.
> Que de soins m'eût coûtés cette tête charmante!

It is difficult to 'place' Racine among the poets. He has affinities with many; but likenesses to few. To balance him rigorously against any other—to ask whether he is better or worse than Shelley or than Virgil—is to attempt impossibilities; but there is one fact which is too often forgotten in comparing his work with that of other poets—with Virgil's for instance—Racine wrote for the stage. Virgil's poetry is intended to be read, Racine's to be declaimed; and it is only in the theatre that one can experience to the full the potency of his art. In a sense we can know him in our library, just as we can hear the music of Mozart with silent eyes. But, when the strings begin, when the whole volume of that divine harmony engulfs us, how differently then we understand and feel! And so, at the theatre, before one of those high tragedies, whose interpretation has taxed to the utmost ten generations of the greatest actresses of France, we realise, with the shock of a new emotion, what we had but half-felt before. To hear the words of Phèdre spoken by the mouth of Bernhardt, to watch, in the culminating horror of crime and of remorse, of jealousy, of rage, of desire, and of despair, all the dark forces of destiny crowd down upon that great spirit, when the heavens and the earth reject her, and Hell opens, and the terrific urn of Minos thunders and crashes to the ground—that indeed is to come close to immortality, to plunge shuddering through infinite abysses, and to look, if only for a moment, upon eternal light.

1908.

SIR THOMAS BROWNE

The life of Sir Thomas Browne does not afford much scope for the biographer. Everyone knows that Browne was a physician who lived at Norwich in the seventeenth century; and, so far as regards what one must call, for want of a better term, his 'life,' that is a sufficient summary of all there is to know. It is obvious that, with such scanty and unexciting materials, no biographer can say very much about what Sir Thomas Browne did; it is quite easy, however, to expatiate about what he wrote. He dug deeply into so many subjects, he touched lightly upon so many more, that his works offer innumerable openings for those half-conversational digressions and excursions of which perhaps the pleasantest kind of criticism is composed.

Mr. Gosse, in his volume on Sir Thomas Browne in the 'English Men of Letters' Series, has evidently taken this view of his subject. He has not attempted to treat it with any great profundity or elaboration; he has simply gone 'about it and about.' The result is a book so full of entertainment, of discrimination, of quiet humour, and of literary tact, that no reader could have the heart to bring up against it the obvious—though surely irrelevant—truth, that the general impression which it leaves upon the mind is in the nature of a composite presentment, in which the features of Sir Thomas have become somehow indissolubly blended with those of his biographer. It would be rash indeed to attempt to improve upon Mr. Gosse's example; after his luminous and suggestive chapters on Browne's life at Norwich, on the *Vulgar Errors*, and on the self-revelations in the *Religio Medici*, there seems to be no room for further comment. One can only admire in silence, and hand on the volume to one's neighbour.

There is, however, one side of Browne's work upon which it may be worth while to dwell at somewhat greater length. Mr. Gosse, who has so much to say on such a variety of topics, has unfortunately limited to a very small number of pages his considerations upon what is, after all, the most important thing about the author of *Urn Burial* and *The Garden of Cyrus*—his style. Mr. Gosse himself confesses that it is chiefly as a master of literary form that Browne deserves to be remembered. Why then does he tell us so little about his literary form, and so much about his family, and his religion, and his scientific opinions, and his porridge, and who fished up the *murex*?

Nor is it only owing to its inadequacy that Mr. Gosse's treatment of Browne as an artist in language is the least satisfactory part of his book: for it is difficult not to think that upon this crucial point Mr. Gosse has for once been deserted by his sympathy and his acumen. In spite of what appears to be a genuine delight in Browne's most splendid and characteristic passages, Mr. Gosse cannot help protesting somewhat acrimoniously against that very method of writing whose effects he is so ready to admire. In practice, he approves; in theory, he condemns. He ranks the *Hydriotaphia* among the gems of English literature; and the prose style of which it is the consummate expression he denounces as fundamentally wrong. The contradiction is obvious; but there can be little doubt that, though Browne has, as it were, extorted a personal homage, Mr. Gosse's real sympathies lie on the other side. His remarks upon Browne's effect upon eighteenth-century prose show clearly enough the true bent of his opinions; and they show, too, how completely misleading a preconceived theory may be.

The study of Sir Thomas Browne, Mr. Gosse says, 'encouraged Johnson, and with him a whole school of rhetorical writers in the eighteenth century, to avoid circumlocution by the invention of superfluous words, learned but pedantic, in which darkness was concentrated without being dispelled.' Such is Mr. Gosse's account of the influence of Browne and Johnson upon the later eighteenth-century writers of prose. But to dismiss Johnson's influence as something altogether deplorable, is surely to misunderstand the whole drift of the great revolution which he brought about in English letters. The characteristics of the pre-Johnsonian prose style—the style which Dryden first established and Swift brought to perfection—are obvious enough. Its advantages are those of clarity and force; but its faults, which, of course, are unimportant in the work of a great master, become glaring in that of the second-rate practitioner. The prose of Locke, for instance, or of Bishop Butler, suffers, in spite of its clarity and vigour, from grave defects. It is very flat and very loose; it has no formal beauty, no elegance, no balance, no trace of the deliberation of art. Johnson, there can be no doubt, determined to remedy these evils by giving a new mould to the texture of English prose; and he went back for a model to Sir Thomas Browne. Now, as Mr. Gosse himself observes, Browne stands out in a remarkable way from among the great mass of his contemporaries and predecessors, by virtue of his highly developed artistic consciousness. He was, says Mr. Gosse, 'never carried away. His effects are closely studied, they are the result of forethought and anxious contrivance'; and no one can doubt the truth or the significance of this dictum who compares, let us say, the last paragraphs of *The Garden of Cyrus* with any page in *The Anatomy of Melancholy*. The peculiarities of Browne's style—the studied pomp of its latinisms, its wealth of allusion, its tendency towards sonorous antithesis—culminated in his last, though not his best, work, the *Christian Morals*, which almost reads like an elaborate and magnificent parody of the Book of Proverbs. With the *Christian Morals* to guide him, Dr. Johnson set about the transformation of the prose of his time. He decorated, he pruned, he balanced; he hung garlands, he draped robes; and he ended by converting the Doric order of Swift into the Corinthian order of Gibbon. Is it quite just to describe this process as one by which 'a whole school of rhetorical writers' was encouraged 'to avoid circumlocution' by the invention 'of superfluous words,' when it was this very process that gave us the peculiar savour of polished ease which characterises nearly all the important prose of the last half of the eighteenth century—that of Johnson himself, of Hume, of Reynolds, of Horace Walpole—which can be traced even in Burke, and which fills the pages of Gibbon? It is, indeed, a curious reflection, but one which is amply justified by the facts, that the *Decline and Fall* could not have been precisely what it is, had Sir Thomas Browne never written the *Christian Morals*.

That Johnson and his disciples had no inkling of the inner spirit of the writer to whose outward form they owed so much, has been pointed out by Mr. Gosse, who adds that Browne's 'genuine merits were rediscovered and asserted by Coleridge and Lamb.' But we have already observed that Mr. Gosse's own assertion of these merits lies a little open to question. His view seems to be, in fact, the precise antithesis of Dr. Johnson's; he swallows the spirit of Browne's writing, and strains at the form. Browne, he says, was 'seduced by a certain obscure romance in the terminology of late Latin writers,' he used 'adjectives of classical extraction, which are neither necessary nor natural,' he forgot that it is better for a writer 'to consult women and people who have not studied, than those who are too learnedly oppressed by a knowledge of Latin and Greek.' He should not have said 'oneiro-criticism,' when he meant the interpretation of dreams, nor 'omneity' instead of 'oneness'; and he had 'no excuse for writing about the "pensile" gardens of Babylon, when all that is required is expressed by "hanging."' Attacks of this kind—attacks upon the elaboration and classicism of Browne's style—are difficult to reply to, because they must seem, to anyone who holds a contrary opinion, to betray such a total lack of sympathy with the subject as to make argument all but impossible. To the true Browne enthusiast, indeed, there is something almost shocking about the state of mind which would exchange 'pensile' for 'hanging,' and 'asperous' for 'rough,' and would do away with 'digladiation' and 'quodlibetically' altogether. The truth is, that there is a great gulf fixed between those who naturally dislike the ornate, and those who naturally love it. There is no remedy; and to attempt to ignore this fact only emphasises it the more. Anyone who is jarred by the expression 'prodigal blazes' had better immediately shut up Sir Thomas Browne. The critic who admits the jar, but continues to appreciate, must present, to the true enthusiast, a spectacle of curious self-contradiction.

If once the ornate style be allowed as a legitimate form of art, no attack such as Mr. Gosse makes on Browne's latinisms can possibly be valid. For it is surely an error to judge and to condemn the latinisms without reference to the whole style of which they form a necessary part. Mr. Gosse, it is true, inclines to treat them as if they were a mere excrescence which could be cut off without difficulty, and might never have existed if Browne's views upon the English language had been a little different. Browne, he says, 'had come to the conclusion that classic words were the only legitimate ones, the only ones which interpreted with elegance the thoughts of a sensitive and cultivated man, and that the rest were barbarous.' We are to suppose, then, that if he had happened to hold the opinion that Saxon words were the only legitimate ones, the *Hydriotaphia* would have been as free from words of classical derivation as the sermons of Latimer. A very little reflection and inquiry will suffice to show how completely mistaken this view really is. In the first place, the theory that Browne considered all unclassical words 'barbarous' and unfit to interpret his thoughts, is clearly untenable, owing to the obvious fact that his writings are full of instances of the deliberate use of such words. So much is this the case, that Pater declares that a dissertation upon style might be written to illustrate Browne's use of the words 'thin' and 'dark.' A striking phrase from the *Christian Morals* will suffice to show the deliberation with which Browne sometimes employed the latter word:—'the areopagy and dark tribunal of our hearts.' If Browne had thought the Saxon epithet 'barbarous,' why should he have gone out of his way to use it, when 'mysterious' or 'secret' would have expressed his meaning? The truth is clear enough. Browne saw that 'dark' was the one word which would give, better than any other, the precise impression of mystery and secrecy which he intended to produce; and so he used it. He did not choose his words according to rule, but according to the effect which he wished them to have. Thus, when he wished to suggest an extreme contrast between simplicity and pomp, we find him using Saxon words in direct antithesis to classical ones. In the last sentence of *Urn Burial*, we are told that the true believer, when he is to be buried, is 'as content with six foot as the Moles of Adrianus.' How could Browne have produced the remarkable sense of contrast which this short phrase conveys, if his vocabulary had been limited, in accordance with a linguistic theory, to words of a single stock?

There is, of course, no doubt that Browne's vocabulary is extraordinarily classical. Why is this? The reason is not far to seek. In his most characteristic moments he was almost entirely occupied with thoughts and emotions which can, owing to their very nature, only be expressed in Latinistic language. The state of mind which he wished to produce in his readers was nearly always a complicated one: they were to be impressed and elevated by a multiplicity of suggestions and a sense of mystery and awe. 'Let thy thoughts,' he says himself, 'be of things which have not entered into the hearts of beasts: think of things long past, and long to come: acquaint thyself with the choragium of the stars, and consider the vast expanse beyond them. Let intellectual tubes give thee a glance of things which visive organs reach not. Have a glimpse of incomprehensibles; and thoughts of things, which thoughts but tenderly touch.' Browne had, in fact, as Dr. Johnson puts it, 'uncommon sentiments'; and how was he to express them unless by a language of pomp, of allusion, and of elaborate rhythm? Not only is the Saxon form of speech devoid of splendour and suggestiveness; its simplicity is still further emphasised by a spondaic rhythm which seems to produce (by some mysterious rhythmic law) an atmosphere of ordinary life, where, though the pathetic may be present, there is no place for the complex or the remote. To understand how unsuitable such conditions would be for the highly subtle and rarefied art of Sir Thomas Browne, it is only necessary to compare one of his periods with a typical passage of Saxon prose.

> Then they brought a faggot, kindled with fire, and laid the same down at Doctor Ridley's feet. To whom Master Latimer spake in this manner: 'Be of good comfort, Master Ridley, and play the man. We shall this day light such a candle, by God's grace, in England, as I trust shall never be put out.'

Nothing could be better adapted to the meaning and sentiment of this passage than the limpid, even flow of its rhythm. But who could conceive of such a rhythm being ever applicable to the meaning and sentiment of these sentences from the *Hydriotaphia*?

> To extend our memories by monuments, whose death we daily pray for, and whose duration we cannot hope without injury to our expectations in the advent of the last day, were a contradiction to our beliefs. We, whose generations are ordained in this setting part of time, are providentially taken off from such imaginations; and, being necessitated to eye the remaining particle of futurity, are naturally constituted unto thoughts of the next world, and cannot excusably decline the consideration of that duration, which maketh pyramids pillars of snow, and all that's past a moment.

Here the long, rolling, almost turgid clauses, with their enormous Latin substantives, seem to carry the reader forward through an immense succession of ages, until at last, with a sudden change of the rhythm, the whole of recorded time crumbles and vanishes before his eyes. The entire effect depends upon the employment of a rhythmical complexity and subtlety which is utterly alien to Saxon prose. It would be foolish to claim a superiority for either of the two styles; it would be still more foolish to suppose that the effects of one might be produced by means of the other.

Wealth of rhythmical elaboration was not the only benefit which a highly Latinised vocabulary conferred on Browne. Without it, he would never have been able to achieve those splendid strokes of stylistic *bravura*, which were evidently so dear to his nature, and occur so constantly in his finest passages. The precise quality cannot be easily described, but is impossible to mistake; and the pleasure which it produces seems to be curiously analogous to that given by a piece of magnificent brushwork in a Rubens or a Velasquez. Browne's 'brushwork' is certainly unequalled in English literature, except by the very greatest masters of sophisticated art, such as Pope and Shakespeare; it is the inspiration of sheer technique. Such expressions as: 'to subsist in bones and be but pyramidally extant'—'sad and sepulchral pitchers which have no joyful voices'—'predicament of chimaeras'—'the irregularities of vain glory, and wild enormities of ancient magnanimity'—are examples of this consummate mastery of language, examples which, with a multitude of others, singly deserve whole hours of delicious gustation, whole days of absorbed and exquisite worship. It is pleasant to start out for a long walk with such a splendid phrase upon one's lips as: 'According to the ordainer of order and mystical mathematicks of the City of Heaven,' to go for miles and miles with the marvellous syllables still rich upon the inward ear, and to return home with them in triumph. It is then that one begins to understand how mistaken it was of Sir Thomas Browne not to have written in simple, short, straightforward Saxon English.

One other function performed by Browne's latinisms must be mentioned, because it is closely connected with the most essential and peculiar of the qualities which distinguish his method of writing. Certain classical words, partly owing to their allusiveness, partly owing to their sound, possess a remarkable flavour which is totally absent from those of Saxon derivation. Such a word, for instance, as 'pyramidally,' gives one at once an immediate sense of something mysterious, something extraordinary, and, at the same time, something almost grotesque. And this subtle blending of mystery and queerness characterises not only Browne's choice of words, but his choice of feelings and of thoughts. The grotesque side of his art, indeed, was apparently all that was visible to the critics of a few generations back, who admired him simply and solely for what they called his 'quaintness'; while Mr. Gosse has flown to the opposite extreme, and will not allow Browne any sense of humour at all. The confusion no doubt arises merely from a difference in the point of view. Mr. Gosse, regarding Browne's most important and general effects, rightly fails to detect anything funny in them. The Early Victorians, however, missed the broad outlines, and were altogether taken up with the obvious grotesqueness of the details. When they found Browne asserting that 'Cato seemed to dote upon Cabbage,' or embroidering an entire paragraph upon the subject of 'Pyrrhus his Toe,' they could not help smiling; and surely they were quite right. Browne, like an impressionist painter, produced his pictures by means of a multitude of details which, if one looks at them in themselves, are discordant, and extraordinary, and even absurd.

There can be little doubt that this strongly marked taste for curious details was one of the symptoms of the scientific bent of his mind. For Browne was scientific just up to the point where the examination of detail ends, and its coordination begins. He knew little or nothing of general laws; but his interest in isolated phenomena was intense. And the more singular the phenomena, the more he was attracted. He was always ready to begin some strange inquiry. He cannot help wondering: 'Whether great-ear'd persons have short necks, long feet, and loose bellies?' 'Marcus Antoninus Philosophus,' he notes in his commonplace book, 'wanted not the advice of the best physicians; yet how warrantable his practice was, to take his repast in the night, and scarce anything but treacle in the day, may admit of great doubt.' To inquire thus is, perhaps, to inquire too curiously; yet such inquiries are the stuff of which great scientific theories are made. Browne, however, used his love of details for another purpose: he co-ordinated them, not into a scientific theory, but into a work of art. His method was one which, to be successful, demanded a self-confidence, an imagination, and a technical power, possessed by only the very greatest artists. Everyone knows Pascal's overwhelming sentence:—'Le silence éternel de ces espaces infinis m'effraie.' It is overwhelming, obviously and immediately; it, so to speak, knocks one down. Browne's ultimate object was to create some such tremendous effect as that, by no knock-down blow, but by a multitude of delicate, subtle, and suggestive touches, by an elaborate evocation of memories and half-hidden things, by a mysterious combination of pompous images and odd unexpected trifles drawn together from the ends of the earth and the four quarters of heaven. His success gives him a place beside Webster and Blake, on one of the very highest peaks of Parnassus. And, if not the highest of all, Browne's peak is—or so at least it seems from the plains below—more difficult of access than some which are no less exalted.

The road skirts the precipice the whole way. If one fails in the style of Pascal, one is merely flat; if one fails in the style of Browne, one is ridiculous. He who plays with the void, who dallies with eternity, who leaps from star to star, is in danger at every moment of being swept into utter limbo, and tossed forever in the Paradise of Fools.

Browne produced his greatest work late in life; for there is nothing in the *Religio Medici* which reaches the same level of excellence as the last paragraphs of *The Garden of Cyrus* and the last chapter of *Urn Burial*. A long and calm experience of life seems, indeed, to be the background from which his most amazing sentences start out into being. His strangest phantasies are rich with the spoils of the real world. His art matured with himself; and who but the most expert of artists could have produced this perfect sentence in *The Garden of Cyrus*, so well known, and yet so impossible not to quote?

> Nor will the sweetest delight of gardens afford much comfort in sleep; wherein the dullness of that sense shakes hands with delectable odours; and though in the bed of Cleopatra, can hardly with any delight raise up the ghost of a rose.

This is Browne in his most exquisite mood. For his most characteristic, one must go to the concluding pages of *Urn Burial*, where, from the astonishing sentence beginning—'Meanwhile Epicurus lies deep in Dante's hell'—to the end of the book, the very quintessence of his work is to be found. The subject—mortality in its most generalised aspect—has brought out Browne's highest powers; and all the resources of his art—elaboration of rhythm, brilliance of phrase, wealth and variety of suggestion, pomp and splendour of imagination—are accumulated in every paragraph. To crown all, he has scattered through these few pages a multitude of proper names, most of them gorgeous in sound, and each of them carrying its own strange freight of reminiscences and allusions from the unknown depths of the past. As one reads, an extraordinary procession of persons seems to pass before one's eyes—Moses, Archimedes, Achilles, Job, Hector and Charles the Fifth, Cardan and Alaric, Gordianus, and Pilate, and Homer, and Cambyses, and the Canaanitish woman. Among them, one visionary figure flits with a mysterious pre-eminence, flickering over every page, like a familiar and ghostly flame. It is Methuselah; and, in Browne's scheme, the remote, almost infinite, and almost ridiculous patriarch is—who can doubt?—the only possible centre and symbol of all the rest. But it would be vain to dwell further upon this wonderful and famous chapter, except to note the extraordinary sublimity and serenity of its general tone. Browne never states in so many words what his own feelings towards the universe actually are. He speaks of everything but that; and yet, with triumphant art, he manages to convey into our minds an indelible impression of the vast and comprehensive grandeur of his soul.

It is interesting—or at least amusing—to consider what are the most appropriate places in which different authors should be read. Pope is doubtless at his best in the midst of a formal garden, Herrick in an orchard, and Shelley in a boat at sea. Sir Thomas Browne demands, perhaps, a more exotic atmosphere. One could read him floating down the Euphrates, or past the shores of Arabia; and it would be pleasant to open the *Vulgar Errors* in Constantinople, or to get by heart a chapter of the *Christian Morals* between the paws of a Sphinx. In England, the most fitting background for his strange ornament must surely be some habitation consecrated to learning, some University which still smells of antiquity and has learnt the habit of repose. The present writer, at any rate, can bear witness to the splendid echo of Browne's syllables amid learned and ancient walls; for he has known, he believes, few happier moments than those in which he has rolled the periods of the *Hydriotaphia* out to the darkness and the nightingales through the studious cloisters of Trinity.

But, after all, who can doubt that it is at Oxford that Browne himself would choose to linger? May we not guess that he breathed in there, in his boyhood, some part of that mysterious and charming spirit which pervades his words? For one traces something of him, often enough, in the old gardens, and down the hidden streets; one has heard his footstep beside the quiet waters of Magdalen; and his smile still hovers amid that strange company of faces which guard, with such a large passivity, the circumference of the Sheldonian.

1906.

SHAKESPEARE'S FINAL PERIOD

The whole of the modern criticism of Shakespeare has been fundamentally affected by one important fact. The chronological order of the plays, for so long the object of the vaguest speculation, of random guesses, or at best of isolated 'points,' has been now discovered and reduced to a coherent law. It is no longer possible to suppose that *The Tempest* was written before *Romeo and 'Juliet*; that *Henry VI.* was produced in succession to *Henry V.*; or that *Antony and Cleopatra* followed close upon the heels of *Julius Caesar*. Such theories were sent to limbo for ever, when a study of those plays of whose date we have external evidence revealed the fact that, as Shakespeare's life advanced, a corresponding development took place in the metrical structure of his verse. The establishment of metrical tests, by which the approximate position and date of any play can be readily ascertained, at once followed; chaos gave way to order; and, for the first time, critics became able to judge, not only of the individual works, but of the whole succession of the works of Shakespeare.

Upon this firm foundation modern writers have been only too eager to build. It was apparent that the Plays, arranged in chronological order, showed something more than a mere development in the technique of verse—a development, that is to say, in the general treatment of characters and subjects, and in the sort of feelings which those characters and subjects were intended to arouse; and from this it was easy to draw conclusions as to the development of the mind of Shakespeare itself. Such conclusions have, in fact, been constantly drawn. But it must be noted that they all rest upon the tacit assumption, that the character of any given drama is, in fact, a true index to the state of mind of the dramatist composing it. The validity of this assumption has never been proved; it has never been shown, for instance, why we should suppose a writer of farces to be habitually merry; or whether we are really justified in concluding, from the fact that Shakespeare wrote nothing but tragedies for six years, that, during that period, more than at any other, he was deeply absorbed in the awful problems of human existence. It is not, however, the purpose of this essay to consider the question of what are the relations between the artist and his art; for it will assume the truth of the generally accepted view, that the character of the one can be inferred from that of the other. What it will attempt to discuss is whether, upon this hypothesis, the most important part of the ordinary doctrine of Shakespeare's mental development is justifiable.

What, then, is the ordinary doctrine? Dr. Furnivall states it as follows:

> Shakespeare's course is thus shown to have run from the amorousness and fun of youth, through the strong patriotism of early manhood, to the wrestlings with the dark problems that beset the man of middle age, to the gloom which weighed on Shakespeare (as on so many men) in later life, when, though outwardly successful, the world seemed all against him, and his mind dwelt with sympathy on scenes of faithlessness of friends, treachery of relations and subjects, ingratitude of children, scorn of his kind; till at last, in his Stratford home again, peace came to him, Miranda and Perdita in their lovely freshness and charm greeted him, and he was laid by his quiet Avon side.

And the same writer goes on to quote with approval Professor Dowden's

> likening of Shakespeare to a ship, beaten and storm-tossed, but yet entering harbour with sails full-set, to anchor in peace.

Such, in fact, is the general opinion of modern writers upon Shakespeare; after a happy youth and a gloomy middle age he reached at last—it is the universal opinion—a state of quiet serenity in which he died. Professor Dowden's book on 'Shakespeare's Mind and Art' gives the most popular expression to this view, a view which is also held by Mr. Ten Brink, by Sir I. Gollancz, and, to a great extent, by Dr. Brandes. Professor Dowden, indeed, has gone so far as to label this final period with the appellation of 'On the Heights,' in opposition to the preceding one, which, he says, was passed 'In the Depths.' Sir Sidney Lee, too, seems to find, in the Plays at least, if not in Shakespeare's mind, the orthodox succession of gaiety, of tragedy, and of the serenity of meditative romance.

Now it is clear that the most important part of this version of Shakespeare's mental history is the end of it. That he did eventually attain to a state of calm content, that he did, in fact, die happy—it is this that gives colour and interest to the whole theory. For some reason or another, the end of a man's life seems naturally to afford the light by which the rest of it should be read; last thoughts do appear in some strange way to be really best and truest; and this is particularly the case when they fit in nicely with the rest of the story, and are, perhaps, just what one likes to think oneself. If it be true that Shakespeare, to quote Professor Dowden, 'did at last attain to the serene self-possession which he had sought with such persistent effort';

that, in the words of Dr. Furnivall, 'forgiven and forgiving, full of the highest wisdom and peace, at one with family and friends and foes, in harmony with Avon's flow and Stratford's level meads, Shakespeare closed his life on earth'—we have obtained a piece of knowledge which is both interesting and pleasant. But if it be not true, if, on the contrary, it can be shown that something very different was actually the case, then will it not follow that we must not only reverse our judgment as to this particular point, but also readjust our view of the whole drift and bearing of Shakespeare's 'inner life'?

The group of works which has given rise to this theory of ultimate serenity was probably entirely composed after Shakespeare's final retirement from London, and his establishment at New Place. It consists of three plays—*Cymbeline*, *The Winter's Tale*, and *The Tempest*—and three fragments—the Shakespearean parts of *Pericles*, *Henry VIII.*, and *The Two Noble Kinsmen*. All these plays and portions of plays form a distinct group; they resemble each other in a multitude of ways, and they differ in a multitude of ways from nearly all Shakespeare's previous work.

One other complete play, however, and one other fragment, do resemble in some degree these works of the final period; for, immediately preceding them in date, they show clear traces of the beginnings of the new method, and they are themselves curiously different from the plays they immediately succeed—that great series of tragedies which began with *Hamlet* in 1601 and ended in 1608 with *Antony and Cleopatra*. In the latter year, indeed, Shakespeare's entire method underwent an astonishing change. For six years he had been persistently occupied with a kind of writing which he had himself not only invented but brought to the highest point of excellence—the tragedy of character. Every one of his masterpieces has for its theme the action of tragic situation upon character; and, without those stupendous creations in character, his greatest tragedies would obviously have lost the precise thing that has made them what they are. Yet, after *Antony and Cleopatra* Shakespeare deliberately turned his back upon the dramatic methods of all his past career. There seems no reason why he should not have continued, year after year, to produce *Othellos*, *Hamlets*, and *Macbeths*; instead, he turned over a new leaf, and wrote *Coriolanus*.

Coriolanus is certainly a remarkable, and perhaps an intolerable play: remarkable, because it shows the sudden first appearance of the Shakespeare of the final period; intolerable, because it is impossible to forget how much better it might have been. The subject is thick with situations; the conflicts of patriotism and pride, the effects of sudden disgrace following upon the very height of fortune, the struggles between family affection on the one hand

and every interest of revenge and egotism on the other—these would have made a tragic and tremendous setting for some character worthy to rank with Shakespeare's best. But it pleased him to ignore completely all these opportunities; and, in the play he has given us, the situations, mutilated and degraded, serve merely as miserable props for the gorgeous clothing of his rhetoric. For rhetoric, enormously magnificent and extraordinarily elaborate, is the beginning and the middle and the end of *Coriolanus*. The hero is not a human being at all; he is the statue of a demi-god cast in bronze, which roars its perfect periods, to use a phrase of Sir Walter Raleigh's, through a melodious megaphone. The vigour of the presentment is, it is true, amazing; but it is a presentment of decoration, not of life. So far and so quickly had Shakespeare already wandered from the subtleties of *Cleopatra*. The transformation is indeed astonishing; one wonders, as one beholds it, what will happen next.

At about the same time, some of the scenes in *Timon of Athens* were in all probability composed: scenes which resemble *Coriolanus* in their lack of characterisation and abundance of rhetoric, but differ from it in the peculiar grossness of their tone. For sheer virulence of foul-mouthed abuse, some of the speeches in Timon are probably unsurpassed in any literature; an outraged drayman would speak so, if draymen were in the habit of talking poetry. From this whirlwind of furious ejaculation, this splendid storm of nastiness, Shakespeare, we are confidently told, passed in a moment to tranquillity and joy, to blue skies, to young ladies, and to general forgiveness.

> From 1604 to 1610 [says Professor Dowden] a show of tragic figures, like the kings who passed before Macbeth, filled the vision of Shakespeare; until at last the desperate image of Timon rose before him; when, as though unable to endure or to conceive a more lamentable ruin of man, he turned for relief to the pastoral loves of Prince Florizel and Perdita; and as soon as the tone of his mind was restored, gave expression to its ultimate mood of grave serenity in *The Tempest*, and so ended.

This is a pretty picture, but is it true? It may, indeed, be admitted at once that Prince Florizel and Perdita are charming creatures, that Prospero is 'grave,' and that Hermione is more or less 'serene'; but why is it that, in our consideration of the later plays, the whole of our attention must always be fixed upon these particular characters? Modern critics, in their eagerness to appraise everything that is beautiful and good at its proper value, seem to have entirely forgotten that there is another side to the medal; and they have omitted to point out that these plays contain a series of portraits of peculiar infamy, whose wickedness finds expression in language of extraordinary force. Coming fresh from their pages to the pages of *Cymbeline*, *The Winter's Tale*, and *The Tempest*, one is astonished and perplexed. How is it possible to fit into their scheme of roses and maidens that 'Italian fiend' the 'yellow Iachimo,' or Cloten, that 'thing too bad for bad report,' or the 'crafty devil,' his mother, or Leontes, or Caliban, or Trinculo? To omit these figures of discord and evil from our consideration, to banish them comfortably to the background of the stage, while Autolycus and Miranda dance before the footlights, is surely a fallacy in proportion; for the presentment of the one group of persons is every whit as distinct and vigorous as that of the other. Nowhere, indeed, is Shakespeare's violence of expression more constantly displayed than in the 'gentle utterances' of his last period; it is here that one finds Paulina, in a torrent of indignation as far from 'grave serenity' as it is from 'pastoral love,' exclaiming to Leontes:

> What studied torments, tyrant, hast for me?
> What wheels? racks? fires? what flaying? Boiling
> In leads or oils? what old or newer torture
> Must I receive, whose every word deserves
> To taste of thy most worst? Thy tyranny,
> Together working with thy jealousies,
> Fancies too weak for boys, too green and idle
> For girls of nine, O! think what they have done,
> And then run mad indeed, stark mad; for all
> Thy by-gone fooleries were but spices of it.
> That thou betray'dst Polixenes, 'twas nothing;
> That did but show thee, of a fool, inconstant
> And damnable ingrateful; nor was't much
> Thou would'st have poison'd good Camillo's honour,
> To have him kill a king; poor trespasses,
> More monstrous standing by; whereof I reckon
> The casting forth to crows thy baby daughter
> To be or none or little; though a devil
> Would have shed water out of fire ere done't.
> Nor is't directly laid to thee, the death
> Of the young prince, whose honourable thoughts,
> Thoughts high for one so tender, cleft the heart
> That could conceive a gross and foolish sire

Blemished his gracious dam.

Nowhere are the poet's metaphors more nakedly material; nowhere does he verge more often upon a sort of brutality of phrase, a cruel coarseness. Iachimo tells us how:

> The cloyed will,
> That satiate yet unsatisfied desire, that tub
> Both filled and running, ravening first the lamb,
> Longs after for the garbage.

and talks of:

> an eye
> Base and unlustrous as the smoky light
> That's fed with stinking tallow.

'The south fog rot him!' Cloten bursts out to Imogen, cursing her husband in an access of hideous rage.

What traces do such passages as these show of 'serene self-possession,' of 'the highest wisdom and peace,' or of 'meditative romance'? English critics, overcome by the idea of Shakespeare's ultimate tranquillity, have generally denied to him the authorship of the brothel scenes in *Pericles* but these scenes are entirely of a piece with the grossnesses of *The Winter's Tale* and *Cymbeline*.

> Is there no way for men to be, but women
> Must be half-workers?

says Posthumus when he hears of Imogen's guilt.

> We are all bastards;
> And that most venerable man, which I
> Did call my father, was I know not where
> When I was stamped. Some coiner with his tools
> Made me a counterfeit; yet my mother seemed
> The Dian of that time; so doth my wife
> The nonpareil of this—O vengeance, vengeance!
> Me of my lawful pleasure she restrained
> And prayed me, oft, forbearance; did it with
> A pudency so rosy, the sweet view on't
> Might well have warmed old Saturn, that I thought her
> As chaste as unsunned snow—O, all the devils!—

> This yellow Iachimo, in an hour,—was't not?
> Or less,—at first: perchance he spoke not; but,
> Like a full-acorned boar, a German one,
> Cried, oh! and mounted: found no opposition
> But what he looked for should oppose, and she
> Should from encounter guard.

And Leontes, in a similar situation, expresses himself in images no less to the point.

> There have been,
> Or I am much deceived, cuckolds ere now,
> And many a man there is, even at this present,
> Now, while I speak this, holds his wife by the arm,
> That little thinks she has been sluiced in's absence
> And his pond fished by his next neighbour, by
> Sir Smile, his neighbour: nay, there's comfort in't,
> Whiles other men have gates, and those gates opened,
> As mine, against their will. Should all despair
> That have revolted wives, the tenth of mankind
> Would hang themselves. Physic for't there's none;
> It is a bawdy planet, that will strike
> Where 'tis predominant; and 'tis powerful, think it,
> From east, west, north and south: be it concluded,
> No barricade for a belly, know't;
> It will let in and out the enemy
> With bag and baggage: many thousand on's
> Have the disease, and feel't not.

It is really a little difficult, in the face of such passages, to agree with Professor Dowden's dictum: 'In these latest plays the beautiful pathetic light is always present.'

But how has it happened that the judgment of so many critics has been so completely led astray? Charm and gravity, and even serenity, are to be found in many other plays of Shakespeare. Ophelia is charming, Brutus is grave, Cordelia is serene; are we then to suppose that *Hamlet*, and *Julius Caesar*, and *King Lear* give expression to the same mood of high tranquillity which is betrayed by *Cymbeline*, *The Tempest*, and *The Winter's Tale*? 'Certainly not,' reply the orthodox writers, 'for you must distinguish. The plays of the last period are not tragedies; they all end happily'—'in scenes,' says Sir I. Gollancz, 'of forgiveness, reconciliation, and peace.' Virtue, in fact, is not only virtuous, it is triumphant; what would you more?

But to this it may be retorted, that, in the case of one of Shakespeare's plays, even the final vision of virtue and beauty triumphant over ugliness and vice fails to dispel a total effect of horror and of gloom. For, in *Measure for Measure* Isabella is no whit less pure and lovely than any Perdita or Miranda, and her success is as complete; yet who would venture to deny that the atmosphere of *Measure for Measure* was more nearly one of despair than of serenity? What is it, then, that makes the difference? Why should a happy ending seem in one case futile, and in another satisfactory? Why does it sometimes matter to us a great deal, and sometimes not at all, whether virtue is rewarded or not?

The reason, in this case, is not far to seek. *Measure for Measure* is, like nearly every play of Shakespeare's before *Coriolanus*, essentially realistic. The characters are real men and women; and what happens to them upon the stage has all the effect of what happens to real men and women in actual life. Their goodness appears to be real goodness, their wickedness real wickedness; and, if their sufferings are terrible enough, we regret the fact, even though in the end they triumph, just as we regret the real sufferings of our friends. But, in the plays of the final period, all this has changed; we are no longer in the real world, but in a world of enchantment, of mystery, of wonder, a world of shifting visions, a world of hopeless anachronisms, a world in which anything may happen next. The pretences of reality are indeed usually preserved, but only the pretences. Cymbeline is supposed to be the king of a real Britain, and the real Augustus is supposed to demand tribute of him; but these are the reasons which his queen, in solemn audience with the Roman ambassador, urges to induce her husband to declare for war:

> Remember, sir, my liege,
> The Kings your ancestors, together with
> The natural bravery of your isle, which stands
> As Neptune's park, ribbed and paled in
> With rocks unscaleable and roaring waters,
> With sands that will not bear your enemies' boats,
> But suck them up to the topmast. A kind of conquest
> Caesar made here; but made not here his brag
> Of 'Came, and saw, and overcame'; with shame—The first
> that ever touched him—he was carried
> From off our coast, twice beaten; and his shipping—
> Poor ignorant baubles!—on our terrible seas,
> Like egg-shells moved upon the surges, crack'd
> As easily 'gainst our rocks; for joy whereof
> The famed Cassibelan, who was once at point—

> O giglot fortune!—to master Caesar's sword,
> Made Lud's town with rejoicing fires bright
> And Britons strut with courage.

It comes with something of a shock to remember that this medley of poetry, bombast, and myth will eventually reach the ears of no other person than the Octavius of *Antony and Cleopatra*; and the contrast is the more remarkable when one recalls the brilliant scene of negotiation and diplomacy in the latter play, which passes between Octavius, Maecenas, and Agrippa on the one side, and Antony and Enobarbus on the other, and results in the reconciliation of the rivals and the marriage of Antony and Octavia.

Thus strangely remote is the world of Shakespeare's latest period; and it is peopled, this universe of his invention, with beings equally unreal, with creatures either more or less than human, with fortunate princes and wicked step-mothers, with goblins and spirits, with lost princesses and insufferable kings. And of course, in this sort of fairy land, it is an essential condition that everything shall end well; the prince and princess are bound to marry and live happily ever afterwards, or the whole story is unnecessary and absurd; and the villains and the goblins must naturally repent and be forgiven. But it is clear that such happy endings, such conventional closes to fantastic tales, cannot be taken as evidences of serene tranquillity on the part of their maker; they merely show that he knew, as well as anyone else, how such stories ought to end.

Yet there can be no doubt that it is this combination of charming heroines and happy endings which has blinded the eyes of modern critics to everything else. Iachimo, and Leontes, and even Caliban, are to be left out of account, as if, because in the end they repent or are forgiven, words need not be wasted on such reconciled and harmonious fiends. It is true they are grotesque; it is true that such personages never could have lived; but who, one would like to know, has ever met Miranda, or become acquainted with Prince Florizel of Bohemia? In this land of faery, is it right to neglect the goblins? In this world of dreams, are we justified in ignoring the nightmares? Is it fair to say that Shakespeare was in 'a gentle, lofty spirit, a peaceful, tranquil mood,' when he was creating the Queen in *Cymbeline*, or writing the first two acts of *The Winter's Tale*?

Attention has never been sufficiently drawn to one other characteristic of these plays, though it is touched upon both by Professor Dowden and Dr. Brandes—the singular carelessness with which great parts of them were obviously written. Could anything drag more wretchedly than the *dénouement* of *Cymbeline*? And with what perversity is the great pastoral scene in *The Winter's Tale* interspersed with long-winded intrigues, and disguises, and homilies! For these blemishes are unlike the blemishes which enrich rather than lessen the beauty of the earlier plays; they are not, like them, interesting or delightful in themselves; they are usually merely necessary to explain the action, and they are sometimes purely irrelevant. One is, it cannot be denied, often bored, and occasionally irritated, by Polixenes and Camillo and Sebastian and Gonzalo and Belarius; these personages have not even the life of ghosts; they are hardly more than speaking names, that give patient utterance to involution upon involution. What a contrast to the minor characters of Shakespeare's earlier works!

It is difficult to resist the conclusion that he was getting bored himself. Bored with people, bored with real life, bored with drama, bored, in fact, with everything except poetry and poetical dreams. He is no longer interested, one often feels, in what happens, or who says what, so long as he can find place for a faultless lyric, or a new, unimagined rhythmical effect, or a grand and mystic speech. In this mood he must have written his share in *The Two Noble Kinsmen*, leaving the plot and characters to Fletcher to deal with as he pleased, and reserving to himself only the opportunities for pompous verse. In this mood he must have broken off half-way through the tedious history of *Henry VIII.*; and in this mood he must have completed, with all the resources of his rhetoric, the miserable archaic fragment of *Pericles*.

Is it not thus, then, that we should imagine him in the last years of his life? Half enchanted by visions of beauty and loveliness, and half bored to death; on the one side inspired by a soaring fancy to the singing of ethereal songs, and on the other urged by a general disgust to burst occasionally through his torpor into bitter and violent speech? If we are to learn anything of his mind from his last works, it is surely this.

And such is the conclusion which is particularly forced upon us by a consideration of the play which is in many ways most typical of Shakespeare's later work, and the one which critics most consistently point to as containing the very essence of his final benignity—*The Tempest*. There can be no doubt that the peculiar characteristics which distinguish *Cymbeline* and *The Winter's Tale* from the dramas of Shakespeare's prime, are present here in a still greater degree. In *The Tempest*, unreality has reached its apotheosis. Two of the principal characters are frankly not human beings at all; and the whole action passes, through a series of impossible occurrences, in a place which can only by courtesy be said to exist. The Enchanted Island, indeed, peopled, for a timeless moment, by this strange fantastic medley of persons and of things, has been cut adrift for ever from common sense, and floats, buoyed up by a sea, not of waters, but of poetry. Never did Shakespeare's magnificence of diction reach more marvellous heights than in some of the speeches of Prospero, or his lyric art a purer beauty than in the songs of Ariel; nor is it only in these ethereal regions that the triumph of his language asserts itself. It finds as splendid a vent in the curses of Caliban:

> All the infection that the sun sucks up
> From bogs, fens, flats, on Prosper fall, and make him
> By inch-meal a disease!

and in the similes of Trinculo:

> Yond' same black cloud, yond' huge one, looks like a foul
> bombard that would shed his liquor.

The *dénouement* itself, brought about by a preposterous piece of machinery, and lost in a whirl of rhetoric, is hardly more than a peg for fine writing.

> O, it is monstrous, monstrous!
> Methought the billows spoke and told me of it;
> The winds did sing it to me; and the thunder,
> That deep and dreadful organ-pipe, pronounced
> The name of Prosper; it did bass my trespass.
> Therefore my son i' th' ooze is bedded, and
> I'll seek him deeper than e'er plummet sounded,
> And with him there lie mudded.

And this gorgeous phantasm of a repentance from the mouth of the pale phantom Alonzo is a fitting climax to the whole fantastic play.

A comparison naturally suggests itself, between what was perhaps the last of Shakespeare's completed works, and that early drama which first gave undoubted proof that his imagination had taken wings. The points of resemblance between *The Tempest* and *A Midsummer Night's Dream*, their common atmosphere of romance and magic, the beautiful absurdities of their intrigues, their studied contrasts of the grotesque with the delicate, the ethereal with the earthly, the charm of their lyrics, the *verve* of their vulgar comedy—these, of course, are obvious enough; but it is the points of difference which really make the comparison striking. One thing, at any rate, is certain about the wood near Athens—it is full of life. The persons that haunt it—though most of them are hardly more than children, and some of them are fairies, and all of them are too agreeable to be true—are nevertheless substantial creatures, whose loves and jokes and quarrels receive our thorough sympathy; and the air they breathe—the lords and the ladies, no less than the mechanics and the elves—is instinct with an exquisite good-humour, which makes us as happy as the night is long. To turn from Theseus and Titania and Bottom to the Enchanted Island, is to step out of a country lane into a conservatory. The roses and the dandelions have vanished before preposterous cactuses, and fascinating orchids too delicate for the open air; and, in the artificial atmosphere, the gaiety of youth has been replaced by the disillusionment of middle age. Prospero is the central figure of *The Tempest*; and it has often been wildly asserted that he is a portrait of the author—an embodiment of that spirit of wise benevolence which is supposed to have thrown a halo over Shakespeare's later life. But, on closer inspection, the portrait seems to be as imaginary as the original. To an irreverent eye, the ex-Duke of Milan would perhaps appear as an unpleasantly crusty personage, in whom a twelve years' monopoly of the conversation had developed an inordinate propensity for talking. These may have been the sentiments of Ariel, safe at the Bermoothes; but to state them is to risk at least ten years in the knotty entrails of an oak, and it is sufficient to point out, that if Prospero is wise, he is also self-opinionated and sour, that his gravity is often another name for pedantic severity, and that there is no character in the play to whom, during some part of it, he is not studiously disagreeable. But his Milanese countrymen are not even disagreeable; they are simply dull. 'This is the silliest stuff that e'er I heard,' remarked Hippolyta of Bottom's amateur theatricals; and one is tempted to wonder what she would have said to the dreary puns and interminable conspiracies of Alonzo, and Gonzalo, and Sebastian, and Antonio, and Adrian, and Francisco, and other shipwrecked noblemen. At all events, there can be little doubt that they would not have had the entrée at Athens.

The depth of the gulf between the two plays is, however, best measured by a comparison of Caliban and his masters with Bottom and his companions. The guileless group of English mechanics, whose sports are interrupted by the mischief of Puck, offers a strange contrast to the hideous trio of the 'jester,' the 'drunken butler,' and the 'savage and deformed slave,' whose designs are thwarted by the magic of Ariel. Bottom was the first of Shakespeare's masterpieces in characterisation, Caliban was the last: and what a world of bitterness and horror lies between them! The charming coxcomb it is easy to know and love; but the 'freckled whelp hag-born' moves us mysteriously to pity and to terror, eluding us for ever in fearful allegories, and strange coils of disgusted laughter and phantasmagorical tears. The physical vigour of the presentment is often so remorseless as to shock us. 'I left them,' says Ariel, speaking of Caliban and his crew:

> I' the filthy-mantled pool beyond your cell,
> There dancing up to the chins, that the foul lake
> O'erstunk their feet.

But at other times the great half-human shape seems to swell like the 'Pan' of Victor Hugo, into something unimaginably vast.

> You taught me language, and my profit on't
> Is, I know how to curse.

Is this Caliban addressing Prospero, or Job addressing God? It may be either; but it is not serene, nor benign, nor pastoral, nor 'On the Heights.'

1906.

THE LIVES OF THE POETS[1]

No one needs an excuse for re-opening the *Lives of the Poets*; the book is too delightful. It is not, of course, as delightful as Boswell; but who re-opens Boswell? Boswell is in another category; because, as every one knows, when he has once been opened he can never be shut. But, on its different level, the *Lives* will always hold a firm and comfortable place in our affections. After Boswell, it is the book which brings us nearer than any other to the mind of Dr. Johnson. That is its primary import. We do not go to it for information or for instruction, or that our tastes may be improved, or that our sympathies may be widened; we go to it to see what Dr. Johnson thought. Doubtless, during the process, we are informed and instructed and improved in various ways; but these benefits are incidental, like the invigoration which comes from a mountain walk. It is not for the sake of the exercise that we set out; but for the sake of the view. The view from the mountain which is Samuel Johnson is so familiar, and has been so constantly analysed and admired, that further description would be superfluous. It is sufficient for us to recognise that he is a mountain, and to pay all the reverence that is due. In one of Emerson's poems a mountain and a squirrel begin to discuss each other's merits; and the squirrel comes to the triumphant conclusion that he is very much the better of the two, since he can crack a nut, while the mountain can do no such thing. The parallel is close enough between this impudence and the attitude—implied, if not expressed—of too much modern criticism towards the sort of qualities—the easy, indolent power, the searching sense of actuality, the combined command of sanity and paradox, the immovable independence of thought—which went to the making of the *Lives of the Poets*. There is only, perhaps, one flaw in the analogy: that, in this particular instance, the mountain was able to crack nuts a great deal better than any squirrel that ever lived.

That the *Lives* continue to be read, admired, and edited, is in itself a high proof of the eminence of Johnson's intellect; because, as serious criticism, they can hardly appear to the modern reader to be very far removed from the futile. Johnson's aesthetic judgments are almost invariably subtle, or solid, or bold; they have always some good quality to recommend them—except one: they are never right. That is an unfortunate deficiency; but no one can doubt that Johnson has made up for it, and that his wit has saved all. He has managed to be wrong so cleverly, that nobody minds. When Gray, for instance, points the moral to his poem on Walpole's cat with a reminder to the fair that all that glisters is not gold, Johnson remarks that this is 'of no relation to the purpose; if *what glistered* had been *gold*, the cat would not have gone into the water; and, if she had, would not less have been drowned.' Could anything be more ingenious, or more neatly put, or more obviously true? But then, to use Johnson's own phrase, could anything be of less 'relation to the purpose'? It is his wit—and we are speaking, of course, of wit in its widest sense—that has sanctified Johnson's peversities and errors, that has embalmed them for ever, and that has put his book, with all its mass of antiquated doctrine, beyond the reach of time.

For it is not only in particular details that Johnson's criticism fails to convince us; his entire point of view is patently out of date. Our judgments differ from his, not only because our tastes are different, but because our whole method of judging has changed. Thus, to the historian of letters, the *Lives* have a special interest, for they afford a standing example of a great dead tradition—a tradition whose characteristics throw more than one curious light upon the literary feelings and ways which have become habitual to ourselves. Perhaps the most striking difference between the critical methods of the eighteenth century and those of the present day, is the difference in sympathy. The most cursory glance at Johnson's book is enough to show that he judged authors as if they were criminals in the dock, answerable for every infraction of the rules and regulations laid down by the laws of art, which it was his business to administer without fear or favour. Johnson never inquired what poets were trying to do; he merely aimed at discovering whether what they had done complied with the canons of poetry. Such a system of criticism was clearly unexceptionable, upon one condition—that the critic was quite certain what the canons of poetry were; but the moment that it became obvious that the only way of arriving at a conclusion upon the subject was by consulting the poets themselves, the whole situation completely changed. The judge had to bow to the prisoner's ruling. In other words, the critic discovered that his first duty was, not to criticise, but to understand the object of his criticism. That is the essential distinction between the school of Johnson and the school of Sainte-Beuve. No one can doubt the greater width and profundity of the modern method; but it is not without its drawbacks. An excessive sympathy with one's author brings its own set of errors: the critic is so happy to explain everything, to show how this was the product of the age, how that was the product of environment, and how the other was the inevitable result of inborn qualities and tastes—that he sometimes forgets to mention whether the work in question has any value. It is then that one cannot help regretting the Johnsonian black cap.

But other defects, besides lack of sympathy, mar the *Lives of the Poets*. One cannot help feeling that no matter how anxious Johnson might have been to enter into the spirit of some of the greatest of the masters with whom he was concerned, he never could have succeeded. Whatever critical method he might have adopted, he still would have been unable to appreciate certain literary qualities, which, to our minds at any rate, appear to be the most important of all. His opinion of *Lycidas* is well known: he found that poem 'easy, vulgar, and therefore disgusting.' Of the songs in *Comus* he remarks: 'they are harsh in their diction, and not very musical in their numbers.' He could see nothing in the splendour and elevation of Gray, but 'glittering accumulations of ungraceful ornaments.' The passionate intensity of Donne escaped him altogether; he could only wonder how so ingenious a writer could be so absurd. Such preposterous judgments can only be accounted for by inherent deficiencies of taste; Johnson had no ear, and he had no imagination. These are, indeed, grievous disabilities in a critic. What could have induced such a man, the impatient reader is sometimes tempted to ask, to set himself up as a judge of poetry?

The answer to the question is to be found in the remarkable change which has come over our entire conception of poetry, since the time when Johnson wrote. It has often been stated that the essential characteristic of that great Romantic Movement which began at the end of the eighteenth century, was the re-introduction of Nature into the domain of poetry. Incidentally, it is curious to observe that nearly every literary revolution has been hailed by its supporters as a return to Nature. No less than the school of Coleridge and Wordsworth, the school of Denham, of Dryden, and of Pope, proclaimed itself as the champion of Nature; and there can be little doubt that Donne himself—the father of all the conceits and elaborations of the seventeenth century—wrote under the impulse of a Naturalistic reaction against the conventional classicism of the Renaissance. Precisely the same contradictions took place in France. Nature was the watchword of Malherbe and of Boileau; and it was equally the watchword of Victor Hugo. To judge by the successive proclamations of poets, the development of literature offers a singular paradox. The further it goes back, the more sophisticated it becomes; and it grows more and more natural as it grows distant from the State of Nature. However this may be, it is at least certain that the Romantic revival peculiarly deserves to be called Naturalistic, because it succeeded in bringing into vogue the operations of the external world—'the Vegetable Universe,' as Blake called it—as subject-matter for poetry. But it would have done very little, if it had done nothing more than this. Thomson, in the full meridian of the eighteenth century, wrote poems upon the subject of Nature; but it would be foolish to suppose that Wordsworth and Coleridge merely carried on a fashion which Thomson had begun. Nature, with them, was something more than a peg for descriptive and didactic verse; it was the manifestation of the vast and mysterious forces of the world. The publication of *The Ancient Mariner* is a landmark in the history of letters, not because of its descriptions of natural objects, but because it swept into the poet's vision a whole new universe of infinite and eternal things; it was the discovery of the Unknown. We are still under the spell of *The Ancient Mariner*; and poetry to us means, primarily, something which suggests, by means of words, mysteries and infinitudes. Thus, music and imagination seem to us the most essential qualities of poetry, because they are the most potent means by which such suggestions may be invoked. But the eighteenth century knew none of these things. To Lord Chesterfield and to Pope, to Prior and to Horace Walpole, there was nothing at all strange about the world; it was charming, it was disgusting, it was ridiculous, and it was just what one might have expected. In such a world, why should poetry, more than anything else, be mysterious? No! Let it be sensible; that was enough.

The new edition of the *Lives*, which Dr. Birkbeck Hill prepared for publication before his death, and which has been issued by the Clarendon Press, with a brief Memoir of the editor, would probably have astonished Dr. Johnson. But, though the elaborate erudition of the notes and appendices might have surprised him, it would not have put him to shame. One can imagine his growling scorn of the scientific conscientiousness of the present day. And indeed, the three tomes of Dr. Hill's edition, with all their solid wealth of information, their voluminous scholarship, their accumulation of vast research, are a little ponderous and a little ugly; the hand is soon wearied with the weight, and the eye is soon distracted by the varying types, and the compressed columns of the notes, and the paragraphic numerals in the margins. This is the price that must be paid for increased efficiency. The wise reader will divide his attention between the new business-like edition and one of the charming old ones, in four comfortable volumes, where the text is supreme upon the page, and the paragraphs follow one another at leisurely intervals. The type may be a little faded, and the paper a little yellow; but what of that? It is all quiet and easy; and, as one reads, the brilliant sentences seem to come to one, out of the Past, with the friendliness of a conversation.

1906.

NOTES:

[1] *Lives of the English Poets.* By Samuel Johnson, LL.D. Edited by George Birkbeck Hill, D.C.L. Oxford: at the Clarendon Press, 1905.

MADAME DU DEFFAND[2]

When Napoleon was starting for his campaign in Russia, he ordered the proof-sheets of a forthcoming book, about which there had been some disagreement among the censors of the press, to be put into his carriage, so that he might decide for himself what suppressions it might be necessary to make. 'Je m'ennuie en route; je lirai ces volumes, et j'écrirai de Mayence ce qu'il y aura à faire.' The volumes thus chosen to beguile the imperial leisure between Paris and Mayence contained the famous correspondence of Madame du Deffand with Horace Walpole. By the Emperor's command a few excisions were made, and the book—reprinted from Miss Berry's original edition which had appeared two years earlier in England—was published almost at once. The sensation in Paris was immense; the excitement of the Russian campaign itself was half forgotten; and for some time the blind old inhabitant of the Convent of Saint Joseph held her own as a subject of conversation with the burning of Moscow and the passage of the Berezina. We cannot wonder that this was so. In the Parisian drawing-room of those days the letters of Madame du Deffand must have exercised a double fascination—on the one hand as a mine of gossip about numberless persons and events still familiar to many a living memory, and, on the other, as a detailed and brilliant record of a state of society which had already ceased to be actual and become historical. The letters were hardly more than thirty years old; but the world which they depicted in all its intensity and all its singularity—the world of the old régime—had vanished for ever into limbo. Between it and the eager readers of the First Empire a gulf was fixed—a narrow gulf, but a deep one, still hot and sulphurous with the volcanic fires of the Revolution. Since then a century has passed; the gulf has widened; and the vision which these curious letters show us to-day seems hardly less remote—from some points of view, indeed, even more—than that which is revealed to us in the Memoirs of Cellini or the correspondence of Cicero. Yet the vision is not simply one of a strange and dead antiquity: there is a personal and human element in the letters which gives them a more poignant interest, and brings them close to ourselves. The soul of man is not subject to the rumour of periods; and these pages, impregnated though they be with the abolished life of the eighteenth century, can never be out of date.

A fortunate chance enables us now, for the first time, to appreciate them in their completeness. The late Mrs. Paget Toynbee, while preparing her edition of Horace Walpole's letters, came upon the trace of the original manuscripts, which had long lain hidden in obscurity in a country house in Staffordshire. The publication of these manuscripts in full, accompanied by notes and indexes in which Mrs. Toynbee's well-known accuracy, industry, and tact are everywhere conspicuous, is an event of no small importance to lovers of French literature. A great mass of new and deeply interesting material makes its appearance. The original edition produced by Miss Berry in 1810, from which all the subsequent editions were reprinted with varying degrees of inaccuracy, turns out to have contained nothing more than a comparatively small fraction of the whole correspondence; of the 838 letters published by Mrs. Toynbee, 485 are entirely new, and of the rest only 52 were printed by Miss Berry in their entirety. Miss Berry's edition was, in fact, simply a selection, and as a selection it deserves nothing but praise. It skims the cream of the correspondence; and it faithfully preserves the main outline of the story which the letters reveal. No doubt that was enough for the readers of that generation; indeed, even for the more exacting reader of to-day, there is something a little overwhelming in the closely packed 2000 pages of Mrs. Toynbee's volumes. Enthusiasm alone will undertake to grapple with them, but enthusiasm will be rewarded. In place of the truthful summary of the earlier editions, we have now the truth itself—the truth in all its subtle gradations, all its long-drawn-out suspensions, all its intangible and irremediable obscurities: it is the difference between a clear-cut drawing in black-and-white and a finished painting in oils. Probably Miss Berry's edition will still be preferred by the ordinary reader who wishes to become acquainted with a celebrated figure in French literature; but Mrs. Toynbee's will always be indispensable for the historical student, and invaluable for anyone with the leisure, the patience, and the taste for a detailed and elaborate examination of a singular adventure of the heart.

The Marquise du Deffand was perhaps the most typical representative of that phase of civilisation which came into existence in Western Europe during the early years of the eighteenth century, and reached its most concentrated and characteristic form about the year 1750 in the drawing-rooms of Paris. She was supremely a woman of her age; but it is important to notice that her age was the first, and not the second, half of the eighteenth century: it was the age of the Regent Orleans, Fontenelle, and the young Voltaire; not that of Rousseau, the 'Encyclopaedia,' and the Patriarch of Ferney. It is true that her letters to Walpole, to which her fame is mainly due, were written between 1766 and 1780; but they are the letters of an old woman, and they bear upon every page of them the traces of a mind to which the whole movement of contemporary life was profoundly distasteful. The new forces to which the eighteenth century gave birth in thought, in art, in sentiment, in action—which for us form its peculiar interest and its peculiar glory—were anathema to Madame du Deffand. In her letters to Walpole, whenever she compares the present with the past her bitterness becomes extreme. 'J'ai eu autrefois,' she writes in 1778, 'des plaisirs indicibles aux opéras de Quinault et de Lulli, et au jeu de Thévenart et de la Lemaur. Pour aujourd'hui, tout me paraît détestable: acteurs, auteurs, musiciens, beaux esprits, philosophes, tout est de mauvais goût, tout est affreux, affreux.' That great movement towards intellectual and political emancipation which centred in the 'Encyclopaedia' and the *Philosophes* was the object of her particular detestation. She saw Diderot once—and that was enough for both of them. She could never understand why it was that M. de Voltaire would persist in wasting his talent for writing over such a dreary subject as religion. Turgot, she confessed, was an honest man, but he was also a 'sot animal.' His dismissal from office—that fatal act, which made the French Revolution inevitable—delighted her: she concealed her feelings from Walpole, who admired him, but she was outspoken enough to the Duchesse de Choiseul. 'Le renvoi du Turgot me plaît extrêmement,' she wrote; 'tout me paraît en bon train.' And then she added, more prophetically than she knew, 'Mais, assurément, nous n'en resterons pas là.' No doubt her dislike of the Encyclopaedists and all their works was in part a matter of personal pique—the result of her famous quarrel with Mademoiselle de Lespinasse, under whose opposing banner d'Alembert and all the intellectual leaders of Parisian society had unhesitatingly ranged themselves. But that quarrel was itself far more a symptom of a deeply rooted spiritual antipathy than a mere vulgar struggle for influence between two rival *salonnières*. There are indications that, even before it took place, the elder woman's friendship for d'Alembert was giving way under the strain of her scorn for his advanced views and her hatred of his proselytising cast of mind. 'Il y a de certains articles,' she complained to Voltaire in 1763—a year before the final estrangement—'qui sont devenus pour lui affaires de parti, et sur lesquels je ne lui trouve pas le sens commun.' The truth is that d'Alembert and his friends were moving, and Madame du Deffand was standing still. Mademoiselle de Lespinasse simply precipitated and intensified an inevitable rupture. She was the younger generation knocking at the door.

Madame du Deffand's generation had, indeed, very little in common with that ardent, hopeful, speculative, sentimental group of friends who met together every evening in the drawing-room of Mademoiselle de Lespinasse. Born at the close of the seventeenth century, she had come into the world in the brilliant days of the Regent, whose witty and licentious reign had suddenly dissipated the atmosphere of gloom and bigotry imposed upon society by the moribund Court of Louis XIV. For a fortnight (so she confessed to Walpole) she was actually the Regent's mistress; and a fortnight, in those days, was a considerable time. Then she became the intimate friend of Madame de Prie—the singular woman who, for a moment, on the Regent's death, during the government of M. le Duc, controlled the destinies of France, and who committed suicide when that amusement was denied her. During her early middle age Madame du Deffand was one of the principal figures in the palace of Sceaux, where the Duchesse du Maine, the grand-daughter of the great Condé and the daughter-in-law of Louis XIV., kept up for many years an almost royal state among the most distinguished men and women of the time. It was at Sceaux, with its endless succession of entertainments and conversations—supper-parties and water-parties, concerts and masked balls, plays in the little theatre and picnics under the great trees of the park—that Madame du Deffand came to her maturity and established her position as one of the leaders of the society in which she moved. The nature of that society is plainly enough revealed in the letters and the memoirs that have come down to us. The days of formal pomp and vast representation had ended for ever when the 'Grand Monarque' was no longer to be seen strutting, in periwig and red-heeled shoes, down the glittering gallery of Versailles; the intimacy and seclusion of modern life had not yet begun. It was an intermediate period, and the comparatively small group formed by the elite of the rich, refined, and intelligent classes led an existence in which the elements of publicity and privacy were curiously combined. Never, certainly, before or since, have any set of persons lived so absolutely and unreservedly with and for their friends as these high ladies and gentlemen of the middle years of the eighteenth century. The circle of one's friends was, in those days, the framework of one's whole being; within which was to be found all that life had to offer, and outside of which no interest, however fruitful, no passion, however profound, no art, however soaring, was of the slightest account. Thus while in one sense the ideal of such a society was an eminently selfish one, it is none the less true that there have been very few societies indeed in which the ordinary forms of personal selfishness have played so small a part. The selfishness of the eighteenth century was a communal selfishness. Each individual was expected to practise, and did in fact practise to a consummate degree, those difficult arts which make the wheels of human intercourse run smoothly—the arts of tact and temper, of frankness and sympathy, of delicate compliment and exquisite self-abnegation—with the result that a condition of living was produced which, in all its superficial and obvious qualities, was one of unparalleled amenity. Indeed, those persons who were privileged to enjoy it showed their appreciation of it in an unequivocal way—by the tenacity with which they clung to the scene of such delights and graces. They refused to grow old; they almost refused to die. Time himself seems to have joined their circle, to have been infected with their politeness, and to have absolved them, to the furthest possible point, from the operation of his laws. Voltaire, d'Argental, Moncrif, Hénault, Madame d'Egmont, Madame du Deffand herself—all were born within a few years of each other, and all lived to be well over eighty, with the full zest of their activities unimpaired. Pont-de-Veyle, it is true, died young—at the age of seventy-seven. Another contemporary, Richelieu, who was famous for his adventures while Louis XIV. was still on the throne, lived till within a year of the opening of the States-General. More typical still of this singular and fortunate generation was Fontenelle, who, one morning in his hundredth year, quietly observed that he felt a difficulty in existing, and forthwith, even more quietly, ceased to do so.

Yet, though the wheels of life rolled round with such an alluring smoothness, they did not roll of themselves; the skill and care of trained mechanicians were needed to keep them going; and the task was no light one. Even Fontenelle himself, fitted as he was for it by being blessed (as one of his friends observed) with two brains and no heart, realised to the full the hard conditions of social happiness. 'Il y a peu de choses,' he wrote, 'aussi difficiles et aussi dangereuses que le commerce des hommes.' The sentence, true for all ages, was particularly true for his own. The graceful, easy motions of that gay company were those of dancers balanced on skates, gliding, twirling, interlacing, over the thinnest ice. Those drawing-rooms, those little circles, so charming with the familiarity of their privacy, were themselves the rigorous abodes of the deadliest kind of public opinion—the kind that lives and glitters in a score of penetrating eyes. They required in their votaries the absolute submission that reigns in religious orders—the willing sacrifice of the entire life. The intimacy of personal passion, the intensity of high endeavour—these things must be left behind and utterly cast away by all who would enter that narrow sanctuary. Friendship might be allowed there, and flirtation disguised as love; but the overweening and devouring influence of love itself should never be admitted to destroy the calm of daily intercourse and absorb into a single channel attentions due to all. Politics were to be tolerated, so long as they remained a game; so soon as they grew serious and envisaged the public good, they became insufferable. As for literature and art, though they might be excellent as subjects for recreation and good talk, what could be more preposterous than to treat such trifles as if they had a value of their own? Only one thing; and that was to indulge, in the day-dreams of religion or philosophy, the inward ardours of the soul. Indeed, the scepticism of that generation was the most uncompromising that the world has known; for it did not even trouble to deny: it simply ignored. It presented a blank wall of perfect indifference alike to the mysteries of the universe and to the solutions of them. Madame du Deffand gave early proof that she shared to the full this propensity of her age. While still a young girl in a convent school, she had shrugged her shoulders when the nuns began to instruct her in the articles of their faith. The matter was considered serious, and the great Massillon, then at the height of his fame as a preacher and a healer of souls, was sent for to deal with the youthful heretic. She was not impressed by his arguments. In his person the generous fervour and the massive piety of an age that could still believe felt the icy and disintegrating touch of a new and strange indifference. 'Mais qu'elle est jolie!' he murmured as he came away. The Abbess ran forward to ask what holy books he recommended. 'Give her a threepenny Catechism,' was Massillon's reply. He had seen that the case was hopeless.

An innate scepticism, a profound levity, an antipathy to enthusiasm that wavered between laughter and disgust, combined with an unswerving devotion to the exacting and arduous ideals of social intercourse—such were the characteristics of the brilliant group of men and women who had spent their youth at the Court of the Regent, and dallied out their middle age down the long avenues of Sceaux. About the middle of the century the Duchesse du Maine died, and Madame du Deffand established herself in Paris at the Convent of Saint Joseph in a set of rooms which still showed traces—in the emblazoned arms over the great mantelpiece—of the occupation of Madame de Montespan. A few years later a physical affliction overtook her: at the age of fifty-seven she became totally blind; and this misfortune placed her, almost without a transition, among the ranks of the old. For the rest of her life she hardly moved from her drawing-room, which speedily became the most celebrated in Europe. The thirty years of her reign there fall into two distinct and almost equal parts. The first, during which d'Alembert was pre-eminent, came to an end with the violent expulsion of Mademoiselle de Lespinasse. During the second, which lasted for the rest of her life, her salon, purged of the Encyclopaedists, took on a more decidedly worldly tone; and the influence of Horace Walpole was supreme.

It is this final period of Madame du Deffand's life that is reflected so minutely in the famous correspondence which the labours of Mrs. Toynbee have now presented to us for the first time in its entirety. Her letters to Walpole form in effect a continuous journal covering the space of fifteen years (1766-1780). They allow us, on the one hand, to trace through all its developments the progress of an extraordinary passion, and on the other to examine, as it were under the microscope of perhaps the bitterest perspicacity on record, the last phase of a doomed society. For the circle which came together in her drawing-room during those years had the hand of death upon it. The future lay elsewhere; it was simply the past that survived there—in the rich trappings of fashion and wit and elaborate gaiety—but still irrevocably the past. The radiant creatures of Sceaux had fallen into the yellow leaf. We see them in these letters, a collection of elderly persons trying hard to amuse themselves, and not succeeding very well. Pont-de-Veyle, the youthful septuagenarian, did perhaps succeed; for he never noticed what a bore he was becoming with his perpetual cough, and continued to go the rounds with indefatigable animation, until one day his cough was heard no more. Hénault—once notorious for his dinner-parties, and for having written an historical treatise—which, it is true, was worthless, but he had written it—Hénault was beginning to dodder, and Voltaire, grinning in Ferney, had already dubbed him 'notre délabré Président.' Various dowagers were engaged upon various vanities. The Marquise de Boufflers was gambling herself to ruin; the Comtesse de Boufflers was wringing out the last drops of her reputation as the mistress of a Royal Prince; the Maréchale de Mirepoix was involved in shady politics; the Maréchale de Luxembourg was obliterating a highly dubious past by a scrupulous attention to 'bon ton,' of which, at last, she became the arbitress: 'Quel ton! Quel effroyable ton!' she is said to have exclaimed after a shuddering glance at the Bible; 'ah, Madame, quel dommage que le Saint Esprit eût aussi peu de goût!' Then there was the floating company of foreign diplomats, some of whom were invariably to be found at Madame du Deffand's: Caraccioli, for instance, the Neapolitan Ambassador—'je perds les trois quarts de ce qu'il dit,' she wrote, 'mais comme il en dit beaucoup, on peut supporter cette perte'; and Bernstorff, the Danish envoy, who became the fashion, was lauded to the skies for his wit and fine manners, until, says the malicious lady, 'à travers tous ces éloges, je m'avisai de l'appeler Puffendorf,' and Puffendorf the poor man remained for evermore. Besides the diplomats, nearly every foreign traveller of distinction found his way to the renowned *salon*; Englishmen were particularly frequent visitors; and among the familiar figures of whom we catch more than one glimpse in the letters to Walpole are Burke, Fox, and Gibbon. Sometimes influential parents in England obtained leave for their young sons to be admitted into the centre of Parisian refinement. The English cub, fresh from Eton, was introduced by his tutor into the red and yellow drawing-room, where the great circle of a dozen or more elderly important persons, glittering in jewels and orders, pompous in powder and rouge, ranged in rigid order round the fireplace, followed with the precision of a perfect orchestra the leading word or smile or nod of an ancient Sibyl, who seemed to survey the company with her eyes shut, from a vast chair by the wall. It is easy to imagine the scene, in all its terrifying politeness. Madame du Deffand could not tolerate young people; she declared that she did not know what to say to them; and they, no doubt, were in precisely the same difficulty. To an English youth, unfamiliar with the language and shy as only English youths can be, a conversation with that redoubtable old lady must have been a grim ordeal indeed. One can almost hear the stumbling, pointless observations, almost see the imploring looks cast, from among the infinitely attentive company, towards the tutor, and the pink ears growing still more pink. But such awkward moments were rare. As a rule the days flowed on in easy monotony—or rather, not the days, but the nights. For Madame du Deffand rarely rose till five o'clock in the evening; at six she began her reception; and at nine or half-past the central moment of the twenty-four hours arrived—the moment of supper. Upon this event the whole of her existence hinged. Supper, she used to say, was one of the four ends of man, and what the other three were she could never remember. She lived up to her dictum. She had an income of £1400 a year, and of this she spent more than half—£720—on food. These figures should be largely increased to give them their modern values; but, economise as she might, she found that she could only just manage to rub along. Her parties varied considerably in size; sometimes only four or five persons sat down to supper—sometimes twenty or thirty. No doubt they were elaborate meals. In a moment of economy we find the hospitable lady making pious resolutions: she would no longer give 'des repas'—only ordinary suppers for six people at the most, at which there should be served nothing more than two entrées, one roast, two sweets, and—mysterious addition—'la pièce du milieu.' This was certainly moderate for those days (Monsieur de Jonsac rarely provided fewer than fourteen entrées), but such resolutions did not last long. A week later she would suddenly begin to issue invitations wildly, and, day after day, her tables would be loaded with provisions for thirty guests. But she did not always have supper at home. From time to time she sallied forth in her vast coach and rattled through the streets of Paris to one of her still extant dowagers—a Maréchale, or a Duchesse—or the more and more 'délabré Président.' There the same company awaited her as that which met in her own house; it was simply a change of decorations; often enough for weeks together she had supper every night with the same half-dozen persons. The entertainment, apart from the supper itself, hardly varied. Occasionally there was a little music, more often there were cards and gambling. Madame du Deffand disliked gambling, but she loathed going to bed, and, if it came to a choice between the two, she did not hesitate: once, at the age of seventy-three, she sat up till seven o'clock in the morning playing vingt-et-un with Charles Fox. But distractions of that kind were merely incidental to the grand business of the night—the conversation. In the circle that, after an eight hours' sitting, broke up reluctantly at two or three every morning to meet again that same evening at six, talk continually flowed. For those strange creatures it seemed to form the very substance of life itself. It was the underlying essence, the circumambient ether, in which alone the pulsations of existence had their being; it was the one eternal reality; men might come and men might go, but talk went on for ever. It is difficult, especially for those born under the Saturnine influence of an English sky, quite to realise the nature of such conversation. Brilliant, charming, easy-flowing, gay and rapid it must have been; never profound, never intimate, never thrilling; but also never emphatic, never affected, never languishing, and never dull. Madame du Deffand herself had a most vigorous flow of language. 'Écoutez! Écoutez!' Walpole used constantly to exclaim, trying to get in his points; but in vain; the sparkling cataract swept on unheeding. And indeed to listen was the wiser part—to drink in deliciously the animation of those quick, illimitable, exquisitely articulated syllables, to surrender one's whole soul to the pure and penetrating precision of those phrases, to follow without a breath the happy swiftness of that fine-spun thread of thought. Then at moments her wit crystallised; the cataract threw off a shower of radiant jewels, which one caught as one might. Some of these have come down to us. Her remark on Montesquieu's great book— 'C'est de l'esprit sur les lois'—is an almost final criticism. Her famous 'mot de Saint Denis,' so dear to the heart of Voltaire, deserves to be once more recorded. A garrulous and credulous Cardinal was describing the martyrdom of Saint Denis the Areopagite: when his head was cut off, he took it up and carried it in his hands. That, said the Cardinal, was well known; what was not well known was the extraordinary fact that he walked with his head under his arm all the way from Montmartre to the Church of Saint Denis—a distance of six miles. 'Ah, Monseigneur!' said Madame du Deffand, 'dans une telle situation, il n'y a que le premier pas qui coûte.' At two o'clock the brilliance began to flag; the guests began to go; the dreadful moment was approaching. If Madame de Gramont happened to be there, there was still some hope, for Madame de Gramont abhorred going to bed almost as much as Madame du Deffand. Or there was just a chance that the Duc de Choiseul might come in at the last moment, and stay on for a couple of hours. But at length it was impossible to hesitate any longer; the chariot was at the door. She swept off, but it was still early; it was only half-past three; and the coachman was ordered to drive about the Boulevards for an hour before going home.

It was, after all, only natural that she should put off going to bed, for she rarely slept for more than two or three hours. The greater part of that empty time, during which conversation was impossible, she devoted to her books. But she hardly ever found anything to read that she really enjoyed. Of the two thousand volumes she possessed—all bound alike, and stamped on the back with her device of a cat—she had only read four or five hundred; the rest were impossible. She perpetually complained to Walpole of the extreme dearth of reading matter. In nothing, indeed, is the contrast more marked between that age and ours than in the quantity of books available for the ordinary reader. How the eighteenth century would envy us our innumerable novels, our biographies, our books of travel, all our easy approaches to knowledge and entertainment, our translations, our cheap reprints! In those days, even for a reader of catholic tastes, there was really very little to read. And, of course, Madame du Deffand's tastes were far from catholic—they were fastidious to the last degree. She considered that Racine alone of writers had reached perfection, and that only once—in *Athalie*. Corneille carried her away for moments, but on the whole he was barbarous. She highly admired 'quelques centaines de vers de M. de Voltaire.' She thought Richardson and Fielding excellent, and she was enraptured by the style—but only by the style—of *Gil Blas*. And that was all. Everything else appeared to her either affected or pedantic or insipid. Walpole recommended to her a History of Malta; she tried it, but she soon gave it up—it mentioned the Crusades. She began Gibbon, but she found him superficial. She tried Buffon, but he was 'd'une monotonie insupportable; il sait bien ce qu'il sait, mais il ne s'occupe que des bêtes; il faut l'être un peu soi-même pour se dévouer à une telle occupation.' She got hold of the memoirs of Saint-Simon in manuscript, and these amused her enormously; but she was so disgusted by the style that she was very nearly sick. At last, in despair, she embarked on a prose translation of Shakespeare. The result was unexpected; she was positively pleased. *Coriolanus*, it is true, 'me semble, sauf votre respect, épouvantable, et n'a pas le sens commun'; and 'pour *La Tempête*, je ne suis pas touchée de ce genre.' But she was impressed by *Othello*; she was interested by *Macbeth*; and she admired *Julius Caesar*, in spite of its bad taste. At *King Lear*, indeed, she had to draw the line. 'Ah, mon Dieu! Quelle pièce! Réellement la trouvez-vous belle? Elle me noircit l'âme à un point que je ne puis exprimer; c'est un amas de toutes les horreurs infernales.' Her reader was an old soldier from the Invalides, who came round every morning early, and took up his position by her bedside. She lay back among the cushions, listening, for long hours. Was there ever a more incongruous company, a queerer trysting-place, for Goneril and Desdemona, Ariel and Lady Macbeth?

Often, even before the arrival of the old pensioner, she was at work dictating a letter, usually to Horace Walpole, occasionally to Madame de Choiseul or Voltaire. Her letters to Voltaire are enchanting; his replies are no less so; and it is much to be regretted that the whole correspondence has never been collected together in chronological order, and published as a separate book. The slim volume would be, of its kind, quite perfect. There was no love lost between the two old friends; they could not understand each other; Voltaire, alone of his generation, had thrown himself into the very vanguard of thought; to Madame du Deffand progress had no meaning, and thought itself was hardly more than an unpleasant necessity. She distrusted him profoundly, and he returned the compliment. Yet neither could do without the other: through her, he kept in touch with one of the most influential circles in Paris; and even she could not be insensible to the glory of corresponding with such a man. Besides, in spite of all their differences, they admired each other genuinely, and they were held together by the habit of a long familiarity. The result was a marvellous display of epistolary art. If they had liked each other any better, they never would have troubled to write so well. They were on their best behaviour—exquisitely courteous and yet punctiliously at ease, like dancers in a minuet. His cajoleries are infinite; his deft sentences, mingling flattery with reflection, have almost the quality of a caress. She replies in the tone of a worshipper, glancing lightly at a hundred subjects, purring out her 'Monsieur de Voltaire,' and seeking his advice on literature and life. He rejoins in that wonderful strain of epicurean stoicism of which he alone possessed the secret: and so the letters go on. Sometimes one just catches the glimpse of a claw beneath the soft pad, a grimace under the smile of elegance; and one remembers with a shock that, after all, one is reading the correspondence of a monkey and a cat.

Madame du Deffand's style reflects, perhaps even more completely than that of Voltaire himself, the common-sense of the eighteenth century. Its precision is absolute. It is like a line drawn in one stroke by a master, with the prompt exactitude of an unerring subtlety. There is no breadth in it—no sense of colour and the concrete mass of things. One cannot wonder, as one reads her, that she hardly regretted her blindness. What did she lose by it? Certainly not

> The sweet approach of even or morn,
> Or sight of vernal bloom, or Summer's rose;

for what did she care for such particulars when her eyes were at their clearest? Her perception was intellectual; and to the penetrating glances of her mental vision the objects of the sensual world were mere irrelevance. The kind of writing produced by such a quality of mind may seem thin and barren to those accustomed to the wealth and variety of the Romantic school. Yet it will repay attention. The vocabulary is very small; but every word is the right one; this old lady of high society, who had never given a thought to her style, who wrote—and spelt—by the light of nature, was a past mistress of that most difficult of literary accomplishments—'l'art de dire en un mot tout ce qu'un mot peut dire.' The object of all art is to make suggestions. The romantic artist attains that end by using a multitude of different stimuli, by calling up image after image, recollection after recollection, until the reader's mind is filled and held by a vivid and palpable evocation; the classic works by the contrary method of a fine economy, and, ignoring everything but what is essential, trusts, by means of the exact propriety of his presentation, to produce the required effect. Madame du Deffand carries the classical ideal to its furthest point. She never strikes more than once, and she always hits the nail on the head. Such is her skill that she sometimes seems to beat the Romantics even on their own ground: her reticences make a deeper impression than all the dottings of their i's. The following passage from a letter to Walpole is characteristic:

> Nous eûmes une musique charmante, une dame qui joue de la harpe à merveille; elle me fit tant de plaisir que j'eus du regret que vous ne l'entendissiez pas; c'est un instrument admirable. Nous eûmes aussi un clavecin, mais quoiqu'il fût touché avec une grande perfection, ce n'est rien en comparaison de la harpe. Je fus fort triste toute la soirée; j'avais appris en partant que Mme. de Luxembourg, qui était allée samedi à Montmorency pour y passer quinze jours, s'était trouvée si mal qu'on avait fait venir Tronchin, et qu'on l'avait ramenée le dimanche à huit heures du soir, qu'on lui croyait de l'eau dans la poitrine. L'ancienneté de la connaissance; une habitude qui a l'air de l'amitié; voir disparaître ceux avec qui l'on vit; un retour sur soi-même; sentir que l'on ne tient à rien, que tout fuit, que tout échappe, qu'on reste seule dans l'univers, et que malgré cela on craint de le quitter; voilà ce qui m'occupa pendant la musique.

Here are no coloured words, no fine phrases—only the most flat and ordinary expressions—'un instrument admirable'—'une grande perfection'—'fort triste.' Nothing is described; and yet how much is suggested! The whole scene is conjured up—one does not know how; one's imagination is switched on to the right rails, as it were, by a look, by a gesture, and then left to run of itself. In the simple, faultless rhythm of that closing sentence, the trembling melancholy of the old harp seems to be lingering still.

While the letters to Voltaire show us nothing but the brilliant exterior of Madame du Deffand's mind, those to Walpole reveal the whole state of her soul. The revelation is not a pretty one. Bitterness, discontent, pessimism, cynicism, boredom, regret, despair—these are the feelings that dominate every page. To a superficial observer Madame du Deffand's lot must have seemed peculiarly enviable; she was well off, she enjoyed the highest consideration, she possessed intellectual talents of the rarest kind which she had every opportunity of displaying, and she was surrounded by a multitude of friends. What more could anyone desire? The harsh old woman would have smiled grimly at such a question. 'A little appetite,' she might have answered. She was like a dyspeptic at a feast; the finer the dishes that were set before her, the greater her distaste; that spiritual gusto which lends a savour to the meanest act of living, and without which all life seems profitless, had gone from her for ever. Yet—and this intensified her wretchedness—though the banquet was loathsome to her, she had not the strength to tear herself away from the table. Once, in a moment of desperation, she had thoughts of retiring to a convent, but she soon realised that such an action was out of the question. Fate had put her into the midst of the world, and there she must remain. 'Je ne suis point assez heureuse,' she said, 'de me passer des choses dont je ne me soucie pas.' She was extremely lonely. As fastidious in friendship as in literature, she passed her life among a crowd of persons whom she disliked and despised, 'Je ne vois que des sots et des fripons,' she said; and she did not know which were the most disgusting. She took a kind of deadly pleasure in analysing 'les nuances des sottises' among the people with whom she lived. The varieties were many, from the foolishness of her companion, Mademoiselle Sanadon, who would do nothing but imitate her—'elle fait des définitions,' she wails—to that of the lady who hoped to prove her friendship by unending presents of grapes and pears—'comme je n'y tâte pas, cela diminue mes scrupules du peu de goût que j'ai pour elle.' Then there were those who were not quite fools but something very near it. 'Tous les Matignon sont des sots,' said somebody one day to the Regent, 'excepté le Marquis de Matignon.' 'Cela est vrai,' the Regent replied, 'il n'est pas sot, mais on voit bien qu'il est le fils d'un sot.' Madame du Deffand was an expert at tracing such affinities. For instance, there was Necker. It was clear that Necker was not a fool, and yet—what was it? Something was the matter—yes, she had it: he made you feel a fool yourself—'l'on est plus bête avec lui que l'on ne l'est tout seul.' As she said of herself: 'elle est toujours tentée d'arracher les masques qu'elle rencontre.' Those blind, piercing eyes of hers spied out unerringly the weakness or the ill-nature or the absurdity that lurked behind the gravest or the most fascinating exterior; then her fingers began to itch, and she could resist no longer—she gave way to her besetting temptation. It is impossible not to sympathise with Rousseau's remark about her—'J'aimai mieux encore m'exposer au fléau de sa haine qu'à celui de son amitié.' There, sitting in her great Diogenes-tub of an armchair—her 'tonneau' as she called it—talking, smiling, scattering her bons mots, she went on through the night, in the remorseless secrecy of her heart, tearing off the masks from the faces that surrounded her. Sometimes the world in which she lived displayed itself before her horrified inward vision like some intolerable and meaningless piece of clock-work mechanism:

> J'admirais hier au soir la nombreuse compagnie qui était chez moi; hommes et femmes me paraissaient des machines à ressorts, qui allaient, venaient, parlaient, riaient, sans penser, sans réfléchir, sans sentir; chacun jouait son rôle par habitude: Madame la Duchesse d'Aiguillon crevait de rire, Mme. de Forcalquier dédaignait tout, Mme. de la Vallière jabotait sur tout. Les hommes ne jouaient pas de meilleurs rôles, et moi j'étais abîmée dans les réflexions les plus noires; je pensai que j'avais passé ma vie dans les illusions; que je m'étais creusée tous les abîmes dans lesquels j'étais tombée.

At other times she could see around her nothing but a mass of mutual hatreds, into which she was plunged herself no less than her neighbours:

> Je ramenai la Maréchale de Mirepoix chez elle; j'y descendis, je causai une heure avec elle; je n'en fus pas mécontente. Elle hait la petite Idole, elle hait la Maréchale de Luxembourg; enfin, sa haine pour tous les gens qui me déplaisent me fit lui pardonner l'indifférence et peut-être la haine qu'elle a pour moi. Convenez que voilà une jolie société, un charmant commerce.

Once or twice for several months together she thought that she had found in the Duchesse de Choiseul a true friend and a perfect companion. But there was one fatal flaw even in Madame de Choiseul: she *was* perfect!—'Elle est parfaite; et c'est un plus grand défaut qu'on ne pense et qu'on ne saurait imaginer.' At last one day the inevitable happened—she went to see Madame de Choiseul, and she was bored. 'Je rentrai chez moi à une heure, pénétrée, persuadée qu'on ne peut être content de personne.'

One person, however, there was who pleased her; and it was the final irony of her fate that this very fact should have been the last drop that caused the cup of her unhappiness to overflow. Horace Walpole had come upon her at a psychological moment. Her quarrel with Mademoiselle de Lespinasse and the Encyclopaedists had just occurred; she was within a few years of seventy; and it must have seemed to her that, after such a break, at such an age, there was little left for her to do but to die quietly. Then the gay, talented, fascinating Englishman appeared, and she suddenly found that, so far from her life being over, she was embarked for good and all upon her greatest adventure. What she experienced at that moment was something like a religious conversion. Her past fell away from her a dead thing; she was overwhelmed by an ineffable vision; she, who had wandered for so many years in the ways of worldly indifference, was uplifted all at once on to a strange summit, and pierced with the intensest pangs of an unknown devotion. Henceforward her life was dedicated; but, unlike the happier saints of a holier persuasion, she was to find no peace on earth. It was, indeed, hardly to be expected that Walpole, a blasé bachelor of fifty, should have reciprocated so singular a passion; yet he might at least have treated it with gentleness and respect. The total impression of him which these letters produce is very damaging. It is true that he was in a difficult position; and it is also true that, since only the merest fragments of his side of the correspondence have been preserved, our knowledge of the precise details of his conduct is incomplete; nevertheless, it is clear that, on the whole, throughout the long and painful episode, the principal motive which actuated him was an inexcusable egoism. He was obsessed by a fear of ridicule. He knew that letters were regularly opened at the French Post Office, and he lived in terror lest some spiteful story of his absurd relationship with a blind old woman of seventy should be concocted and set afloat among his friends, or his enemies, in England, which would make him the laughing-stock of society for the rest of his days. He was no less terrified by the intensity of the sentiment of which he had become the object. Thoroughly superficial and thoroughly selfish, immersed in his London life of dilettantism and gossip, the weekly letters from France with their burden of a desperate affection appalled him and bored him by turns. He did not know what to do; and his perplexity was increased by the fact that he really liked Madame du Deffand—so far as he could like anyone—and also by the fact that his vanity was highly flattered by her letters. Many courses were open to him, but the one he took was probably the most cruel that he could have taken: he insisted with an absolute rigidity on their correspondence being conducted in the tone of the most ordinary friendship—on those terms alone, he said, would he consent to continue it. And of course such terms were impossible to Madame du Deffand. She accepted them—what else could she do?—but every line she wrote was a denial of them. Then, periodically, there was an explosion. Walpole stormed, threatened, declared he would write no more; and on her side there were abject apologies, and solemn promises of amendment. Naturally, it was all in vain. A few months later he would be attacked by a fit of the gout, her solicitude would be too exaggerated, and the same fury was repeated, and the same submission. One wonders what the charm could have been that held that proud old spirit in such a miserable captivity. Was it his very coldness that subdued her? If he had cared for her a little more, perhaps she would have cared for him a good deal less. But it is clear that what really bound her to him was the fact that they so rarely met. If he had lived in Paris, if he had been a member of her little clique, subject to the unceasing searchlight of her nightly scrutiny, who can doubt that, sooner or later, Walpole too would have felt 'le fléau de son amitié'? His mask, too, would have been torn to tatters like the rest. But, as it was, his absence saved him; her imagination clothed him with an almost mythic excellence; his brilliant letters added to the impression; and then, at intervals of about two years, he appeared in Paris for six weeks— just long enough to rivet her chains, and not long enough to loosen them. And so it was that she fell before him with that absolute and unquestioning devotion of which only the most dominating and fastidious natures are capable. Once or twice, indeed, she did attempt a revolt, but only succeeded in plunging herself into a deeper subjection. After one of his most violent and cruel outbursts, she refused to communicate with him further, and for three or four weeks she kept her word; then she crept back and pleaded for forgiveness. Walpole graciously granted it. It is with some satisfaction that one finds him, a few weeks later, laid up with a peculiarly painful attack of the gout.

About half-way through the correspondence there is an acute crisis, after which the tone of the letters undergoes a marked change. After seven years of struggle, Madame du Deffand's indomitable spirit was broken; henceforward she would hope for nothing; she would gratefully accept the few crumbs that might be thrown her; and for the rest she resigned herself to her fate. Gradually sinking into extreme old age, her self-repression and her bitterness grew ever more and more complete. She was always bored; and her later letters are a series of variations on the perpetual theme of 'ennui.' 'C'est une maladie de l'âme,' she says, 'dont nous afflige la nature en nous donnant l'existence; c'est le ver solitaire qui absorbe tout.' And again, 'l'ennui est l'avant-goût du néant, mais le néant lui est préférable.' Her existence had become a hateful waste—a garden, she said, from which all the flowers had been uprooted and which had been sown with salt. 'Ah! Je le répète sans cesse, il n'y a qu'un malheur, celui d'être né.' The grasshopper had become a burden; and yet death seemed as little desirable as life. 'Comment est-il possible,' she asks, 'qu'on craigne la fin d'une vie aussi triste?' When Death did come at last, he came very gently. She felt his approaches, and dictated a letter to Walpole, bidding him, in her strange fashion, an infinitely restrained farewell: 'Divertissez-vous, mon ami, le plus que vous pourrez; ne vous affligez point de mon état, nous étions presque perdus l'un pour l'autre; nous ne nous devions jamais revoir; vous me regretterez, parce qu'on est bien aise de se savoir aimé.' That was her last word to him. Walpole might have reached her before she finally lost consciousness, but, though he realised her condition and knew well enough what his presence would have been to her, he did not trouble to move. She died as she had lived—her room crowded with acquaintances and the sound of a conversation in her ears. When one reflects upon her extraordinary tragedy, when one attempts to gauge the significance of her character and of her life, it is difficult to know whether to pity most, to admire, or to fear. Certainly there is something at once pitiable and magnificent in such an unflinching perception of the futilities of living, such an uncompromising refusal to be content with anything save the one thing that it is impossible to have. But there is something alarming too; was she perhaps right after all?

NOTES:

[2] *Lettres de la Marquise du Deffand à Horace Walpole* (1766-80). Première Edition complète, augmentée d'environ 500 Lettres inédites, publiées, d'après les originaux, avec une introduction, des notes, et une table des noms, par Mrs. Paget Toynbee. 3 vols. Methuen, 1912.

VOLTAIRE AND ENGLAND[3]

The visit of Voltaire to England marks a turning-point in the history of civilisation. It was the first step in a long process of interaction—big with momentous consequences—between the French and English cultures. For centuries the combined forces of mutual ignorance and political hostility had kept the two nations apart: Voltaire planted a small seed of friendship which, in spite of a thousand hostile influences, grew and flourished mightily. The seed, no doubt, fell on good ground, and no doubt, if Voltaire had never left his native country, some chance wind would have carried it over the narrow seas, so that history in the main would have been unaltered. But actually his was the hand which did the work.

It is unfortunate that our knowledge of so important a period in Voltaire's life should be extremely incomplete. Carlyle, who gave a hasty glance at it in his life of Frederick, declared that he could find nothing but 'mere inanity and darkness visible'; and since Carlyle's day the progress has been small. A short chapter in Desnoiresterres' long Biography and an essay by Churton Collins did something to co-ordinate the few known facts. Another step was taken a few years ago with the publication of M. Lanson's elaborate and exhaustive edition of the *Lettres Philosophiques*, the work in which Voltaire gave to the world the distilled essence of his English experiences. And now M. Lucien Foulet has brought together all the extant letters concerning the period, which he has collated with scrupulous exactitude and to which he has added a series of valuable appendices upon various obscure and disputed points. M. Lanson's great attainments are well known, and to say that M. Foulet's work may fitly rank as a supplementary volume to the edition of the *Lettres Philosophiques* is simply to say that he is a worthy follower of that noble tradition of profound research and perfect lucidity which has made French scholarship one of the glories of European culture.

Upon the events in particular which led up to Voltaire's departure for England, M. Foulet has been able to throw considerable light. The story, as revealed by the letters of contemporary observers and the official documents of the police, is an instructive and curious one. In the early days of January 1726 Voltaire, who was thirty-one years of age, occupied a position which, so far as could be seen upon the surface, could hardly have been more fortunate. He was recognised everywhere as the rising poet of the day; he was a successful dramatist; he was a friend of Madame de Prie, who was all-powerful at Court, and his talents had been rewarded by a pension from the royal purse. His brilliance, his gaiety, his extraordinary capacity for being agreeable had made him the pet of the narrow and aristocratic circle which dominated France. Dropping his middle-class antecedents as completely as he had dropped his middle-class name, young Arouet, the notary's offspring, floated at his ease through the palaces of dukes and princes, with whose sons he drank and jested, and for whose wives—it was *de rigueur* in those days—he expressed all the ardours of a passionate and polite devotion. Such was his roseate situation when, all at once, the catastrophe came. One night at the Opéra the Chevalier de Rohan-Chabot, of the famous and powerful family of the Rohans, a man of forty-three, quarrelsome, blustering, whose reputation for courage left something to be desired, began to taunt the poet upon his birth—'Monsieur Arouet, Monsieur Voltaire—what *is* your name?' To which the retort came quickly—'Whatever my name may be, I know how to preserve the honour of it.' The Chevalier muttered something and went off, but the incident was not ended. Voltaire had let his high spirits and his sharp tongue carry him too far, and he was to pay the penalty. It was not an age in which it was safe to be too witty with lords. 'Now mind, Dancourt,' said one of those *grands seigneurs* to the leading actor of the day, 'if you're more amusing than I am at dinner to-night, *je te donnerai cent coups de bâtons.*' It was dangerous enough to show one's wits at all in the company of such privileged persons, but to do so at their expense——! A few days later Voltaire and the Chevalier met again, at the Comédie, in Adrienne Lecouvreur's dressing-room. Rohan repeated his sneering question, and 'the Chevalier has had his answer' was Voltaire's reply. Furious, Rohan lifted his stick, but at that moment Adrienne very properly fainted, and the company dispersed. A few days more and Rohan had perfected the arrangements for his revenge. Voltaire, dining at the Duc de Sully's, where, we are told, he was on the footing of a son of the house, received a message that he was wanted outside in the street. He went out, was seized by a gang of lackeys, and beaten before the eyes of Rohan, who directed operations from a cab. 'Epargnez la tête,' he shouted, 'elle est encore bonne pour faire rire le public'; upon which, according to one account, there were exclamations from the crowd which had gathered round of 'Ah! le bon seigneur!' The sequel is known to everyone: how Voltaire rushed back, dishevelled and agonised, into Sully's dining-room, how he poured out his story in an agitated flood of words, and how that high-born company, with whom he had been living up to that moment on terms of the closest intimacy, now only displayed the signs of a frigid indifference. The caste-feeling had suddenly asserted itself. Poets, no doubt, were all very well in their way, but really, if they began squabbling with noblemen, what could they expect? And then the callous and stupid convention of that still half-barbarous age—the convention which made misfortune the proper object of ridicule—came into play no less powerfully. One might take a poet seriously, perhaps—until he was whipped; then, of course, one could only laugh at him. For the next few days, wherever Voltaire went he was received with icy looks, covert smiles, or exaggerated politeness. The Prince de Conti, who, a month or two before, had written an ode in which he placed the author of *Oedipe* side by side with the authors of *Le Cid* and *Phèdre*, now remarked, with a shrug of the shoulders, that 'ces coups de bâtons étaient bien reçus et mal donnés.' 'Nous serions bien malheureux,' said another well-bred personage, as he took a pinch of snuff, 'si les poètes n'avaient pas des épaules.' Such friends as remained faithful were helpless. Even Madame de Prie could do nothing. 'Le pauvre Voltaire me fait grande pitié,' she said; 'dans le fond il a raison.' But the influence of the Rohan family was too much for her, and she could only advise him to disappear for a little into the country, lest worse should befall. Disappear he did, remaining for the next two months concealed in the outskirts of Paris, where he practised swordsmanship against his next meeting with his enemy. The situation was cynically topsy-turvy. As M. Foulet points out, Rohan had legally rendered himself liable, under the edict against duelling, to a long term of imprisonment, if not to the penalty of death. Yet the law did not move, and Voltaire was left to take the only course open in those days to a man of honour in such circumstances—to avenge the insult by a challenge and a fight. But now the law, which had winked at Rohan, began to act against Voltaire. The police were instructed to arrest him so soon as he should show any sign of an intention to break the peace. One day he suddenly appeared at Versailles, evidently on the lookout for Rohan, and then as suddenly vanished. A few weeks later, the police reported that he was in Paris, lodging with a fencing-master, and making no concealment of his desire to 'insulter incessamment et avec éclat M. le chevalier de Rohan.' This decided the authorities, and accordingly on the night of the 17th of April, as we learn from the *Police Gazette*, 'le sieur Arrouët de Voltaire, fameux poète,' was arrested, and conducted 'par ordre du Roi' to the Bastille.

A letter, written by Voltaire to his friend Madame de Bernières while he was still in hiding, reveals the effect which these events had produced upon his mind. It is the first letter in the series of his collected correspondence which is not all Epicurean elegance and caressing wit. The wit, the elegance, the finely turned phrase, the shifting smile—these things are still visible there no doubt, but they are informed and overmastered by a new, an almost ominous spirit: Voltaire, for the first time in his life, is serious.

> J'ai été à l'extrémité; je n'attends que ma convalescence pour abandonner à jamais ce pays-ci. Souvenez-vous de l'amitié tendre que vous avez eue pour moi; au nom de cette amitié informez-moi par un mot de votre main de ce qui se passe, ou parlez à l'homme que je vous envoi, en qui vous pouvez prendre une entière confiance. Présentez mes respects à Madame du Deffand; dites à Thieriot que je veux absolument qu'il m'aime, ou quand je serai mort, ou quand je serai heureux; jusque-là, je lui pardonne son indifférence. Dites à M. le chevalier des Alleurs que je n'oublierai jamais la générosité de ses procédés pour moi. Comptez que tout détrompé que je suis de la vanité des amitiés humaines, la vôtre me sera à jamais précieuse. Je ne souhaite de revenir à Paris que pour vous voir, vous embrasser encore une fois, et vous faire voir ma constance dans mon amitié et dans mes malheurs.

'Présentez mes respects à Madame du Deffand!' Strange indeed are the whirligigs of Time! Madame de Bernières was then living in none other than that famous house at the corner of the Rue de Beaune and the Quai des Théatins (now Quai Voltaire) where, more than half a century later, the writer of those lines was to come, bowed down under the weight of an enormous celebrity, to look for the last time upon Paris and the world; where, too, Madame du Deffand herself, decrepit, blind, and bitter with the disillusionments of a strange lifetime, was to listen once more to the mellifluous enchantments of that extraordinary intelligence, which—so it seemed to her as she sat entranced—could never, never grow old.[4]

Voltaire was not kept long in the Bastille. For some time he had entertained a vague intention of visiting England, and he now begged for permission to leave the country. The authorities, whose one object was to prevent an unpleasant *fracas*, were ready enough to substitute exile for imprisonment; and thus, after a fortnight's detention, the 'fameux poète' was released on condition that he should depart forthwith, and remain, until further permission, at a distance of at least fifty leagues from Versailles.

It is from this point onwards that our information grows scanty and confused. We know that Voltaire was in Calais early in May, and it is generally agreed that he crossed over to England shortly afterwards. His subsequent movements are uncertain. We find him established at Wandsworth in the middle of October, but it is probable that in the interval he had made a secret journey to Paris with the object—in which he did not succeed—of challenging the Chevalier de Rohan to a duel. Where he lived during these months is unknown, but apparently it was not in London. The date of his final departure from England is equally in doubt; M. Foulet adduces some reasons for supposing that he returned secretly to France in November 1728, and in that case the total length of the English visit was just two and a half years. Churton Collins, however, prolongs it until March 1729. A similar obscurity hangs over all the details of Voltaire's stay. Not only are his own extant letters during this period unusually few, but allusions to him in contemporary English correspondences are almost entirely absent. We have to depend upon scattered hints, uncertain inferences, and conflicting rumours. We know that he stayed for some time at Wandsworth with a certain Everard Falkener in circumstances which he described to Thieriot in a letter in English—an English quaintly flavoured with the gay impetuosity of another race. 'At my coming to London,' he wrote, 'I found my damned Jew was broken.' (He had depended upon some bills of exchange drawn upon a Jewish broker.)

> I was without a penny, sick to dye of a violent ague, stranger, alone, helpless, in the midst of a city wherein I was known to nobody; my Lord and Lady Bolingbroke were into the country; I could not make bold to see our ambassadour in so wretched a condition. I had never undergone such distress; but I am born to run through all the misfortunes of life. In these circumstances my star, that among all its direful influences pours allways on me some kind refreshment, sent to me an English gentleman unknown to me, who forced me to receive some money that I wanted. Another London citisen that I had seen but once at Paris, carried me to his own country house, wherein I lead an obscure and charming life since that time, without going to London, and quite given over to the pleasures of indolence and friendshipp. The true and generous affection of this man who soothes the bitterness of my life brings me to love you more and more. All the instances of friendshipp indear my friend Tiriot to me. I have seen often mylord and mylady Bolinbroke; I have found their affection still the same, even increased in proportion to my unhappiness; they offered me all, their money, their house; but I have refused all, because they are lords, and I have accepted all from Mr. Faulknear because he is a single gentleman.

We know that the friendship thus begun continued for many years, but as to who or what Everard Falkener was—besides the fact that he was a 'single gentleman'—we have only just information enough to make us wish for more.

'I am here,' he wrote after Voltaire had gone, 'just as you left me, neither merrier nor sadder, nor richer nor poorer, enjoying perfect health, having everything that makes life agreeable, without love, without avarice, without ambition, and without envy; and as long as all this lasts I shall take the liberty to call myself a very happy man.' This stoical Englishman was a merchant who eventually so far overcame his distaste both for ambition and for love, as to become first Ambassador at Constantinople and then Postmaster-General—has anyone, before or since, ever held such a singular succession of offices?—and to wind up by marrying, as we are intriguingly told, at the age of sixty-three, 'the illegitimate daughter of General Churchill.'

We have another glimpse of Voltaire at Wandsworth in a curious document brought to light by M. Lanson. Edward Higginson, an assistant master at a Quaker's school there, remembered how the excitable Frenchman used to argue with him for hours in Latin on the subject of 'water-baptism,' until at last Higginson produced a text from St. Paul which seemed conclusive.

> Some time after, Voltaire being at the Earl Temple's seat in Fulham, with Pope and others such, in their conversation fell on the subject of water-baptism. Voltaire assumed the part of a quaker, and at length came to mention that assertion of Paul. They questioned there being such an assertion in all his writings; on which was a large wager laid, as near as I remember of £500: and Voltaire, not retaining where it was, had one of the Earl's horses, and came over the ferry from Fulham to Putney.... When I came he desired me to give him in writing the place where Paul said, *he was not sent to baptize*; which I presently did. Then courteously taking his leave, he mounted and rode back—

and, we must suppose, won his wager.

> He seemed so taken with me (adds Higginson) as to offer to buy out the remainder of my time. I told him I expected my master would be very exorbitant in his demand. He said, let his demand be what it might, he would give it on condition I would yield to be his companion, keeping the same company, and I should always, in every respect, fare as he fared, wearing my clothes like his and of equal value: telling

me then plainly, he was a Deist; adding, so were most of the noblemen in France and in England; deriding the account given by the four Evangelists concerning the birth of Christ, and his miracles, etc., so far that I desired him to desist: for I could not bear to hear my Saviour so reviled and spoken against. Whereupon he seemed under a disappointment, and left me with some reluctance.

In London itself we catch fleeting visions of the eager gesticulating figure, hurrying out from his lodgings in Billiter Square—'Belitery Square' he calls it—or at the sign of the 'White Whigg' in Maiden Lane, Covent Garden, to go off to the funeral of Sir Isaac Newton in Westminster Abbey, or to pay a call on Congreve, or to attend a Quaker's Meeting. One would like to know in which street it was that he found himself surrounded by an insulting crowd, whose jeers at the 'French dog' he turned to enthusiasm by jumping upon a milestone, and delivering a harangue beginning—'Brave Englishmen! Am I not sufficiently unhappy in not having been born among you?' Then there are one or two stories of him in the great country houses—at Bubb Dodington's where he met Dr. Young and disputed with him upon the episode of Sin and Death in *Paradise Lost* with such vigour that at last Young burst out with the couplet:

You are so witty, profligate, and thin,
At once we think you Milton, Death, and Sin;

and at Blenheim, where the old Duchess of Marlborough hoped to lure him into helping her with her decocted memoirs, until she found that he had scruples, when in a fury she snatched the papers out of his hands. 'I thought,' she cried, 'the man had sense; but I find him at bottom either a fool or a philosopher.'

It is peculiarly tantalising that our knowledge should be almost at its scantiest in the very direction in which we should like to know most, and in which there was most reason to hope that our curiosity might have been gratified. Of Voltaire's relations with the circle of Pope, Swift, and Bolingbroke only the most meagre details have reached us. His correspondence with Bolingbroke, whom he had known in France and whose presence in London was one of his principal inducements in coming to England—a correspondence which must have been considerable—has completely disappeared. Nor, in the numerous published letters which passed about between the members of that distinguished group, is there any reference to Voltaire's name. Now and then some chance remark raises our expectations, only to make our disappointment more acute. Many years later, for instance, in 1765, a certain Major Broome paid a visit to Ferney, and made the following entry in his diary:

> Dined with Mons. Voltaire, who behaved very politely. He is very old, was dressed in a robe-de-chambre of blue sattan and gold spots on it, with a sort of blue sattan cap and tassle of gold. He spoke all the time in English.... His house is not very fine, but genteel, and stands upon a mount close to the mountains. He is tall and very thin, has a very piercing eye, and a look singularly vivacious. He told me of his acquaintance with Pope, Swift (with whom he lived for three months at Lord Peterborough's) and Gay, who first showed him the *Beggar's Opera* before it was acted. He says he admires Swift, and loved Gay vastly. He said that Swift had a great deal of the ridiculum acre.

And then Major Broome goes on to describe the 'handsome new church' at Ferney, and the 'very neat water-works' at Geneva. But what a vision has he opened out for us, and, in that very moment, shut away for ever from our gaze in that brief parenthesis—'with whom he lived for three months at Lord Peterborough's'! What would we not give now for no more than one or two of the bright intoxicating drops from that noble river of talk which flowed then with such a careless abundance!—that prodigal stream, swirling away, so swiftly and so happily, into the empty spaces of forgetfulness and the long night of Time!

So complete, indeed, is the lack of precise and well-authenticated information upon this, by far the most obviously interesting side of Voltaire's life in England, that some writers have been led to adopt a very different theory from that which is usually accepted, and to suppose that his relations with Pope's circle were in reality of a purely superficial, or even of an actually disreputable, kind. Voltaire himself, no doubt, was anxious to appear as the intimate friend of the great writers of England; but what reason is there to believe that he was not embroidering upon the facts, and that his true position was not that of a mere literary hanger-on, eager simply for money and *réclame*, with, perhaps, no particular scruples as to his means of getting hold of those desirable ends? The objection to this theory is that there is even less evidence to support it than there is to support Voltaire's own story. There are a few rumours and anecdotes; but that is all. Voltaire was probably the best-hated man in the eighteenth century, and it is only natural that, out of the enormous mass of mud that was thrown at him, some handfuls should have been particularly aimed at his life in England. Accordingly, we learn that somebody was told by somebody else—'avec des détails que je ne rapporterai point'—that 'M. de Voltaire se conduisit très-irrégulièrement en Angleterre: qu'il s'y est fait beaucoup d'ennemis, par des procédés qui n'accordaient pas avec les principes d'une morale exacte.' And we are told that he left England 'under a cloud'; that before he went he was 'cudgelled' by an infuriated publisher; that he swindled Lord Peterborough out of large sums of money, and that the outraged nobleman drew his sword upon the miscreant, who only escaped with his life by a midnight flight. A more circumstantial story has been given currency by Dr. Johnson. Voltaire, it appears, was a spy in the pay of Walpole, and was in the habit of betraying Bolingbroke's political secrets to the Government. The tale first appears in a third-rate life of Pope by Owen Ruffhead, who had it from Warburton, who had it from Pope himself. Oddly enough Churton Collins apparently believed it, partly from the evidence afforded by the 'fulsome flattery' and 'exaggerated compliments' to be found in Voltaire's correspondence, which, he says, reveal a man in whom 'falsehood and hypocrisy are of the very essence of his composition. There is nothing, however base, to which he will not stoop: there is no law in the code of social honour which he is not capable of violating.' Such an extreme and sweeping conclusion, following from such shadowy premises, seems to show that some of the mud thrown in the eighteenth century was still sticking in the twentieth. M. Foulet, however, has examined Ruffhead's charge in a very different spirit, with conscientious minuteness, and has concluded that it is utterly without foundation.

It is, indeed, certain that Voltaire's acquaintanceship was not limited to the extremely bitter Opposition circle which centred about the disappointed and restless figure of Bolingbroke. He had come to London with letters of introduction from Horace Walpole, the English Ambassador at Paris, to various eminent persons in the Government. 'Mr. Voltaire, a poet and a very ingenious one,' was recommended by Walpole to the favour and protection of the Duke of Newcastle, while Dodington was asked to support the subscription to 'an excellent poem, called "Henry IV.," which, on account of some bold strokes in it against persecution and the priests, cannot be printed here.' These letters had their effect, and Voltaire rapidly made friends at Court. When he brought out his London edition of the *Henriade*, there was hardly a great name in England which was not on the subscription list. He was allowed to dedicate the poem to Queen Caroline, and he received a royal gift of £240. Now it is also certain that just before this time Bolingbroke and Swift were suspicious of a 'certain pragmatical spy of quality, well known to act in that capacity by those into whose company he insinuates himself,' who, they believed, were betraying their plans to the Government. But to conclude that this detected spy was Voltaire, whose favour at Court was known to be the reward of treachery to his friends, is, apart from the inherent improbability of the supposition, rendered almost impossible, owing to the fact that Bolingbroke and Swift were themselves subscribers to the *Henriade*—Bolingbroke took no fewer than twenty copies—and that Swift was not only instrumental in obtaining a large number of Irish subscriptions, but actually wrote a preface to the Dublin edition of another of Voltaire's works. What inducement could Bolingbroke have had for such liberality towards a man who had betrayed him? Who can conceive of the redoubtable Dean of St. Patrick, then at the very summit of his fame, dispensing such splendid favours to a wretch whom he knew to be engaged in the shabbiest of all traffics at the expense of himself and his friends?

Voltaire's literary activities were as insatiable while he was in England as during every other period of his career. Besides the edition of the *Henriade*, which was considerably altered and enlarged—one of the changes was the silent removal of the name of Sully from its pages—he brought out a volume of two essays, written in English, upon the French Civil Wars and upon Epic Poetry, he began an adaptation of *Julius Caesar* for the French stage, he wrote the opening acts of his tragedy of *Brutus*, and he collected a quantity of material for his History of Charles XII. In addition to all this, he was busily engaged with the preparations for his *Lettres Philosophiques*. The *Henriade* met with a great success. Every copy of the magnificent quarto edition was sold before publication; three octavo editions were exhausted in as many weeks; and Voltaire made a profit of at least ten thousand francs. M. Foulet thinks that he left England shortly after this highly successful transaction, and that he established himself secretly in some town in Normandy, probably Rouen, where he devoted himself to the completion of the various works which he had in hand. Be this as it may, he was certainly in France early in April 1729; a few days later he applied for permission to return to Paris; this was granted on the 9th of April, and the remarkable incident which had begun at the Opera more than three years before came to a close.

It was not until five years later that the *Lettres Philosophiques* appeared. This epoch-making book was the lens by means of which Voltaire gathered together the scattered rays of his English impressions into a focus of brilliant and burning intensity. It so happened that the nation into whose midst he had plunged, and whose characteristics he had scrutinised with so avid a curiosity, had just reached one of the culminating moments in its history. The great achievement of the Revolution and the splendid triumphs of Marlborough had brought to England freedom, power, wealth, and that sense of high exhilaration which springs from victory and self-confidence. Her destiny was in the hands of an aristocracy which was not only capable and enlightened, like most successful aristocracies, but which possessed the peculiar attribute of being deep-rooted in popular traditions and popular sympathies and of drawing its life-blood from the popular will. The agitations of the reign of Anne were over; the stagnation of the reign of Walpole had not yet begun. There was a great outburst of intellectual activity and aesthetic energy. The amazing discoveries of Newton seemed to open out boundless possibilities of speculation; and in the meantime the great nobles were building palaces and reviving the magnificence of the Augustan Age, while men of letters filled the offices of State. Never, perhaps, before or since, has England been so thoroughly English; never have the national qualities of solidity and sense, independence of judgment and idiosyncrasy of temperament, received a more forcible and complete expression. It was the England of Walpole and Carteret, of Butler and Berkeley, of Swift and Pope. The two works which, out of the whole range of English literature, contain in a supreme degree those elements of power, breadth, and common sense, which lie at the root of the national genius— 'Gulliver's Travels' and the 'Dunciad'—both appeared during Voltaire's visit. Nor was it only in the high places of the nation's consciousness that these signs were manifest; they were visible everywhere, to every stroller through the London streets—in the Royal Exchange, where all the world came crowding to pour its gold into English purses, in the Meeting Houses of the Quakers, where the Holy Spirit rushed forth untrammelled to clothe itself in the sober garb of English idiom, and in the taverns of Cheapside, where the brawny fellow-countrymen of Newton and Shakespeare sat, in an impenetrable silence, over their English beef and English beer.

It was only natural that such a society should act as a powerful stimulus upon the vivid temperament of Voltaire, who had come to it with the bitter knowledge fresh in his mind of the medieval futility, the narrow-minded cynicism of his own country. Yet the book which was the result is in many ways a surprising one. It is almost as remarkable for what it does not say as for what it does. In the first place, Voltaire makes no attempt to give his readers an account of the outward surface, the social and spectacular aspects of English life. It is impossible not to regret this, especially since we know, from a delightful fragment which was not published until after his death, describing his first impressions on arriving in London, in how brilliant and inimitable a fashion he would have accomplished the task. A full-length portrait of Hanoverian England from the personal point of view, by Voltaire, would have been a priceless possession for posterity; but it was never to be painted. The first sketch revealing in its perfection the hand of the master, was lightly drawn, and then thrown aside for ever. And in reality it is better so. Voltaire decided to aim at something higher and more important, something more original and more profound. He determined to write a book which should be, not the sparkling record of an ingenious traveller, but a work of propaganda and a declaration of faith. That new mood, which had come upon him first in Sully's dining-room and is revealed to us in the quivering phrases of the note to Madame de Bernières, was to grow, in the congenial air of England, into the dominating passion of his life. Henceforth, whatever quips and follies, whatever flouts and mockeries might play upon the surface, he was to be in deadly earnest at heart. He was to live and die a fighter in the ranks of progress, a champion in the mighty struggle which was now beginning against the powers of darkness in France. The first great blow in that struggle had been struck ten years earlier by Montesquieu in his *Lettres Persanes*; the second was struck by Voltaire in the *Lettres Philosophiques*. The intellectual freedom, the vigorous precision, the elegant urbanity which characterise the earlier work appear in a yet more perfect form in the later one. Voltaire's book, as its title indicates, is in effect a series of generalised reflections upon a multitude of important topics, connected together by a common point of view. A description of the institutions and manners of England is only an incidental part of the scheme: it is the fulcrum by means of which the lever of Voltaire's philosophy is brought into operation. The book is an extremely short one—it fills less than two hundred small octavo pages; and its tone and style have just that light and airy gaiety which befits the ostensible form of it—a set of private letters to a friend. With an extraordinary width of comprehension, an extraordinary pliability of intelligence, Voltaire touches upon a hundred subjects of the most varied interest and importance—from the theory of gravitation to the satires of Lord Rochester, from the effects of inoculation to the immortality of the soul—and every touch tells. It is the spirit of Humanism carried to its furthest, its quintessential point; indeed, at first sight, one is tempted to think that this quality of rarefied universality has been exaggerated into a defect. The matters treated of are so many and so vast, they are disposed of and dismissed so swiftly, so easily, so unemphatically, that one begins to wonder whether, after all, anything of real significance can have been expressed. But, in reality, what, in those few small pages, has been expressed is simply the whole philosophy of Voltaire. He offers one an exquisite dish of whipped cream; one swallows down the unsubstantial trifle, and asks impatiently if that is all? At any rate, it is enough. Into that frothy sweetness his subtle hand has insinuated a single drop of some strange liquor—is it a poison or is it an elixir of life?—whose penetrating influence will spread and spread until the remotest fibres of the system have felt its power. Contemporary French readers, when they had shut the book, found somehow that they were looking out upon a new world; that a process of disintegration had begun among their most intimate beliefs and feelings; that the whole rigid frame-work of society—of life itself—the hard, dark, narrow, antiquated structure of their existence—had suddenly, in the twinkling of an eye, become a faded, shadowy thing.

It might have been expected that, among the reforms which such a work would advocate, a prominent place would certainly have been given to those of a political nature. In England a political revolution had been crowned with triumph, and all that was best in English life was founded upon the political institutions which had been then established. The moral was obvious: one had only to compare the state of England under a free government with the state of France, disgraced, bankrupt, and incompetent, under autocratic rule. But the moral is never drawn by Voltaire. His references to political questions are slight and vague; he gives a sketch of English history, which reaches Magna Charta, suddenly mentions Henry VII., and then stops; he has not a word to say upon the responsibility of Ministers, the independence of the judicature, or even the freedom of the press. He approves of the English financial system, whose control by the Commons he mentions, but he fails to indicate the importance of the fact. As to the underlying principles of the constitution, the account which he gives of them conveys hardly more to the reader than the famous lines in the *Henriade*:

> Aux murs de Westminster on voit paraître ensemble
> Trois pouvoirs étonnés du noeud qui les rassemble.

Apparently Voltaire was aware of these deficiencies, for in the English edition of the book he caused the following curious excuses to be inserted in the preface:

> Some of his *English* Readers may perhaps be dissatisfied at his not expatiating farther on their Constitution and their Laws, which most of them revere almost to Idolatry; but, this Reservedness is an effect of *M. de Voltaire's* Judgment. He contented himself with giving his opinion of them in general Reflexions, the Cast of which is entirely new, and which prove that he had made this Part of the *British* Polity his particular Study. Besides, how was it possible for a Foreigner to pierce thro' their Politicks, that gloomy Labyrinth, in which such of the *English* themselves as are best acquainted with it, confess daily that they are bewilder'd and lost?

Nothing could be more characteristic of the attitude, not only of Voltaire himself, but of the whole host of his followers in the later eighteenth century, towards the actual problems of politics. They turned away in disgust from the 'gloomy labyrinth' of practical fact to take refuge in those charming 'general Reflexions' so dear to their hearts, 'the Cast of which was entirely new'—and the conclusion of which was also entirely new, for it was the French Revolution.

It was, indeed, typical of Voltaire and of his age that the *Lettres Philosophiques* should have been condemned by the authorities, not for any political heterodoxy, but for a few remarks which seemed to call in question the immortality of the soul. His attack upon the *ancien régime* was, in the main, a theoretical attack; doubtless its immediate effectiveness was thereby diminished, but its ultimate force was increased. And the *ancien régime* itself was not slow to realise the danger: to touch the ark of metaphysical orthodoxy was in its eyes the unforgiveable sin. Voltaire knew well enough that he must be careful.

> Il n'y a qu'une lettre touchant M. Loke [he wrote to a friend]. La seule matière philosophique que j'y traite est la petite bagatelle de l'immortalité de l'âme; mais la chose a trop de conséquence pour la traiter sérieusement. Il a fallu l'égorger pour ne pas heurter de front nos seigneurs les théologiens, gens qui voient si clairement la spiritualité de l'âme qu'ils feraient brûler, s'ils pouvaient, les corps de ceux qui en doutent.

Nor was it only 'M. Loke' whom he felt himself obliged to touch so gingerly; the remarkable movement towards Deism, which was then beginning in England, Voltaire only dared to allude to in a hardly perceivable hint. He just mentions, almost in a parenthesis, the names of Shaftesbury, Collins, and Toland, and then quickly passes on. In this connexion, it may be noticed that the influence upon Voltaire of the writers of this group has often been exaggerated. To say, as Lord Morley says, that 'it was the English onslaught which sowed in him the seed of the idea ... of a systematic and reasoned attack' upon Christian theology, is to misjudge the situation. In the first place it is certain both that Voltaire's opinions upon those matters were fixed, and that his proselytising habits had begun, long before he came to England. There is curious evidence of this in an anonymous letter, preserved among the archives of the Bastille, and addressed to the head of the police at the time of Voltaire's imprisonment.

> Vous venez de mettre à la Bastille [says the writer, who, it is supposed, was an ecclesiastic] un homme que je souhaitais y voir il y a plus de 15 années.

The writer goes on to speak of the

> métier que faisait l'homme en question, prêchant le déisme tout à découvert aux toilettes de nos jeunes seigneurs ... L'Ancien Testament, selon lui, n'est qu'un tissu de contes et

de fables, les apôtres étaient de bonnes gens idiots, simples, et crédules, et les pères de l'Eglise, Saint Bernard surtout, auquel il en veut le plus, n'étaient que des charlatans et des suborneurs.

'Je voudrais être homme d'authorité,' he adds, 'pour un jour seulement, afin d'enfermer ce poète entre quatre murailles pour toute sa vie.' That Voltaire at this early date should have already given rise to such pious ecclesiastical wishes shows clearly enough that he had little to learn from the deists of England. And, in the second place, the deists of England had very little to teach a disciple of Bayle, Fontenelle, and Montesquieu. They were, almost without exception, a group of second-rate and insignificant writers whose 'onslaught' upon current beliefs was only to a faint extent 'systematic and reasoned.' The feeble and fluctuating rationalism of Toland and Wollaston, the crude and confused rationalism of Collins, the half-crazy rationalism of Woolston, may each and all, no doubt, have furnished Voltaire with arguments and suggestions, but they cannot have seriously influenced his thought. Bolingbroke was a more important figure, and he was in close personal relation with Voltaire; but his controversial writings were clumsy and superficial to an extraordinary degree. As Voltaire himself said, 'in his works there are many leaves and little fruit; distorted expressions and periods intolerably long.' Tindal and Middleton were more vigorous; but their work did not appear until a later period. The masterly and far-reaching speculations of Hume belong, of course, to a totally different class.

Apart from politics and metaphysics, there were two directions in which the *Lettres Philosophiques* did pioneer work of a highly important kind: they introduced both Newton and Shakespeare to the French public. The four letters on Newton show Voltaire at his best—succinct, lucid, persuasive, and bold. The few paragraphs on Shakespeare, on the other hand, show him at his worst. Their principal merit is that they mention his existence—a fact hitherto unknown in France; otherwise they merely afford a striking example of the singular contradiction in Voltaire's nature which made him a revolutionary in intellect and kept him a high Tory in taste. Never was such speculative audacity combined with such aesthetic timidity; it is as if he had reserved all his superstition for matters of art. From his account of Shakespeare, it is clear that he had never dared to open his eyes and frankly look at what he should see before him. All was 'barbare, dépourvu de bienséances, d'ordre, de vraisemblance'; in the hurly-burly he was dimly aware of a figured and elevated style, and of some few 'lueurs étonnantes'; but to the true significance of Shakespeare's genius he remained utterly blind.

Characteristically enough, Voltaire, at the last moment, did his best to reinforce his tentative metaphysical observations on 'M. Loke' by slipping into his book, as it were accidentally, an additional letter, quite disconnected from the rest of the work, containing reflexions upon some of the *Pensées* of Pascal. He no doubt hoped that these reflexions, into which he had distilled some of his most insidious venom, might, under cover of the rest, pass unobserved. But all his subterfuges were useless. It was in vain that he pulled wires and intrigued with high personages; in vain that he made his way to the aged Minister, Cardinal Fleury, and attempted, by reading him some choice extracts on the Quakers, to obtain permission for the publication of his book. The old Cardinal could not help smiling, though Voltaire had felt that it would be safer to skip the best parts—'the poor man!' he said afterwards, 'he didn't realise what he had missed'—but the permission never came. Voltaire was obliged to have recourse to an illicit publication; and then the authorities acted with full force. The *Lettres Philosophiques* were officially condemned; the book was declared to be scandalous and 'contraire à la religion, aux bonnes moeurs, et au respect dû aux puissances,' and it was ordered to be publicly burned by the executioner. The result was precisely what might have been expected: the prohibitions and fulminations, so far from putting a stop to the sale of such exciting matter, sent it up by leaps and bounds. England suddenly became the fashion; the theories of M. Loke and Sir Newton began to be discussed; even the plays of 'ce fou de Shakespeare' began to be read. And, at the same time, the whispered message of tolerance, of free inquiry, of enlightened curiosity, was carried over the land. The success of Voltaire's work was complete.

He himself, however, had been obliged to seek refuge from the wrath of the government in the remote seclusion of Madame du Châtelet's country house at Cirey. In this retirement he pursued his studies of Newton, and a few years later produced an exact and brilliant summary of the work of the great English philosopher. Once more the authorities intervened, and condemned Voltaire's book. The Newtonian system destroyed that of Descartes, and Descartes still spoke in France with the voice of orthodoxy; therefore, of course, the voice of Newton must not be heard. But, somehow or other, the voice of Newton *was* heard. The men of science were converted to the new doctrine; and thus it is not too much to say that the wonderful advances in the study of mathematics which took place in France during the later years of the eighteenth century were the result of the illuminating zeal of Voltaire.

With his work on Newton, Voltaire's direct connexion with English influences came to an end. For the rest of his life, indeed, he never lost his interest in England; he was never tired of reading English books, of being polite to English travellers, and of doing his best, in the intervals of more serious labours, to destroy the reputation of that deplorable English buffoon, whom, unfortunately, he himself had been so foolish as first to introduce to the attention of his countrymen. But it is curious to notice how, as time went on, the force of Voltaire's nature inevitably carried him further and further away from the central standpoints of the English mind. The stimulus which he had received in England only served to urge him into a path which no Englishman has ever trod. The movement of English thought in the eighteenth century found its perfect expression in the profound, sceptical, and yet essentially conservative, genius of Hume. How different was the attitude of Voltaire! With what a reckless audacity, what a fierce uncompromising passion he charged and fought and charged again! He had no time for the nice discriminations of an elaborate philosophy, and no desire for the careful balance of the judicial mind; his creed was simple and explicit, and it also possessed the supreme merit of brevity: 'Écrasez l'infâme!' was enough for him.

1914.

NOTES:

[3] *Correspondance de Voltaire* (1726-1729). By Lucien Foulet. Paris: Hachette, 1913.

[4] 'Il est aussi animé qu'il ait jamais été. Il a quatre-vingt-quatre ans, et en vérité je le crois immortel; il jouit de tous ses sens, aucun même n'est affaibli; c'est un être bien singulier, et en vérité fort supérieur.' Madame du Deffand to Horace Walpole, 12 Avril 1778.

A DIALOGUE

BETWEEN
MOSES, DIOGENES, AND MR. LOKE

DIOGENES

Confess, oh *Moses*! Your Miracles were but conjuring-tricks, your Prophecies lucky Hazards, and your Laws a *Gallimaufry* of Commonplaces and Absurdities.

MR. LOKE

Confess that you were more skill'd in flattering the Vulgar than in ascertaining the Truth, and that your Reputation in the World would never have been so high, had your Lot fallen among a Nation of Philosophers.

DIOGENES

Confess that when you taught the *Jews* to spoil the *Egyptians* you were a sad rogue.

MR. LOKE

Confess that it was a Fable to give Horses to Pharaoh and an uncloven hoof to the Hare.

DIOGENES

Confess that you did never see the *Back Parts* of the Lord.

MR. LOKE

Confess that your style had too much Singularity and too little Taste to be that of the Holy Ghost.

MOSES

All this may be true, my good Friends; but what are the Conclusions you would draw from your Raillery? Do you suppose that I am ignorant of all that a Wise Man might urge against my Conduct, my Tales, and my Language? But alas! my path was chalk'd out for me not by Choice but by Necessity. I had not the Happiness of living in *England* or a *Tub*. I was the Leader of an ignorant and superstitious People, who would never have heeded the sober Counsels of Good Sense and Toleration, and who would have laughed at the Refinements of a nice Philosophy. It was necessary to flatter their Vanity by telling them that they were the favour'd Children of God, to satisfy their Passions by allowing them to be treacherous and cruel to their Enemies, and to tickle their Ears by Stories and Farces by turns ridiculous and horrible, fit either for a Nursery or *Bedlam*. By such Contrivances I was able to attain my Ends and to establish the Welfare of my Countrymen. Do you blame me? It is not the business of a Ruler to be truthful, but to be politick; he must fly even from Virtue herself, if she sit in a different Quarter from Expediency. It is his Duty to *sacrifice* the Best, which is impossible, to a *little Good*, which is close at hand. I was willing to lay down a Multitude of foolish Laws, so that, under their Cloak, I might slip in a few Wise ones; and, had I not shown myself to be both Cruel and Superstitious, the *Jews* would never have escaped from the Bondage of the *Egyptians*.

DIOGENES.

Perhaps that would not have been an overwhelming Disaster. But, in truth, you are right. There is no viler Profession than the Government of Nations. He who dreams that he can lead a great Crowd of Fools without a great Store of Knavery is a Fool himself.

MR. LOKE

Are not you too hasty? Does not History show that there have been great Rulers who were good Men? Solon, Henry of *Navarre*, and Milord Somers were certainly not Fools, and yet I am unwilling to believe that they were Knaves either.

MOSES

No, not Knaves; but Dissemblers. In their different degrees, they all juggled; but 'twas not because Jugglery pleas'd 'em; 'twas because Men cannot be governed without it.

MR. LOKE

I would be happy to try the Experiment. If Men were told the Truth, might they not believe it? If the Opportunity of Virtue and Wisdom is never to be offer'd 'em, how can we be sure that they would not be willing to take it? Let Rulers be *bold* and *honest*, and it is possible that the Folly of their Peoples will disappear.

DIOGENES

A pretty phantastick Vision! But History is against you.

MOSES

And Prophecy.

DIOGENES

And Common Observation. Look at the World at this moment, and what do we see? It is as it has always been, and always will be. So long as it endures, the World will continue to be rul'd by Cajolery, by Injustice, and by Imposture.

MR. LOKE

If that be so, I must take leave to lament the *Destiny* of the Human Race.

VOLTAIRE'S TRAGEDIES

The historian of Literature is little more than a historian of exploded reputations. What has he to do with Shakespeare, with Dante, with Sophocles? Has he entered into the springs of the sea? Or has he walked in the search of the depth? The great fixed luminaries of the firmament of Letters dazzle his optic glass; and he can hardly hope to do more than record their presence, and admire their splendours with the eyes of an ordinary mortal. His business is with the succeeding ages of men, not with all time; but *Hyperion* might have been written on the morrow of Salamis, and the Odes of Pindar dedicated to George the Fourth. The literary historian must rove in other hunting grounds. He is the geologist of literature, whose study lies among the buried strata of forgotten generations, among the fossil remnants of the past. The great men with whom he must deal are the great men who are no longer great—mammoths and ichthyosauri kindly preserved to us, among the siftings of so many epochs, by the impartial benignity of Time. It is for him to unravel the jokes of Erasmus, and to be at home among the platitudes of Cicero. It is for him to sit up all night with the spectral heroes of Byron; it is for him to exchange innumerable alexandrines with the faded heroines of Voltaire.

The great potentate of the eighteenth century has suffered cruelly indeed at the hands of posterity. Everyone, it is true, has heard of him; but who has read him? It is by his name that ye shall know him, and not by his works. With the exception of his letters, of *Candide*, of *Akakia*, and of a few other of his shorter pieces, the vast mass of his productions has been already consigned to oblivion. How many persons now living have travelled through *La Henriade* or *La Pucelle*? How many have so much as glanced at the imposing volumes of *L'Esprit des Moeurs*? *Zadig* and *Zaïre*, *Mérope* and *Charles XII*. still linger, perhaps, in the schoolroom; but what has become of *Oreste*, and of *Mahomet*, and of *Alzire*? *Où sont les neiges d'antan*?

Though Voltaire's reputation now rests mainly on his achievements as a precursor of the Revolution, to the eighteenth century he was as much a poet as a reformer. The whole of Europe beheld at Ferney the oracle, not only of philosophy, but of good taste; for thirty years every scribbler, every rising genius, and every crowned head, submitted his verses to the censure of Voltaire; Voltaire's plays were performed before crowded houses;

his epic was pronounced superior to Homer's, Virgil's, and Milton's; his epigrams were transcribed by every letter-writer, and got by heart by every wit. Nothing, perhaps, shows more clearly the gulf which divides us from our ancestors of the eighteenth century, than a comparison between our thoughts and their thoughts, between our feelings and their feelings, with regard to one and the same thing—a tragedy by Voltaire. For us, as we take down the dustiest volume in our bookshelf, as we open it vaguely at some intolerable tirade, as we make an effort to labour through the procession of pompous commonplaces which meets our eyes, as we abandon the task in despair, and hastily return the book to its forgotten corner—to us it is well-nigh impossible to imagine the scene of charming brilliance which, five generations since, the same words must have conjured up. The splendid gaiety, the refined excitement, the pathos, the wit, the passion—all these things have vanished as completely from our perceptions as the candles, the powder, the looking-glasses, and the brocades, among which they moved and had their being. It may be instructive, or at least entertaining, to examine one of these forgotten masterpieces a little more closely; and we may do so with the less hesitation, since we shall only be following in the footsteps of Voltaire himself. His examination of *Hamlet* affords a precedent which is particularly applicable, owing to the fact that the same interval of time divided him from Shakespeare as that which divides ourselves from him. One point of difference, indeed, does exist between the relative positions of the two authors. Voltaire, in his study of Shakespeare, was dealing with a living, and a growing force; our interest in the dramas of Voltaire is solely an antiquarian interest. At the present moment,[5] a literal translation of *King Lear* is drawing full houses at the Théâtre Antoine. As a rule it is rash to prophesy; but, if that rule has any exceptions, this is certainly one of them—hundred years hence a literal translation of *Zaïre* will not be holding the English boards.

It is not our purpose to appreciate the best, or to expose the worst, of Voltaire's tragedies. Our object is to review some specimen of what would have been recognised by his contemporaries as representative of the average flight of his genius. Such a specimen is to be found in *Alzire, ou Les Américains*, first produced with great success in 1736, when Voltaire was forty-two years of age and his fame as a dramatist already well established.

Act I.—The scene is laid in Lima, the capital of Peru, some years after the Spanish conquest of America. When the play opens, Don Gusman, a Spanish grandee, has just succeeded his father, Don Alvarez, in the Governorship of Peru. The rule of Don Alvarez had been beneficent and just; he had spent his life in endeavouring to soften the cruelty of his countrymen; and his only remaining wish was to see his son carry on the work which he had begun. Unfortunately, however, Don Gusman's temperament was the very opposite of his father's; he was tyrannical, harsh, headstrong, and bigoted.

> L'Américain farouche est un monstre sauvage
> Qui mord en frémissant le frein de l'esclavage ...
> Tout pouvoir, en un mot, périt par l'indulgence,
> Et la sévérité produit l'obéissance.

Such were the cruel maxims of his government—maxims which he was only too ready to put into practice. It was in vain that Don Alvarez reminded his son that the true Christian returns good for evil, and that, as he epigrammatically put it, 'Le vrai Dieu, mon fils, est un Dieu qui pardonne.' To enforce his argument, the good old man told the story of how his own life had been spared by a virtuous American, who, as he said, 'au lieu de me frapper, embrassa mes genoux.' But Don Gusman remained unmoved by such narratives, though he admitted that there was one consideration which impelled him to adopt a more lenient policy. He was in love with Alzire, Alzire the young and beautiful daughter of Montèze, who had ruled in Lima before the coming of the Spaniards. 'Je l'aime, je l'avoue,' said Gusman to his father, 'et plus que je ne veux.' With these words, the dominating situation of the play becomes plain to the spectator. The wicked Spanish Governor is in love with the virtuous American princess. From such a state of affairs, what interesting and romantic developments may not follow? Alzire, we are not surprised to learn, still fondly cherished the memory of a Peruvian prince, who had been slain in an attempt to rescue his country from the tyranny of Don Gusman. Yet, for the sake of Montèze, her ambitious and scheming father, she consented to give her hand to the Governor. She consented; but, even as she did so, she was still faithful to Zamore. 'Sa foi me fut promise,' she declared to Don Gusman, 'il eut pour moi des charmes.'

> Il m'aima: son trépas me coûte encore des larmes:
> Vous, loin d'oser ici condamner ma douleur,
> Jugez de ma constance, et connaissez mon coeur.

The ruthless Don did not allow these pathetic considerations to stand in the way of his wishes, and gave orders that the wedding ceremony should be immediately performed. But, at the very moment of his apparent triumph, the way was being prepared for the overthrow of all his hopes.

Act II.—It was only natural to expect that a heroine affianced to a villain should turn out to be in love with a hero. The hero adored by Alzire had, it is true, perished; but then what could be more natural than his resurrection? The noble Zamore was not dead; he had escaped with his life from the torture-chamber of Don Gusman, had returned to avenge himself, had been immediately apprehended, and was lying imprisoned in the lowest dungeon of the castle, while his beloved princess was celebrating her nuptials with his deadly foe.

In this distressing situation, he was visited by the venerable Alvarez, who had persuaded his son to grant him an order for the prisoner's release. In the gloom of the dungeon, it was at first difficult to distinguish the features of Zamore; but the old man at last discovered that he was addressing the very American who, so many years ago, instead of hitting him, had embraced his knees. He was overwhelmed by this extraordinary coincidence. 'Approach. O heaven! O Providence! It is he, behold the object of my gratitude. ... My benefactor! My son!' But let us not pry further into so affecting a passage; it is sufficient to state that Don Alvarez, after promising his protection to Zamore, hurried off to relate this remarkable occurrence to his son, the Governor.

Act III.—Meanwhile, Alzire had been married. But she still could not forget her Peruvian lover. While she was lamenting her fate, and imploring the forgiveness of the shade of Zamore, she was informed that a released prisoner begged a private interview. 'Admit him.' He was admitted. 'Heaven! Such were his features, his gait, his voice: Zamore!' She falls into the arms of her confidante. 'Je succombe; à peine je respire.'

ZAMORE: Reconnais ton amant.
ALZIRE: Zamore aux pieds d'Alzire!
Est-ce une illusion?

It was no illusion; and the unfortunate princess was obliged to confess to her lover that she was already married to Don Gusman. Zamore was at first unable to grasp the horrible truth, and, while he was still struggling with his conflicting emotions, the door was flung open, and Don Gusman, accompanied by his father, entered the room.

A double recognition followed. Zamore was no less horrified to behold in Don Gusman the son of the venerable Alvarez, than Don Gusman was infuriated at discovering that the prisoner to whose release he had consented was no other than Zamore. When the first shock of surprise was over, the Peruvian hero violently insulted his enemy, and upbraided him with the tortures he had inflicted. The Governor replied by ordering the instant execution of the prince. It was in vain that Don Alvarez reminded his son of Zamore's magnanimity; it was in vain that Alzire herself offered to sacrifice her life for that of her lover. Zamore was dragged from the apartment; and Alzire and Don Alvarez were left alone to bewail the fate of the Peruvian hero. Yet some faint hopes still lingered in the old man's breast. 'Gusman fut inhumain,' he admitted, 'je le sais, j'en frémis;

> Mais il est ton époux, il t'aime, il est mon fils:
> Son âme à la pitié se peut ouvrir encore.'

'Hélas!' (replied Alzire), 'que n'êtes-vous le père de Zamore!'

Act IV.—Even Don Gusman's heart was, in fact, unable to steel itself entirely against the prayers and tears of his father and his wife; and he consented to allow a brief respite to Zamore's execution. Alzire was not slow to seize this opportunity of doing her lover a good turn; for she immediately obtained his release by the ingenious stratagem of bribing the warder of the dungeon. Zamore was free. But alas! Alzire was not; was she not wedded to the wicked Gusman? Her lover's expostulations fell on unheeding ears. What mattered it that her marriage vow had been sworn before an alien God? 'J'ai promis; il suffit; il n'importe à quel dieu!'

> ZAMORE: Ta promesse est un crime; elle est ma perte; adieu.
> Périssent tes serments et ton Dieu que j'abhorre!
> ALZIRE: Arrête; quels adieux! arrête, cher Zamore!

But the prince tore himself away, with no further farewell upon his lips than an oath to be revenged upon the Governor. Alzire, perplexed, deserted, terrified, tortured by remorse, agitated by passion, turned for comfort to that God, who, she could not but believe, was, in some mysterious way, the Father of All.

> Great God, lead Zamore in safety through the desert places. ... Ah! can it be true that thou art but the Deity of another universe? Have the Europeans alone the right to please thee? Art thou after all the tyrant of one world and the father of another? ... No! The conquerors and the conquered, miserable mortals as they are, all are equally the work of thy hands....

Her reverie was interrupted by an appalling sound. She heard shrieks; she heard a cry of 'Zamore!' And her confidante, rushing in, confusedly informed her that her lover was in peril of his life.

> Ah, chère Emire [she exclaimed], allons le secourir!
> EMIRE: Que pouvez-vous, Madame? O Ciel!
> ALZIRE: Je puis mourir.

Hardly was the epigram out of her mouth when the door opened, and an emissary of Don Gusman announced to her that she must consider herself under arrest. She demanded an explanation in vain, and was immediately removed to the lowest dungeon.

Act V.—It was not long before the unfortunate princess learnt the reason of her arrest. Zamore, she was informed, had rushed straight from her apartment into the presence of Don Gusman, and had plunged a dagger into his enemy's breast. The hero had then turned to Don Alvarez and, with perfect tranquillity, had offered him the bloodstained poniard.

> J'ai fait ce que j'ai dû, j'ai vengé mon injure;
> Fais ton devoir, dit-il, et venge la nature.

Before Don Alvarez could reply to this appeal, Zamore had been haled off by the enraged soldiery before the Council of Grandees. Don Gusman had been mortally wounded; and the Council proceeded at once to condemn to death, not only Zamore, but also Alzire, who, they found, had been guilty of complicity in the murder. It was the unpleasant duty of Don Alvarez to announce to the prisoners the Council's sentence. He did so in the following manner:

> Good God, what a mixture of tenderness and horror! My own liberator is the assassin of my son. Zamore!... Yes, it is to thee that I owe this life which I detest; how dearly didst thou sell me that fatal gift.... I am a father, but I am also a man; and, in spite of thy fury, in spite of the voice of that blood which demands vengeance from my agitated soul, I can still hear the voice of thy benefactions. And thou, who wast my daughter, thou whom in our misery I yet call by a name which makes our tears to flow, ah! how far is it from thy father's wishes to add to the agony which he already feels the horrible pleasure of vengeance. I must lose, by an unheard-of catastrophe, at once my liberator, my daughter, and my son. The Council has sentenced you to death.

Upon one condition, however, and upon one alone, the lives of the culprits were to be spared—that of Zamore's conversion to Christianity. What need is there to say that the noble Peruvians did not hesitate for a moment? 'Death, rather than dishonour!' exclaimed Zamore, while Alzire added some elegant couplets upon the moral degradation entailed by hypocritical conversion. Don Alvarez was in complete despair, and was just beginning to make another speech, when Don Gusman, with the pallor of death upon his features, was carried into the room. The implacable Governor was about to utter his last words. Alzire was resigned; Alvarez was plunged in misery; Zamore was indomitable to the last. But lo! when the Governor spoke, it was seen at once that an extraordinary change had come over his mind. He was no longer proud, he was no longer cruel, he was no longer unforgiving; he was kind, humble, and polite; in short, he had repented. Everybody was pardoned, and everybody recognised the truth of Christianity. And their faith was particularly strengthened when Don Gusman, invoking a final blessing upon Alzire and Zamore, expired in the arms of Don Alvarez. For thus were the guilty punished, and the virtuous rewarded. The noble Zamore, who had murdered his enemy in cold blood, and the gentle Alzire who, after bribing a sentry, had allowed her lover to do away with her husband, lived happily ever afterwards. That they were able to do so was owing entirely to the efforts of the wicked Don Gusman; and the wicked Don Gusman very properly descended to the grave.

Such is the tragedy of *Alzire*, which, it may be well to repeat, was in its day one of the most applauded of its author's productions. It was upon the strength of works of this kind that his contemporaries recognised Voltaire's right to be ranked in a sort of dramatic triumvirate, side by side with his great predecessors, Corneille and Racine. With Racine, especially, Voltaire was constantly coupled; and it is clear that he himself firmly believed that the author of *Alzire* was a worthy successor of the author of *Athalie*. At first sight, indeed, the resemblance between the two dramatists is obvious enough; but a closer inspection reveals an ocean of differences too vast to be spanned by any superficial likeness.

A careless reader is apt to dismiss the tragedies of Racine as mere *tours de force*; and, in one sense, the careless reader is right. For, as mere displays of technical skill, those works are certainly unsurpassed in the whole range of literature. But the notion of 'a mere *tour de force*' carries with it something more than the idea of technical perfection; for it denotes, not simply a work which is technically perfect, but a work which is technically perfect and nothing more. The problem before a writer of a Chant Royal is to overcome certain technical difficulties of rhyme and rhythm; he performs his *tour de force*, the difficulties are overcome, and his task is accomplished. But Racine's problem was very different. The technical restrictions he laboured under were incredibly great; his vocabulary was cribbed, his versification was cabined, his whole power of dramatic movement was scrupulously confined; conventional rules of every conceivable denomination hurried out to restrain his genius, with the alacrity of Lilliputians pegging down a Gulliver; wherever he turned he was met by a hiatus or a pitfall, a blind-alley or a *mot bas*. But his triumph was not simply the conquest of these refractory creatures; it was something much more astonishing. It was the creation, in spite of them, nay, by their very aid, of a glowing, living, soaring, and enchanting work of art. To have brought about this amazing combination, to have erected, upon a structure of Alexandrines, of Unities, of Noble Personages, of stilted diction, of the whole intolerable paraphernalia of the Classical stage, an edifice of subtle psychology, of exquisite poetry, of overwhelming passion—that is a *tour de force* whose achievement entitles Jean Racine to a place among the very few consummate artists of the world.

Voltaire, unfortunately, was neither a poet nor a psychologist; and, when he took up the mantle of Racine, he put it, not upon a human being, but upon a tailor's block. To change the metaphor, Racine's work resembled one of those elaborate paper transparencies which delighted our grandmothers, illuminated from within so as to present a charming tinted picture with varying degrees of shadow and of light. Voltaire was able to make the transparency, but he never could light the candle; and the only result of his efforts was some sticky pieces of paper, cut into curious shapes, and roughly daubed with colour. To take only one instance, his diction is the very echo of Racine's. There are the same pompous phrases, the same inversions, the same stereotyped list of similes, the same poor bedraggled company of words. It is amusing to note the exclamations which rise to the lips of Voltaire's characters in moments of extreme excitement— *Qu'entends-je? Que vois-je? Où suis-je? Grands Dieux! Ah, c'en est trop, Seigneur! Juste Ciel! Sauve-toi de ces lieux! Madame, quelle horreur* ... &c. And it is amazing to discover that these are the very phrases with which Racine has managed to express all the violence of human terror, and rage, and love. Voltaire at his best never rises above the standard of a sixth-form boy writing hexameters in the style of Virgil; and, at his worst, he certainly falls within measurable distance of a flogging. He is capable, for instance, of writing lines as bad as the second of this couplet—

> C'est ce même guerrier dont la main tutélaire,
> De Gusman, votre époux, sauva, dit-on, le père,

or as

> Qui les font pour un temps rentrer tous en eux-mêmes,

or

> Vous comprenez, seigneur, que je ne comprends pas.

Voltaire's most striking expressions are too often borrowed from his predecessors. Alzire's 'Je puis mourir,' for instance, is an obvious reminiscence of the 'Qu'il mourût!' of le vieil Horace; and the cloven hoof is shown clearly enough by the 'O ciel!' with which Alzire's confidante manages to fill out the rest of the line. Many of these blemishes are, doubtless, the outcome of simple carelessness; for Voltaire was too busy a man to give over-much time to his plays. 'This tragedy was the work of six days,' he wrote to d'Alembert, enclosing *Olympie*. 'You should not have rested on the seventh,' was d'Alembert's reply. But, on the whole, Voltaire's verses succeed in keeping up to a high level of mediocrity; they are the verses, in fact, of a very clever man. It is when his cleverness is out of its depth, that he most palpably fails. A human being by Voltaire bears the same relation to a real human being that stage scenery bears to a real landscape; it can only be looked at from in front. The curtain rises, and his villains and his heroes, his good old men and his exquisite princesses, display for a moment their one thin surface to the spectator; the curtain falls, and they are all put back into their box. The glance which the reader has taken into the little case labelled *Alzire* has perhaps given him a sufficient notion of these queer discarded marionettes.

Voltaire's dramatic efforts were hampered by one further unfortunate incapacity; he was almost completely devoid of the dramatic sense. It is only possible to write good plays without the power of character-drawing, upon one condition—that of possessing the power of creating dramatic situations. The *Oedipus Tyrannus* of Sophocles, for instance, is not a tragedy of character; and its vast crescendo of horror is produced by a dramatic treatment of situation, not of persons. One of the principal elements in this stupendous example of the manipulation of a great dramatic theme has been pointed out by Voltaire himself. The guilt of Oedipus, he says, becomes known to the audience very early in the play; and, when the *dénouement* at last arrives, it comes as a shock, not to the audience, but to the King. There can be no doubt that Voltaire has put his finger upon the very centre of those underlying causes which make the *Oedipus* perhaps the most awful of tragedies. To know the hideous truth, to watch its gradual dawn upon one after another of the characters, to see Oedipus at last alone in ignorance, to recognise clearly that he too must know, to witness his struggles, his distraction, his growing terror, and, at the inevitable moment, the appalling revelation— few things can be more terrible than this. But Voltaire's comment upon the master-stroke by which such an effect has been obtained illustrates, in a remarkable way, his own sense of the dramatic. 'Nouvelle preuve,' he remarks, 'que Sophocle n'avait pas perfectionné son art.'

More detailed evidence of Voltaire's utter lack of dramatic insight is to be found, of course, in his criticisms of Shakespeare. Throughout these, what is particularly striking is the manner in which Voltaire seems able to get into such intimate contact with his great predecessor, and yet to remain as absolutely unaffected by him as Shakespeare himself was by Voltaire. It is unnecessary to dwell further upon so hackneyed a subject; but one instance may be given of the lengths to which this dramatic insensibility of Voltaire's was able to go—his adaptation of *Julius Caesar* for the French stage. A comparison of the two pieces should be made by anyone who wishes to realise fully, not only the degradation of the copy, but the excellence of the original. Particular attention should be paid to the transmutation of

Antony's funeral oration into French alexandrines. In Voltaire's version, the climax of the speech is reached in the following passage; it is an excellent sample of the fatuity of the whole of his concocted rigmarole:—

> ANTOINE: Brutus ... où suis-je? O ciel! O crime! O barbarie!'
> Chers amis, je succombe; et mes sens interdits ...
> Brutus, son assassin!... ce monstre était son fils!
> ROMAINS: Ah dieux!

If Voltaire's demerits are obvious enough to our eyes, his merits were equally clear to his contemporaries, whose vision of them was not perplexed and retarded by the conventions of another age. The weight of a reigning convention is like the weight of the atmosphere—it is so universal that no one feels it; and an eighteenth-century audience came to a performance of *Alzire* unconscious of the burden of the Classical rules. They found instead an animated procession of events, of scenes just long enough to be amusing and not too long to be dull, of startling incidents, of happy *mots*. They were dazzled by an easy display of cheap brilliance, and cheap philosophy, and cheap sentiment, which it was very difficult to distinguish from the real thing, at such a distance, and under artificial light. When, in *Mérope*, one saw La Dumesnil; 'lorsque,' to quote Voltaire himself, 'les yeux égarés, la voix entrecoupée, levant une main tremblante, elle allait immoler son propre fils; quand Narbas l'arrêta; quand, laissant tomber son poignard, on la vit s'évanouir entre les bras de ses femmes, et qu'elle sortit de cet état de mort avec les transports d'une mère; lorsque, ensuite, s'élançant aux yeux de Polyphonte, traversant en un clin d'oeil tout le théâtre, les larmes dans les yeux, la pâleur sur le front, les sanglots à la bouche, les bras étendus, elle s'écria: "Barbare, il est mon fils!"'—how, face to face with splendours such as these, could one question for a moment the purity of the gem from which they sparkled? Alas! to us, who know not La Dumesnil, to us whose *Mérope* is nothing more than a little sediment of print, the precious stone of our forefathers has turned out to be a simple piece of paste. Its glittering was the outcome of no inward fire, but of a certain adroitness in the manufacture; to use our modern phraseology, Voltaire was able to make up for his lack of genius by a thorough knowledge of 'technique,' and a great deal of 'go.'

And to such titles of praise let us not dispute his right. His vivacity, indeed, actually went so far as to make him something of an innovator. He introduced new and imposing spectacular effects; he ventured to write tragedies in which no persons of royal blood made their appearance; he was so bold as to rhyme 'père' with 'terre.' The wild diversity of his incidents shows a trend towards the romantic, which, doubtless, under happier influences, would have led him much further along the primrose path which ended in the bonfire of 1830.

But it was his misfortune to be for ever clogged by a tradition of decorous restraint; so that the effect of his plays is as anomalous as would be—let us say—that of a shilling shocker written by Miss Yonge. His heroines go mad in epigrams, while his villains commit murder in inversions. Amid the hurly-burly of artificiality, it was all his cleverness could do to keep its head to the wind; and he was only able to remain afloat at all by throwing overboard his humour. The Classical tradition has to answer for many sins; perhaps its most infamous achievement was that it prevented Molière from being a great tragedian. But there can be no doubt that its most astonishing one was to have taken—if only for some scattered moments—the sense of the ridiculous from Voltaire.

NOTES:

[5]   April, 1905.

VOLTAIRE AND FREDERICK THE GREAT

At the present time,[6] when it is so difficult to think of anything but of what is and what will be, it may yet be worth while to cast occasionally a glance backward at what was. Such glances may at least prove to have the humble merit of being entertaining: they may even be instructive as well. Certainly it would be a mistake to forget that Frederick the Great once lived in Germany. Nor is it altogether useless to remember that a curious old gentleman, extremely thin, extremely active, and heavily bewigged, once decided that, on the whole, it would be as well for him *not* to live in France. For, just as modern Germany dates from the accession of Frederick to the throne of Prussia, so modern France dates from the establishment of Voltaire on the banks of the Lake of Geneva. The intersection of those two momentous lives forms one of the most curious and one of the most celebrated incidents in history. To English readers it is probably best known through the few brilliant paragraphs devoted to it by Macaulay; though Carlyle's masterly and far more elaborate narrative is familiar to every lover of *The History of Friedrich II*. Since Carlyle wrote, however, fifty years have passed. New points of view have arisen, and a certain amount of new material—including the valuable edition of the correspondence between Voltaire and Frederick published from the original documents in the Archives at Berlin—has become available. It seems, therefore, in spite of the familiarity of the main outlines of the story, that another rapid review of it will not be out of place.

Voltaire was forty-two years of age, and already one of the most famous men of the day, when, in August 1736, he received a letter from the Crown Prince of Prussia. This letter was the first in a correspondence which was to last, with a few remarkable intervals, for a space of over forty years. It was written by a young man of twenty-four, of whose personal qualities very little was known, and whose importance seemed to lie simply in the fact that he was heir-apparent to one of the secondary European monarchies. Voltaire, however, was not the man to turn up his nose at royalty, in whatever form it might present itself; and it was moreover clear that the young prince had picked up at least a smattering of French culture, that he was genuinely anxious to become acquainted with the tendencies of modern thought, and, above all, that his admiration for the author of the *Henriade* and *Zaïre* was unbounded.

> La douceur et le support [wrote Frederick] que vous marquez pour tous ceux qui se vouent aux arts et aux sciences, me font espérer que vous ne m'excluerez pas du nombre de ceux que vous trouvez dignes de vos instructions. Je nomme ainsi votre commerce de lettres, qui ne peut être que profitable à tout être pensant. J'ose même avancer, sans déroger au mérite d'autrui, que dans l'univers entier il n'y aurait pas d'exception à faire de ceux dont vous ne pourriez être le maître.

The great man was accordingly delighted; he replied with all that graceful affability of which he was a master, declared that his correspondent was 'un prince philosophe qui rendra les hommes heureux,' and showed that he meant business by plunging at once into a discussion of the metaphysical doctrines of 'le sieur Wolf,' whom Frederick had commended as 'le plus célèbre philosophe de nos jours.' For the next four years the correspondence continued on the lines thus laid down. It was a correspondence between a master and a pupil: Frederick, his passions divided between German philosophy and French poetry, poured out with equal copiousness disquisitions upon Free Will and *la raison suffisante*, odes *sur la Flatterie*, and epistles *sur l'Humanité*, while Voltaire kept the ball rolling with no less enormous philosophical replies, together with minute criticisms of His Royal Highness's mistakes in French metre and French orthography. Thus, though the interest of these early letters must have been intense to the young Prince, they have far too little personal flavour to be anything but extremely tedious to the reader of to-day. Only very occasionally is it possible to detect, amid the long and careful periods, some faint signs of feeling or of character. Voltaire's *empressement* seems to take on, once or twice, the colours of something like a real enthusiasm; and one notices that, after two years, Frederick's letters begin no longer with 'Monsieur' but with 'Mon cher ami,' which glides at last insensibly into 'Mon cher Voltaire'; though the careful poet continues with his 'Monseigneur' throughout. Then, on one occasion, Frederick makes a little avowal, which reads oddly in the light of future events.

> Souffrez [he says] que je vous fasse mon caractère, afin que vous ne vous y mépreniez plus ... J'ai peu de mérite et peu de savoir; mais j'ai beaucoup de bonne volonté, et un fonds inépuisable d'estime et d'amitié pour les personnes d'une vertu distinguée, et avec cela je suis capable de toute la constance que la vraie amitié exige. J'ai assez de jugement

pour vous rendre toute la justice que vous méritez; mais je
n'en ai pas assez pour m'empêcher de faire de mauvais vers.

But this is exceptional; as a rule, elaborate compliments take the place of personal confessions; and, while Voltaire is never tired of comparing Frederick to Apollo, Alcibiades, and the youthful Marcus Aurelius, of proclaiming the rebirth of 'les talents de Virgile et les vertus d'Auguste,' or of declaring that 'Socrate ne m'est rien, c'est Frédéric que j'aime,' the Crown Prince is on his side ready with an equal flow of protestations, which sometimes rise to singular heights. 'Ne croyez pas,' he says, 'que je pousse mon scepticisime à outrance ... Je crois, par exemple, qu'il n'y a qu'un Dieu et qu'un Voltaire dans le monde; je crois encore que ce Dieu avait besoin dans ce siècle d'un Voltaire pour le rendre aimable.' Decidedly the Prince's compliments were too emphatic, and the poet's too ingenious; as Voltaire himself said afterwards, 'les épithètes ne nous coûtaient rien'; yet neither was without a little residue of sincerity. Frederick's admiration bordered upon the sentimental; and Voltaire had begun to allow himself to hope that some day, in a provincial German court, there might be found a crowned head devoting his life to philosophy, good sense, and the love of letters. Both were to receive a curious awakening.

In 1740 Frederick became King of Prussia, and a new epoch in the relations between the two men began. The next ten years were, on both sides, years of growing disillusionment. Voltaire very soon discovered that his phrase about 'un prince philosophe qui rendra les hommes heureux' was indeed a phrase and nothing more. His *prince philosophe* started out on a career of conquest, plunged all Europe into war, and turned Prussia into a great military power. Frederick, it appeared, was at once a far more important and a far more dangerous phenomenon than Voltaire had suspected. And, on the other hand, the matured mind of the King was not slow to perceive that the enthusiasm of the Prince needed a good deal of qualification. This change of view, was, indeed, remarkably rapid. Nothing is more striking than the alteration of the tone in Frederick's correspondence during the few months which followed his accession: the voice of the raw and inexperienced youth is heard no more, and its place is taken—at once and for ever—by the self-contained caustic utterance of an embittered man of the world. In this transformation it was only natural that the wondrous figure of Voltaire should lose some of its glitter—especially since Frederick now began to have the opportunity of inspecting that figure in the flesh with his own sharp eyes. The friends met three or four times, and it is noticeable that after each meeting there is a distinct coolness on the part of Frederick. He writes with a sudden brusqueness to accuse Voltaire of showing about his manuscripts, which, he says, had only been sent him on the condition of *un secret inviolable.* He writes to Jordan complaining of Voltaire's avarice in very stringent terms. 'Ton avare boira la lie de son insatiable désir de s'enrichir ... Son apparition de six jours me coûtera par journée cinq cent cinquante écus. C'est bien payer un fou; jamais bouffon de grand seigneur n'eut de pareils gages.' He declares that 'la cervelle du poète est aussi légère que le style de ses ouvrages,' and remarks sarcastically that he is indeed a man *extraordinaire en tout.*

Yet, while his opinion of Voltaire's character was rapidly growing more and more severe, his admiration of his talents remained undiminished. For, though he had dropped metaphysics when he came to the throne, Frederick could never drop his passion for French poetry; he recognised in Voltaire the unapproachable master of that absorbing art; and for years he had made up his mind that, some day or other, he would *posséder*—for so he put it—the author of the *Henriade,* would keep him at Berlin as the brightest ornament of his court, and, above all, would have him always ready at hand to put the final polish on his own verses. In the autumn of 1743 it seemed for a moment that his wish would be gratified. Voltaire spent a visit of several weeks in Berlin; he was dazzled by the graciousness of his reception and the splendour of his surroundings; and he began to listen to the honeyed overtures of the Prussian Majesty. The great obstacle to Frederick's desire was Voltaire's relationship with Madame du Châtelet. He had lived with her for more than ten years; he was attached to her by all the ties of friendship and gratitude; he had constantly declared that he would never leave her—no, not for all the seductions of princes. She would, it is true, have been willing to accompany Voltaire to Berlin; but such a solution would by no means have suited Frederick. He was not fond of ladies—even of ladies like Madame du Châtelet—learned enough to translate Newton and to discuss by the hour the niceties of the Leibnitzian philosophy; and he had determined to *posséder* Voltaire either completely or not at all. Voltaire, in spite of repeated temptations, had remained faithful; but now, for the first time, poor Madame du Châtelet began to be seriously alarmed. His letters from Berlin grew fewer and fewer, and more and more ambiguous; she knew nothing of his plans; 'il est ivre absolument' she burst out in her distress to d'Argental, one of his oldest friends. By every post she dreaded to learn at last that he had deserted her for ever. But suddenly Voltaire returned. The spell of Berlin had been broken, and he was at her feet once more.

What had happened was highly characteristic both of the Poet and of the King. Each had tried to play a trick on the other, and each had found the other out. The French Government had been anxious to obtain an insight into the diplomatic intentions of Frederick, in an unofficial way; Voltaire had offered his services, and it had been agreed that he should write to Frederick declaring that he was obliged to leave France for a time owing to the hostility of a member of the Government, the Bishop of Mirepoix, and asking for Frederick's hospitality. Frederick had not been taken in: though he had not disentangled the whole plot, he had perceived clearly enough that Voltaire's visit was in reality that of an agent of the French Government; he also thought he saw an opportunity of securing the desire of his heart. Voltaire, to give verisimilitude to his story, had, in his letter to Frederick, loaded the Bishop of Mirepoix with ridicule and abuse; and Frederick now secretly sent this letter to Mirepoix himself. His calculation was that Mirepoix would be so outraged that he would make it impossible for Voltaire ever to return to France; and in that case—well, Voltaire would have no other course open to him but to stay where he was, in Berlin, and Madame du Châtelet would have to make the best of it. Of course, Frederick's plan failed, and Voltaire was duly informed by Mirepoix of what had happened. He was naturally very angry. He had been almost induced to stay in Berlin of his own accord, and now he found that his host had been attempting, by means of treachery and intrigue, to force him to stay there whether he liked it or not. It was a long time before he forgave Frederick. But the King was most anxious to patch up the quarrel; he still could not abandon the hope of ultimately securing Voltaire; and besides, he was now possessed by another and a more immediate desire—to be allowed a glimpse of that famous and scandalous work which Voltaire kept locked in the innermost drawer of his cabinet and revealed to none but the most favoured of his intimates—*La Pucelle*.

Accordingly the royal letters became more frequent and more flattering than ever; the royal hand cajoled and implored. 'Ne me faites point injustice sur mon caractère; d'ailleurs il vous est permis de badiner sur mon sujet comme il vous plaira.' '*La Pucelle! La Pucelle! La Pucelle!* et encore *La Pucelle!*' he exclaims. 'Pour l'amour de Dieu, ou plus encore pour l'amour de vous-même, envoyez-la-moi.' And at last Voltaire was softened. He sent off a few fragments of his *Pucelle*—just enough to whet Frederick's appetite—and he declared himself reconciled, 'Je vous ai aimé tendrement,' he wrote in March 1749; 'j'ai été fâché contre vous, je vous ai pardonné, et actuellement je vous aime à la folie.' Within a year of this date his situation had undergone a complete change. Madame du Châtelet was dead; and his position at Versailles, in spite of the friendship of Madame de Pompadour, had become almost as impossible as he had pretended it to have been in 1743. Frederick eagerly repeated his invitation; and this time Voltaire did not refuse. He was careful to make a very good bargain; obliged Frederick to pay for his journey; and arrived at Berlin in July 1750. He was given rooms in the royal palaces both at Berlin and Potsdam; he was made a Court Chamberlain, and received the Order of Merit, together with a pension of £800 a year. These arrangements caused considerable amusement in Paris; and for some days hawkers, carrying prints of Voltaire dressed in furs, and crying 'Voltaire le prussien! Six sols le fameux prussien!' were to be seen walking up and down the Quays.

The curious drama that followed, with its farcical περιπετέια and its tragi-comic *dénouement*, can hardly be understood without a brief consideration of the feelings and intentions of the two chief actors in it. The position of Frederick is comparatively plain. He had now completely thrown aside the last lingering remnants of any esteem which he may once have entertained for the character of Voltaire. He frankly thought him a scoundrel. In September 1749, less than a year before Voltaire's arrival, and at the very period of Frederick's most urgent invitations, we find him using the following language in a letter to Algarotti: 'Voltaire vient de faire un tour qui est indigne.' (He had been showing to all his friends a garbled copy of one of Frederick's letters).

> Il mériterait d'être fleurdelisé au Parnasse. C'est bien dommage qu'une âme aussi lâche soit unie à un aussi beau génie. Il a les gentillesses et les malices d'un singe. Je vous conterai ce que c'est, lorsque je vous reverrai; cependant je ne ferai semblant de rien, car j'en ai besoin pour l'étude de l'élocution française. On peut apprendre de bonnes choses d'un scélérat. Je veux savoir son français; que m'importe sa morale? Cet homme a trouvé le moyen de réunir tous les contraires. On admire son esprit, en même temps qu'on méprise son caractère.

There is no ambiguity about this. Voltaire was a scoundrel; but he was a scoundrel of genius. He would make the best possible teacher of *l'élocution française*; therefore it was necessary that he should come and live in Berlin. But as for anything more—as for any real interchange of sympathies, any genuine feeling of friendliness, of respect, or even of regard—all that was utterly out of the question. The avowal is cynical, no doubt; but it is at any rate straightforward, and above all it is peculiarly devoid of any trace of self-deception. In the face of these trenchant sentences, the view of Frederick's attitude which is suggested so assiduously by Carlyle—that he was the victim of an elevated misapprehension, that he was always hoping for the best, and that, when the explosion came he was very much surprised and profoundly disappointed—becomes obviously untenable. If any man ever acted with his eyes wide open, it was Frederick when he invited Voltaire to Berlin.

Yet, though that much is clear, the letter to Algarotti betrays, in more than one direction, a very singular state of mind. A warm devotion to l'élocution française is easy enough to understand; but Frederick's devotion was much more than warm; it was so absorbing and so intense that it left him no rest until, by hook or by crook, by supplication, or by trickery, or by paying down hard cash, he had obtained the close and constant proximity of—what?—of a man whom he himself described as a 'singe' and a 'scélérat,' a man of base soul and despicable character. And Frederick appears to see nothing surprising in this. He takes it quite as a matter of course that he should be, not merely willing, but delighted to run all the risks involved by Voltaire's undoubted roguery, so long as he can be sure of benefiting from Voltaire's no less undoubted mastery of French versification. This is certainly strange; but the explanation of it lies in the extraordinary vogue—a vogue, indeed, so extraordinary that it is very difficult for the modern reader to realise it—enjoyed throughout Europe by French culture and literature during the middle years of the eighteenth century. Frederick was merely an extreme instance of a universal fact. Like all Germans of any education, he habitually wrote and spoke in French; like every lady and gentleman from Naples to Edinburgh, his life was regulated by the social conventions of France; like every amateur of letters from Madrid to St. Petersburg, his whole conception of literary taste, his whole standard of literary values, was French. To him, as to the vast majority of his contemporaries, the very essence of civilisation was concentrated in French literature, and especially in French poetry; and French poetry meant to him, as to his contemporaries, that particular kind of French poetry which had come into fashion at the court of Louis XIV. For this curious creed was as narrow as it was all-pervading. The *Grand Siècle* was the Church Infallible; and it was heresy to doubt the Gospel of Boileau.

Frederick's library, still preserved at Potsdam, shows us what literature meant in those days to a cultivated man: it is composed entirely of the French Classics, of the works of Voltaire, and of the masterpieces of antiquity translated into eighteenth-century French. But Frederick was not content with mere appreciation; he too would create; he would write alexandrines on the model of Racine, and madrigals after the manner of Chaulieu; he would press in person into the sacred sanctuary, and burn incense with his own hands upon the inmost shrine. It was true that he was a foreigner; it was true that his knowledge of the French language was incomplete and incorrect; but his sense of his own ability urged him forward, and his indefatigable pertinacity kept him at his strange task throughout the whole of his life. He filled volumes, and the contents of those volumes afford probably the most complete illustration in literature of the very trite proverb—*Poeta nascitur, non fit*. The spectacle of that heavy German Muse, with her feet crammed into pointed slippers, executing, with incredible conscientiousness, now the stately measure of a Versailles minuet, and now the spritely steps of a Parisian jig, would be either ludicrous or pathetic—one hardly knows which—were it not so certainly neither the one nor the other, but simply dreary with an unutterable dreariness, from which the eyes of men avert themselves in shuddering dismay. Frederick himself felt that there was something wrong—something, but not really very much. All that was wanted was a little expert advice; and obviously Voltaire was the man to supply it—Voltaire, the one true heir of the Great Age, the dramatist who had revived the glories of Racine (did not Frederick's tears flow almost as copiously over *Mahomet* as over *Britannicus*?), the epic poet who had eclipsed Homer and Virgil (had not Frederick every right to judge, since he had read the 'Iliad' in French prose and the 'Aeneid' in French verse?), the lyric master whose odes and whose epistles occasionally even surpassed (Frederick Confessed it with amazement) those of the Marquis de la Fare. Voltaire, there could be no doubt, would do just what was needed; he would know how to squeeze in a little further the waist of the German Calliope, to apply with his deft fingers precisely the right dab of rouge to her cheeks, to instil into her movements the last *nuances* of correct deportment. And, if he did that, of what consequence were the blemishes of his personal character? 'On peut apprendre de bonnes choses d'un scélérat.'

And, besides, though Voltaire might be a rogue, Frederick felt quite convinced that he could keep him in order. A crack or two of the master's whip—a coldness in the royal demeanour, a hint at a stoppage of the pension—and the monkey would put an end to his tricks soon enough. It never seems to have occurred to Frederick that the possession of genius might imply a quality of spirit which was not that of an ordinary man. This was his great, his fundamental error. It was the ingenuous error of a cynic. He knew that he was under no delusion as to Voltaire's faults, and so he supposed that he could be under no delusion as to his merits. He innocently imagined that the capacity for great writing was something that could be as easily separated from the owner of it as a hat or a glove. 'C'est bien dommage qu'une âme aussi lâche soit unie à un aussi beau génie.' *C'est bien dommage!*—as if there was nothing more extraordinary in such a combination than that of a pretty woman and an ugly dress. And so Frederick held his whip a little tighter, and reminded himself once more that, in spite of that *beau génie*, it was a monkey that he had to deal with. But he was wrong: it was not a monkey; it was a devil, which is a very different thing.

A devil—or perhaps an angel? One cannot be quite sure. For, amid the complexities of that extraordinary spirit, where good and evil were so mysteriously interwoven, where the elements of darkness and the elements of light lay crowded together in such ever-deepening ambiguity, fold within fold, the clearer the vision the greater the bewilderment, the more impartial the judgment the profounder the doubt. But one thing at least is certain: that spirit, whether it was admirable or whether it was odious, was moved by a terrific force. Frederick had failed to realise this; and indeed, though Voltaire was fifty-six when he went to Berlin, and though his whole life had been spent in a blaze of publicity, there was still not one of his contemporaries who understood the true nature of his genius; it was perhaps hidden even from himself. He had reached the threshold of old age, and his life's work was still before him; it was not as a writer of tragedies and epics that he was to take his place in the world. Was he, in the depths of his consciousness, aware that this was so? Did some obscure instinct urge him forward, at this late hour, to break with the ties of a lifetime, and rush forth into the unknown?

What his precise motives were in embarking upon the Berlin adventure it is very difficult to say. It is true that he was disgusted with Paris—he was ill-received at Court, and he was pestered by endless literary quarrels and jealousies; it would be very pleasant to show his countrymen that he had other strings to his bow, that, if they did not appreciate him, Frederick the Great did. It is true, too, that he admired Frederick's intellect, and that he was flattered by his favour. 'Il avait de l'esprit,' he said afterwards, 'des grâces, et, de plus, il était roi; ce qui fait toujours une grande séduction, attendu la faiblesse humaine.' His vanity could not resist the prestige of a royal intimacy; and no doubt he relished to the full even the increased consequence which came to him with his Chamberlain's key and his order— to say nothing of the addition of £800 to his income. Yet, on the other hand, he was very well aware that he was exchanging freedom for servitude, and that he was entering into a bargain with a man who would make quite sure that he was getting his money's worth; and he knew in his heart that he had something better to do than to play, however successfully, the part of a courtier. Nor was he personally attached to Frederick; he was personally attached to no one on earth. Certainly he had never been a man of feeling, and now that he was old and hardened by the uses of the world he had grown to be completely what in essence he always was—a fighter, without tenderness, without scruples, and without remorse. No, he went to Berlin for his own purposes—however dubious those purposes may have been.

And it is curious to observe that in his correspondence with his niece, Madame Denis, whom he had left behind him at the head of his Paris establishment and in whom he confided—in so far as he can be said to have confided in anyone—he repeatedly states that there is nothing permanent about his visit to Berlin. At first he declares that he is only making a stay of a few weeks with Frederick, that he is going on to Italy to visit 'sa Sainteté' and to inspect 'la ville souterraine,' that he will be back in Paris in the autumn. The autumn comes, and the roads are too muddy to travel by; he must wait till the winter, when they will be frozen hard. Winter comes, and it is too cold to move; but he will certainly return in the spring. Spring comes, and he is on the point of finishing his *Siècle de Louis XIV.*; he really must wait just a few weeks more. The book is published; but then how can he appear in Paris until he is quite sure of its success? And so he lingers on, delaying and prevaricating, until a whole year has passed, and still he lingers on, still he is on the point of going, and still he does not go. Meanwhile, to all appearances, he was definitely fixed, a salaried official, at Frederick's court; and he was writing to all his other friends, to assure them that he had never been so happy, that he could see no reason why he should ever come away. What were his true intentions? Could he himself have said? Had he perhaps, in some secret corner of his brain, into which even he hardly dared to look, a premonition of the future? At times, in this Berlin adventure, he seems to resemble some great buzzing fly, shooting suddenly into a room through an open window and dashing frantically from side to side; when all at once, as suddenly, he swoops away and out through another window which opens in quite a different direction, towards wide and flowery fields; so that perhaps the reckless creature knew where he was going after all.

In any case, it is evident to the impartial observer that Voltaire's visit could only have ended as it did—in an explosion. The elements of the situation were too combustible for any other conclusion. When two confirmed egotists decide, for purely selfish reasons, to set up house together, everyone knows what will happen. For some time their sense of mutual advantage may induce them to tolerate each other, but sooner or later human nature will assert itself, and the *ménage* will break up. And, with Voltaire and Frederick, the difficulties inherent in all such cases were intensified by the fact that the relationship between them was, in effect, that of servant and master; that Voltaire, under a very thin disguise, was a paid menial, while Frederick, condescend as he might, was an autocrat whose will was law. Thus the two famous and perhaps mythical sentences, invariably repeated by historians of the incident, about orange-skins and dirty linen, do in fact sum up the gist of the matter. 'When one has sucked the orange, one throws away the skin,' somebody told Voltaire that the King had said, on being asked how much longer he would put up with the poet's vagaries. And Frederick, on his side, was informed that Voltaire, when a batch of the royal verses were brought to him for correction, had burst out with 'Does the man expect me to go on washing his dirty linen for ever?'

Each knew well enough the weak spot in his position, and each was acutely and uncomfortably conscious that the other knew it too. Thus, but a very few weeks after Voltaire's arrival, little clouds of discord become visible on the horizon; electrical discharges of irritability began to take place, growing more and more frequent and violent as time goes on; and one can overhear the pot and the kettle, in strictest privacy, calling each other black. 'The monster,' whispers Voltaire to Madame Denis, 'he opens all our letters in the post'—Voltaire, whose light-handedness with other people's correspondence was only too notorious. 'The monkey,' mutters Frederick, 'he shows my private letters to his friends'—Frederick, who had thought nothing of betraying Voltaire's letters to the Bishop of Mirepoix. 'How happy I should be here,' exclaims the callous old poet, 'but for one thing—his Majesty is utterly heartless!' And meanwhile Frederick, who had never let a farthing escape from his close fist without some very good reason, was busy concocting an epigram upon the avarice of Voltaire.

It was, indeed, Voltaire's passion for money which brought on the first really serious storm. Three months after his arrival in Berlin, the temptation to increase his already considerable fortune by a stroke of illegal stock-jobbing proved too strong for him; he became involved in a series of shady financial transactions with a Jew; he quarrelled with the Jew; there was an acrimonious lawsuit, with charges and countercharges of the most discreditable kind; and, though the Jew lost his case on a technical point, the poet certainly did not leave the court without a stain upon his character. Among other misdemeanours, it is almost certain—the evidence is not quite conclusive—that he committed forgery in order to support a false oath. Frederick was furious, and for a moment was on the brink of dismissing Voltaire from Berlin. He would have been wise if he had done so. But he could not part with his *beau génie* so soon. He cracked his whip, and, setting the monkey to stand in the corner, contented himself with a shrug of the shoulders and the exclamation 'C'est l'affaire d'un fripon qui a voulu tromper un filou.' A few weeks later the royal favour shone forth once more, and Voltaire, who had been hiding himself in a suburban villa, came out and basked again in those refulgent beams.

And the beams were decidedly refulgent—so much so, in fact, that they almost satisfied even the vanity of Voltaire. Almost, but not quite. For, though his glory was great, though he was the centre of all men's admiration, courted by nobles, flattered by princesses—there is a letter from one of them, a sister of Frederick's, still extant, wherein the trembling votaress ventures to praise the great man's works, which, she says, 'vous rendent si célèbre et immortel'—though he had ample leisure for his private activities, though he enjoyed every day the brilliant conversation of the King, though he could often forget for weeks together that he was the paid servant of a jealous despot—yet, in spite of all, there was a crumpled rose-leaf amid the silken sheets, and he lay awake o' nights. He was not the only Frenchman at Frederick's court. That monarch had surrounded himself with a small group of persons—foreigners for the most part—whose business it was to instruct him when he wished to improve his mind, to flatter him when he was out of temper, and to entertain him when he was bored. There was hardly one of them that was not thoroughly second-rate. Algarotti was an elegant dabbler in scientific matters—he had written a book to explain Newton to the ladies; d'Argens was an amiable and erudite writer of a dull free-thinking turn; Chasot was a retired military man with too many debts, and Darget was a good-natured secretary with too many love affairs; La Mettrie was a doctor who had been exiled from France for atheism and bad manners; and Pöllnitz was a decaying baron who, under stress of circumstances, had unfortunately been obliged to change his religion six times.

These were the boon companions among whom Frederick chose to spend his leisure hours. Whenever he had nothing better to do, he would exchange rhymed epigrams with Algarotti, or discuss the Jewish religion with d'Argens, or write long improper poems about Darget, in the style of *La Pucelle*. Or else he would summon La Mettrie, who would forthwith prove the irrefutability of materialism in a series of wild paradoxes, shout with laughter, suddenly shudder and cross himself on upsetting the salt, and eventually pursue his majesty with his buffooneries into a place where even royal persons are wont to be left alone. At other times Frederick would amuse himself by first cutting down the pension of Pöllnitz, who was at the moment a Lutheran, and then writing long and serious letters to him suggesting that if he would only become a Catholic again he might be made a Silesian Abbot. Strangely enough, Frederick was not popular, and one or other of the inmates of his little menagerie was constantly escaping and running away. Darget and Chasot both succeeded in getting through the wires; they obtained leave to visit Paris, and stayed there. Poor d'Argens often tried to follow their example; more than once he set off for France, secretly vowing never to return; but he had no money, Frederick was blandishing, and the wretch was always lured back to captivity. As for La Mettrie, he made his escape in a different manner—by dying after supper one evening of a surfeit of pheasant pie. 'Jésus! Marie!' he gasped, as he felt the pains of death upon him. 'Ah!' said a priest who had been sent for, 'vous voilà enfin retourné à ces noms consolateurs.' La Mettrie, with an oath, expired; and Frederick, on hearing of this unorthodox conclusion, remarked, 'J'en suis bien aise, pour le repos de son âme.'

Among this circle of down-at-heel eccentrics there was a single figure whose distinction and respectability stood out in striking contrast from the rest—that of Maupertuis, who had been, since 1745, the President of the Academy of Sciences at Berlin. Maupertuis has had an unfortunate fate: he was first annihilated by the ridicule of Voltaire, and then recreated by the humour of Carlyle; but he was an ambitious man, very anxious to be famous, and his desire has been gratified in over-flowing measure. During his life he was chiefly known for his voyage to Lapland, and his observations there, by which he was able to substantiate the Newtonian doctrine of the flatness of the earth at the poles. He possessed considerable scientific attainments, he was honest, he was energetic; he appeared to be just the man to revive the waning glories of Prussian science; and when Frederick succeeded in inducing him to come to Berlin as President of his Academy the choice seemed amply justified. Maupertuis had, moreover, some pretensions to wit; and in his earlier days his biting and elegant sarcasms had more than once overwhelmed his scientific adversaries. Such accomplishments suited Frederick admirably. Maupertuis, he declared, was an *homme d'esprit*, and the happy President became a constant guest at the royal supper-parties. It was the happy—the too happy—President who was the rose-leaf in the bed of Voltaire. The two men had known each other slightly for many years, and had always expressed the highest admiration for each other; but their mutual amiability was now to be put to a severe test. The sagacious Buffon observed the danger from afar: 'ces deux hommes,' he wrote to a friend, 'ne sont pas faits pour demeurer ensemble dans la même chambre.' And indeed to the vain and sensitive poet, uncertain of Frederick's cordiality, suspicious of hidden enemies, intensely jealous of possible rivals, the spectacle of Maupertuis at supper, radiant, at his ease, obviously protected, obviously superior to the shady mediocrities who sat around—that sight was gall and wormwood; and he looked closer, with a new malignity; and then those piercing eyes began to make discoveries, and that relentless brain began to do its work.

Maupertuis had very little judgment; so far from attempting to conciliate Voltaire, he was rash enough to provoke hostilities. It was very natural that he should have lost his temper. He had been for five years the dominating figure in the royal circle, and now suddenly he was deprived of his pre-eminence and thrown completely into the shade. Who could attend to Maupertuis while Voltaire was talking?—Voltaire, who as obviously outshone Maupertuis as Maupertuis outshone La Mettrie and Darget and the rest. In his exasperation the President went to the length of openly giving his protection to a disreputable literary man, La Beaumelle, who was a declared enemy of Voltaire. This meant war, and war was not long in coming.

Some years previously Maupertuis had, as he believed, discovered an important mathematical law—the 'principle of least action.' The law was, in fact, important, and has had a fruitful history in the development of mechanical theory; but, as Mr. Jourdain has shown in a recent monograph, Maupertuis enunciated it incorrectly without realising its true import, and a far more accurate and scientific statement of it was given, within a few months, by Euler. Maupertuis, however, was very proud of his discovery, which, he considered, embodied one of the principal reasons for believing in the existence of God; and he was therefore exceedingly angry when, shortly after Voltaire's arrival in Berlin, a Swiss mathematician, Koenig, published a polite memoir attacking both its accuracy and its originality, and quoted in support of his contention an unpublished letter by Leibnitz, in which the law was more exactly expressed. Instead of arguing upon the merits of the case, Maupertuis declared that the letter of Leibnitz was a forgery, and that therefore Koenig's remarks deserved no further consideration. When Koenig expostulated, Maupertuis decided upon a more drastic step. He summoned a meeting of the Berlin Academy of Sciences, of which Koenig was a member, laid the case before it, and moved that it should solemnly pronounce Koenig a forger, and the letter of Leibnitz supposititious and false. The members of the Academy were frightened; their pensions depended upon the President's good will; and even the illustrious Euler was not ashamed to take part in this absurd and disgraceful condemnation.

Voltaire saw at once that his opportunity had come. Maupertuis had put himself utterly and irretrievably in the wrong. He was wrong in attributing to his discovery a value which it did not possess; he was wrong in denying the authenticity of the Leibnitz letter; above all he was wrong in treating a purely scientific question as the proper subject for the disciplinary jurisdiction of an Academy. If Voltaire struck now, he would have his enemy on the hip. There was only one consideration to give him pause, and that was a grave one: to attack Maupertuis upon this matter was, in effect, to attack the King. Not only was Frederick certainly privy to Maupertuis' action, but he was extremely sensitive of the reputation of his Academy and of its President, and he would certainly consider any interference on the part of Voltaire, who himself drew his wages from the royal purse, as a flagrant act of disloyalty. But Voltaire decided to take the risk. He had now been more than two years in Berlin, and the atmosphere of a Court was beginning to weigh upon his spirit; he was restless, he was reckless, he was spoiling for a fight; he would take on Maupertuis singly or Maupertuis and Frederick combined—he did not much care which, and in any case he flattered himself that he would settle the hash of the President.

As a preparatory measure, he withdrew all his spare cash from Berlin, and invested it with the Duke of Wurtemberg. 'Je mets tout doucement ordre à mes affaires,' he told Madame Denis. Then, on September 18, 1752, there appeared in the papers a short article entitled 'Réponse d'un Académicien de Berlin à un Académicien de Paris.' It was a statement, deadly in its bald simplicity, its studied coldness, its concentrated force, of Koenig's case against Maupertuis. The President must have turned pale as he read it; but the King turned crimson. The terrible indictment could, of course only have been written by one man, and that man was receiving a royal pension of £800 a year and carrying about a Chamberlain's gold key in his pocket. Frederick flew to his writing-table, and composed an indignant pamphlet which he caused to be published with the Prussian arms on the title-page. It was a feeble work, full of exaggerated praises of Maupertuis, and of clumsy invectives against Voltaire: the President's reputation was gravely compared to that of Homer; the author of the 'Réponse d'un Académicien de Berlin' was declared to be a 'faiseur de libelles sans génie,' an 'imposteur effronté,' a 'malheureux écrivain' while the 'Réponse' itself was a 'grossièreté plate,' whose publication was an 'action malicieuse, lâche, infâme,' a 'brigandage affreux.' The presence of the royal insignia only intensified the futility of the outburst. 'L'aigle, le sceptre, et la couronne,' wrote Voltaire to Madame Denis, 'sont bien étonnés de se trouver là.' But one thing was now certain: the King had joined the fray. Voltaire's blood was up, and he was not sorry. A kind of exaltation seized him; from this moment his course was clear—he would do as much damage as he could, and then leave Prussia for ever. And it so happened that just then an unexpected opportunity occurred for one of those furious onslaughts so dear to his heart, with that weapon which he knew so well how to wield. 'Je n'ai point de sceptre,' he ominously shot out to Madame Denis, 'mais j'ai une plume.'

Meanwhile the life of the Court—which passed for the most part at Potsdam, in the little palace of Sans Souci which Frederick had built for himself—proceeded on its accustomed course. It was a singular life, half military, half monastic, rigid, retired, from which all the ordinary pleasures of society were strictly excluded. 'What do you do here?' one of the royal princes was once asked. 'We conjugate the verb *s'ennuyer*,' was the reply. But, wherever he might be, that was a verb unknown to Voltaire. Shut up all day in the strange little room, still preserved for the eyes of the curious, with its windows opening on the formal garden, and its yellow walls thickly embossed with the brightly coloured shapes of fruits, flowers, birds, and apes, the indefatigable old man worked away at his histories, his tragedies, his *Pucelle*, and his enormous correspondence. He was, of course, ill—very ill; he was probably, in fact, upon the brink of death; but he had grown accustomed to that situation; and the worse he grew the more furiously he worked. He was a victim, he declared, of erysipelas, dysentery, and scurvy; he was constantly attacked by fever, and all his teeth had fallen out. But he continued to work. On one occasion a friend visited him, and found him in bed. 'J'ai quatre maladies mortelles,' he wailed. 'Pourtant,' remarked the friend, 'vous avez l'oeil fort bon.' Voltaire leapt up from the pillows: 'Ne savez-vous pas,' he shouted, 'que les scorbutiques meurent l'oeil enflammé?' When the evening came it was time to dress, and, in all the pomp of flowing wig and diamond order, to proceed to the little music-room, where his Majesty, after the business of the day, was preparing to relax himself upon the flute. The orchestra was gathered together; the audience was seated; the concerto began. And then the sounds of beauty flowed and trembled, and seemed, for a little space, to triumph over the pains of living and the hard hearts of men; and the royal master poured out his skill in some long and elaborate cadenza, and the adagio came, the marvellous adagio, and the conqueror of Rossbach drew tears from the author of *Candide*. But a moment later it was supper-time; and the night ended in the oval dining-room, amid laughter and champagne, the ejaculations of La Mettrie, the epigrams of Maupertuis, the sarcasms of Frederick, and the devastating coruscations of Voltaire.

Yet, in spite of all the jests and roses, everyone could hear the rumbling of the volcano under the ground. Everyone could hear, but nobody would listen; the little flames leapt up through the surface, but still the gay life went on; and then the irruption came. Voltaire's enemy had written a book. In the intervals of his more serious labours, the President had put together a series of 'Letters,' in which a number of miscellaneous scientific subjects were treated in a mildly speculative and popular style. The volume was rather dull, and very unimportant; but it happened to appear at this particular moment, and Voltaire pounced upon it with the swift swoop of a hawk on a mouse. The famous *Diatribe du Docteur Akakia* is still fresh with a fiendish gaiety after a hundred and fifty years; but to realise to the full the skill and malice which went to the making of it, one must at least have glanced at the flat insipid production which called it forth, and noted with what a diabolical art the latent absurdities in poor Maupertuis' *rêveries* have been detected, dragged forth into the light of day, and nailed to the pillory of an immortal ridicule. The *Diatribe*, however, is not all mere laughter; there is a real criticism in it, too. For instance, it was not simply a farcical exaggeration to say that Maupertuis had set out to prove the existence of God by 'A plus B divided by Z'; in substance, the charge was both important and well founded. 'Lorsque la métaphysique entre dans la géometrie,' Voltaire wrote in a private letter some months afterwards, 'c'est Arimane qui entre dans le royaume d'Oromasde, et qui y apporte des ténèbres'; and Maupertuis had in fact vitiated his treatment of the 'principle of least action' by his metaphysical pre-occupations. Indeed, all through Voltaire's pamphlet, there is an implied appeal to true scientific principles, an underlying assertion of the paramount importance of the experimental method, a consistent attack upon *a priori* reasoning, loose statement, and vague conjecture. But of course, mixed with all this, and covering it all, there is a bubbling, sparkling fountain of effervescent raillery—cruel, personal, insatiable—the raillery of a demon with a grudge. The manuscript was shown to Frederick, who laughed till the tears ran down his cheeks. But, between his gasps, he forbade Voltaire to publish it on pain of his most terrible displeasure. Naturally Voltaire was profuse with promises, and a few days later, under a royal licence obtained for another work, the little book appeared in print. Frederick still managed to keep his wrath within bounds: he collected all the copies of the edition and had them privately destroyed; he gave a furious wigging to Voltaire; and he flattered himself that he had heard the last of the business.

> Ne vous embarrassez de rien, mon cher Maupertuis [he wrote to the President in his singular orthography]; l'affaire des libelles est finie. J'ai parlé si vrai à l'hôme, je lui ai lavé si bien la tête que je ne crois pas qu'il y retourne, et je connais son âme lache, incapable de sentiments d'honneur. Je l'ai intimidé du côté de la boursse, ce qui a fait tout l'effet que j'attendais. Je lui ai déclaré enfin nettement que ma maison devait être un sanctuaire et non une retraite de brigands ou de célérats qui distillent des poissons.

Apparently it did not occur to Frederick that this declaration had come a little late in the day. Meanwhile Maupertuis, overcome by illness and by rage, had taken to his bed. 'Un peu trop d'amour-propre,' Frederick wrote to Darget, 'l'a rendu trop sensible aux manoeuvres d'un singe qu'il devait mépriser après qu'on l'avait fouetté.' But now the monkey *had* been whipped, and doubtless all would be well. It seems strange that Frederick should still, after more than two years of close observation, have had no notion of the material he was dealing with. He might as well have supposed that he could stop a mountain torrent in spate with a wave of his hand, as have imagined that he could impose obedience upon Voltaire in such a crisis by means of a lecture and a threat 'du côté de la boursse.' Before the month was out all Germany was swarming with *Akakias*; thousands of copies were being printed in Holland; and editions were going off in Paris like hot cakes. It is difficult to withold one's admiration from the audacious old spirit who thus, on the mere strength of his mother-wits, dared to defy the enraged master of a powerful state. 'Votre effronterie m'étonne,' fulminated Frederick in a furious note, when he suddenly discovered that all Europe was ringing with the absurdity of the man whom he had chosen to be the President of his favourite Academy, whose cause he had publicly espoused, and whom he had privately assured of his royal protection. 'Ah! Mon Dieu, Sire,' scribbled Voltaire on the same sheet of paper, 'dans l'état où je suis!' (He was, of course, once more dying.) 'Quoi! vous me jugeriez sans entendre! Je demande justice et la mort.' Frederick replied by having copies of *Akakia* burnt by the common hangman in the streets of Berlin. Voltaire thereupon returned his Order, his gold key, and his pension. It might have been supposed that the final rupture had now really come at last. But three months elapsed before Frederick could bring himself to realise that all was over, and to agree to the departure of his extraordinary guest. Carlyle's suggestion that this last delay arose from the unwillingness of Voltaire to go, rather than from Frederick's desire to keep him, is plainly controverted by the facts. The King not only insisted on Voltaire's accepting once again the honours which he had surrendered, but actually went so far as to write him a letter of forgiveness and reconciliation. But the poet would not relent; there was a last week of suppers at Potsdam—'soupers de Damoclès' Voltaire called them; and then, on March 26, 1753, the two men parted for ever.

The storm seemed to be over; but the tail of it was still hanging in the wind. Voltaire, on his way to the waters of Plombières, stopped at Leipzig, where he could not resist, in spite of his repeated promises to the contrary, the temptation to bring out a new and enlarged edition of *Akakia*. Upon this Maupertuis utterly lost his head: he wrote to Voltaire, threatening him with personal chastisement. Voltaire issued yet another edition of *Akakia*, appended a somewhat unauthorised version of the President's letter, and added that if the dangerous and cruel man really persisted in his threat he would be received with a vigorous discharge from those instruments of intimate utility which figure so freely in the comedies of Molière. This stroke was the *coup de grâce* of Maupertuis. Shattered in body and mind, he dragged himself from Berlin to die at last in Basle under the ministration of a couple of Capuchins and a Protestant valet reading aloud the Genevan Bible. In the meantime Frederick had decided on a violent measure. He had suddenly remembered that Voltaire had carried off with him one of the very few privately printed copies of those poetical works upon which he had spent so much devoted labour; it occurred to him that they contained several passages of a highly damaging kind; and he could feel no certainty that those passages would not be given to the world by the malicious Frenchman. Such, at any rate, were his own excuses for the step which he now took; but it seems possible that he was at least partly swayed by feelings of resentment and revenge which had been rendered uncontrollable by the last onslaught upon Maupertuis. Whatever may have been his motives, it is certain that he ordered the Prussian Resident in Frankfort, which was Voltaire's next stopping-place, to hold the poet in arrest until he delivered over the royal volume. A multitude of strange blunders and ludicrous incidents followed, upon which much controversial and patriotic ink has been spilt by a succession of French and German biographers. To an English reader it is clear that in this little comedy of errors none of the parties concerned can escape from blame—that Voltaire was hysterical, undignified, and untruthful, that the Prussian Resident was stupid and domineering, that Frederick was careless in his orders and cynical as to their results. Nor, it is to be hoped, need any Englishman be reminded that the consequences of a system of government in which the arbitrary will of an individual takes the place of the rule of law are apt to be disgraceful and absurd.

After five weeks' detention at Frankfort, Voltaire was free—free in every sense of the word—free from the service of Kings and the clutches of Residents, free in his own mind, free to shape his own destiny. He hesitated for several months, and then settled down by the Lake of Geneva. There the fires, which had lain smouldering so long in the profundities of his spirit, flared up, and flamed over Europe, towering and inextinguishable. In a few years letters began to flow once more to and from Berlin. At first the old grievances still rankled; but in time even the wrongs of Maupertuis and the misadventures of Frankfort were almost forgotten. Twenty years passed, and the King of Prussia was submitting his verses as anxiously as ever to Voltaire, whose compliments and cajoleries were pouring out in their accustomed stream. But their relationship was no longer that of master and pupil, courtier and King; it was that of two independent and equal powers. Even Frederick the Great was forced to see at last in the Patriarch of Ferney something more than a monkey with a genius for French versification. He actually came to respect the author of *Akakia*, and to cherish his memory. 'Je lui fais tous les matins ma prière,' he told d'Alembert, when Voltaire had been two years in the grave; 'je lui dis, Divin Voltaire, *ora pro nobis.*'

1915.

NOTES:

[6] October 1915.

THE ROUSSEAU AFFAIR

No one who has made the slightest expedition into that curious and fascinating country, Eighteenth-Century France, can have come away from it without at least *one* impression strong upon him—that in no other place and at no other time have people ever squabbled so much. France in the eighteenth century, whatever else it may have been—however splendid in genius, in vitality, in noble accomplishment and high endeavour—was certainly not a quiet place to live in. One could never have been certain, when one woke up in the morning, whether, before the day was out, one would not be in the Bastille for something one had said at dinner, or have quarrelled with half one's friends for something one had never said at all.

Of all the disputes and agitations of that agitated age none is more remarkable than the famous quarrel between Rousseau and his friends, which disturbed French society for so many years, and profoundly affected the life and the character of the most strange and perhaps the most potent of the precursors of the Revolution. The affair is constantly cropping up in the literature of the time; it occupies a prominent place in the later books of the *Confessions*; and there is an account of its earlier phases—an account written from the anti-Rousseau point of view—in the *Mémoires* of Madame d'Epinay. The whole story is an exceedingly complex one, and all the details of it have never been satisfactorily explained; but the general verdict of subsequent writers has been decidedly hostile to Rousseau, though it has not subscribed to all the virulent abuse poured upon him by his enemies at the time of the quarrel. This, indeed, is precisely the conclusion which an unprejudiced reader of the *Confessions* would naturally come to. Rousseau's story, even as he himself tells it, does not carry conviction. He would have us believe that he was the victim of a vast and diabolical conspiracy, of which Grimm and Diderot were the moving spirits, which succeeded in alienating from him his dearest friends, and which eventually included all the ablest and most distinguished persons of the age. Not only does such a conspiracy appear, upon the face of it, highly improbable, but the evidence which Rousseau adduces to prove its existence seems totally insufficient; and the reader is left under the impression that the unfortunate Jean-Jacques was the victim, not of a plot contrived by rancorous enemies, but of his own perplexed, suspicious, and deluded mind. This conclusion is supported by the account of the affair given by contemporaries, and it is still further strengthened by Rousseau's own writings subsequent to the *Confessions*, where his endless recriminations, his elaborate hypotheses, and his wild inferences bear all the appearance of mania. Here the matter has rested for many years; and it seemed improbable that any fresh reasons would arise for reopening the question. Mrs. F. Macdonald, however, in a recently-published work[7], has produced some new and important evidence, which throws entirely fresh light upon certain obscure parts of this doubtful history; and is possibly of even greater interest. For it is Mrs. Macdonald's contention that her new discovery completely overturns the orthodox theory, establishes the guilt of Grimm, Diderot, and the rest of the anti-Rousseau party, and proves that the story told in the *Confessions* is simply the truth.

If these conclusions really do follow from Mrs. Macdonald's newly-discovered data, it would be difficult to over-estimate the value of her work, for the result of it would be nothing less than a revolution in our judgments upon some of the principal characters of the eighteenth century. To make it certain that Diderot was a cad and a cheat, that d'Alembert was a dupe, and Hume a liar—that, surely, were no small achievement. And, even if these conclusions do not follow from Mrs. Macdonald's data, her work will still be valuable, owing to the data themselves. Her discoveries are important, whatever inferences may be drawn from them; and for this reason her book, 'which represents,' as she tells us, 'twenty years of research,' will be welcome to all students of that remarkable age.

Mrs. Macdonald's principal revelations relate to the *Mémoires* of Madame d'Epinay. This work was first printed in 1818, and the concluding quarter of it contains an account of the Rousseau quarrel, the most detailed of all those written from the anti-Rousseau point of view. It has, however, always been doubtful how far the *Mémoires* were to be trusted as accurate records of historical fact. The manuscript disappeared; but it was known that the characters who, in the printed book, appear under the names of real persons, were given pseudonyms in the original document; and many of the minor statements contradicted known events. Had Madame d'Epinay merely intended to write a *roman à clef*? What seemed, so far as concerned the Rousseau narrative, to put this hypothesis out of court was the fact that the story of the quarrel as it appears in the *Mémoires* is, in its main outlines, substantiated both by Grimm's references to Rousseau in his *Correspondance Littéraire*, and by a brief memorandum of Rousseau's misconduct, drawn up by Diderot for his private use, and not published until many years after Madame d'Epinay's death. Accordingly most writers on the subject have taken the accuracy of the *Mémoires* for granted; Sainte-Beuve, for instance, prefers the word of Madame d'Epinay to that of

Rousseau, when there is a direct conflict of testimony; and Lord Morley, in his well-known biography, uses the *Mémoires* as an authority for many of the incidents which he relates. Mrs. Macdonald's researches, however, have put an entirely different complexion on the case. She has discovered the manuscript from which the *Mémoires* were printed, and she has examined the original draft of this manuscript, which had been unearthed some years ago, but whose full import had been unaccountably neglected by previous scholars. From these researches, two facts have come to light. In the first place, the manuscript differs in many respects from the printed book, and, in particular, contains a conclusion of two hundred sheets, which has never been printed at all; the alterations were clearly made in order to conceal the inaccuracies of the manuscript; and the omitted conclusion is frankly and palpably a fiction. And in the second place, the original draft of the manuscript turns out to be the work of several hands; it contains, especially in those portions which concern Rousseau, many erasures, corrections, and notes, while several pages have been altogether cut out; most of the corrections were made by Madame d'Epinay herself; but in nearly every case these corrections carry out the instructions in the notes; and the notes themselves are in the handwriting of Diderot and Grimm. Mrs. Macdonald gives several facsimiles of pages in the original draft, which amply support her description of it; but it is to be hoped that before long she will be able to produce a new and complete edition of the *Mémoires*, with all the manuscript alterations clearly indicated; for until then it will be difficult to realise the exact condition of the text. However, it is now beyond dispute both that Madame d'Epinay's narrative cannot be regarded as historically accurate, and that its agreement with the statements of Grimm and Diderot is by no means an independent confirmation of its truth, for Grimm and Diderot themselves had a hand in its compilation.

Thus far we are on firm ground. But what are the conclusions which Mrs. Macdonald builds up from these foundations? The account, she says, of Rousseau's conduct and character, as it appears in the printed version, is hostile to him, but it was not the account which Madame d'Epinay herself originally wrote. The hostile narrative was, in effect, composed by Grimm and Diderot, who induced Madame d'Epinay to substitute it for her own story; and thus her own story could not have agreed with theirs. Madame d'Epinay knew the truth; she knew that Rousseau's conduct had been honourable and wise; and so she had described it in her book; until, falling completely under the influence of Grimm and Diderot, she had allowed herself to become the instrument for blackening the reputation of her old friend. Mrs. Macdonald paints a lurid picture of the conspirators at work—of Diderot penning his false and malignant instructions, of Madame d'Epinay's half-unwilling hand putting the last touches to the fraud, of Grimm, rushing back to Paris at the time of the Revolution, and risking his life in order to make quite certain that the result of all these efforts should reach posterity. Well! it would be difficult—perhaps it would be impossible—to prove conclusively that none of these things ever took place. The facts upon which Mrs. Macdonald lays so much stress—the mutilations, the additions, the instructing notes, the proved inaccuracy of the story the manuscripts tell— these facts, no doubt, may be explained by Mrs. Macdonald's theories; but there are other facts—no less important, and no less certain—which are in direct contradiction to Mrs. Macdonald's view, and over which she passes as lightly as she can. Putting aside the question of the *Mémoires*, we know nothing of Diderot which would lead us to entertain for a moment the supposition that he was a dishonourable and badhearted man; we do know that his writings bear the imprint of a singularly candid, noble, and fearless mind; we do know that he devoted his life, unflinchingly and unsparingly, to a great cause. We know less of Grimm; but it is at least certain that he was the intimate friend of Diderot, and of many more of the distinguished men of the time. Is all this evidence to be put on one side as of no account? Are we to dismiss it, as Mrs. Macdonald dismisses it, as merely 'psychological'? Surely Diderot's reputation as an honest man is as much a fact as his notes in the draft of the *Mémoires*. It is quite true that his reputation *may* have been ill-founded, that d'Alembert, and Turgot, and Hume *may* have been deluded, or *may* have been bribed, into admitting him to their friendship; but is it not clear that we ought not to believe any such hypotheses as these until we have before us such convincing proof of Diderot's guilt that we *must* believe them? Mrs. Macdonald declares that she has produced such proof; and she points triumphantly to her garbled and concocted manuscripts. If there is indeed no explanation of these garblings and concoctions other than that which Mrs. Macdonald puts forward—that they were the outcome of a false and malicious conspiracy to blast the reputation of Rousseau—then we must admit that she is right, and that all our general 'psychological' considerations as to Diderot's reputation in the world must be disregarded. But, before we come to this conclusion, how careful must we be to examine every other possible explanation of Mrs. Macdonald's facts, how rigorously must we sift her own explanation of them, how eagerly must we seize upon every loophole of escape!

It is, I believe, possible to explain the condition of the d'Epinay manuscript without having recourse to the iconoclastic theory of Mrs. Macdonald. To explain everything, indeed, would be out of the question, owing to our insufficient data, and the extreme complexity of the events; all that we can hope to do is to suggest an explanation which will account for the most important of the known facts. Not the least interesting of Mrs. Macdonald's discoveries went to show that the *Mémoires*, so far from being historically accurate, were in reality full of unfounded statements, that they concluded with an entirely imaginary narrative, and that, in short, they might be described, almost without exaggeration, in the very words with which Grimm himself actually did describe them in his *Correspondance Littéraire*, as 'l'ébauche d'un long roman.' Mrs. Macdonald eagerly lays emphasis upon this discovery, because she is, of course, anxious to prove that the most damning of all the accounts of Rousseau's conduct is an untrue one. But she has proved too much. The *Mémoires*, she says, are a fiction; therefore the writers of them were liars. The answer is obvious: why should we not suppose that the writers were not liars at all, but simply novelists? Will not this hypothesis fit into the facts just as well as Mrs. Macdonald's? Madame d'Epinay, let us suppose, wrote a narrative, partly imaginary and partly true, based upon her own experiences, but without any strict adherence to the actual course of events, and filled with personages whose actions were, in many cases, fictitious, but whose characters were, on the whole, moulded upon the actual characters of her friends. Let us suppose that when she had finished her work—a work full of subtle observation and delightful writing—she showed it to Grimm and Diderot. They had only one criticism to make: it related to her treatment of the character which had been moulded upon that of Rousseau. 'Your Rousseau, chère Madame, is a very poor affair indeed! The most salient points in his character seem to have escaped you. We know what that man really was. We know how he behaved at that time. *C'était un homme à faire peur*. You have missed a great opportunity of drawing a fine picture of a hypocritical rascal.' Whereupon they gave her their own impressions of Rousseau's conduct, they showed her the letters that had passed between them, and they jotted down some notes for her guidance. She rewrote the story in accordance with their notes and their anecdotes; but she rearranged the incidents, she condensed or amplified the letters, as she thought fit—for she was not writing a history, but 'l'ébauche d'un long roman.' If we suppose that this, or something like this, was what occurred, shall we not have avoided the necessity for a theory so repugnant to common-sense as that which would impute to a man of recognised integrity the meanest of frauds?

To follow Mrs. Macdonald into the inner recesses and elaborations of her argument would be a difficult and tedious task. The circumstances with which she is principally concerned—the suspicions, the accusations, the anonymous letters, the intrigues, the endless problems as to whether Madame d'Epinay was jealous of Madame d'Houdetot, whether Thérèse told fibs, whether, on the 14th of the month, Grimm was grossly impertinent, and whether, on the 15th, Rousseau was outrageously rude, whether Rousseau revealed a secret to Diderot, which Diderot revealed to Saint-Lambert, and whether, if Diderot revealed it, he believed that Rousseau had revealed it before—these circumstances form, as Lord Morley says, 'a tale of labyrinthine nightmares,' and Mrs. Macdonald has done very little to mitigate either the contortions of the labyrinths or the horror of the dreams. Her book is exceedingly ill-arranged; it is enormously long, filling two large volumes, with an immense apparatus of appendices and notes; it is full of repetitions and of irrelevant matter; and the argument is so indistinctly set forth that even an instructed reader finds great difficulty in following its drift. Without, however, plunging into the abyss of complications which yawns for us in Mrs. Macdonald's pages, it may be worth while to touch upon one point with which she has dealt (perhaps wisely for her own case!) only very slightly—the question of the motives which could have induced Grimm and Diderot to perpetuate a series of malignant lies.

It is, doubtless, conceivable that Grimm, who was Madame d'Epinay's lover, was jealous of Rousseau, who was Madame d'Epinay's friend. We know very little of Grimm's character, but what we do know seems to show that he was a jealous man and an ambitious man; it is possible that a close alliance with Madame d'Epinay may have seemed to him a necessary step in his career; and it is conceivable that he may have determined not to rest until his most serious rival in Madame d'Epinay's affections was utterly cast out. He was probably prejudiced against Rousseau from the beginning, and he may have allowed his prejudices to colour his view of Rousseau's character and acts. The violence of the abuse which Grimm and the rest of the Encyclopaedists hurled against the miserable Jean-Jacques was certainly quite out of proportion to the real facts of the case. Whenever he is mentioned one is sure of hearing something about *traître* and *mensonge* and *scélératesse*. He is referred to as often as not as if he were some dangerous kind of wild beast. This was Grimm's habitual language with regard to him; and this was the view of his character which Madame d'Epinay finally expressed in her book. The important question is—did Grimm know that Rousseau was in reality an honourable man, and, knowing this, did he deliberately defame him in order to drive him out of Madame d'Epinay's affections? The answer, I think, must be in the negative, for the following reason. If Grimm had known that there was something to be ashamed of in the notes with which he had supplied Madame d'Epinay, and which led to the alteration of her *Mémoires*, he certainly would have destroyed the draft of the manuscript, which was the only record of those notes having ever been made. As it happens, we know that he had the opportunity of destroying the draft, and he did not do so. He came to Paris at the risk of his life in 1791, and stayed there for four months, with the object, according to his own account, of collecting papers belonging to the Empress Catherine, or, according to Mrs. Macdonald's account, of having the rough draft of the *Mémoires* copied out by his secretary. Whatever his object, it is certain that the copy—that from which ultimately the *Mémoires* were printed—was made either at that time, or earlier; and that there was nothing on earth to prevent him, during the four months of his stay in Paris, from destroying the draft. Mrs. Macdonald's explanation of this difficulty is lamentably weak. Grimm, she says, must have wished to get away from Paris 'without arousing suspicion by destroying papers.' This is indeed an 'exquisite reason,' which would have delighted that good knight Sir Andrew Aguecheek. Grimm had four months at his disposal; he was undisturbed in his own house; why should he not have burnt the draft page by page as it was copied out? There can be only one reply: Why *should* he?

If it is possible to suggest some fairly plausible motives which might conceivably have induced Grimm to blacken Rousseau's character, the case of Diderot presents difficulties which are quite insurmountable. Mrs. Macdonald asserts that Diderot was jealous of Rousseau. Why? Because he was tired of hearing Rousseau described as 'the virtuous'; that is all. Surely Mrs. Macdonald should have been the first to recognise that such an argument is a little too 'psychological.' The truth is that Diderot had nothing to gain by attacking Rousseau. He was not, like Grimm, in love with Madame d'Epinay; he was not a newcomer who had still to win for himself a position in the Parisian world. His acquaintance with Madame d'Epinay was slight; and, if there were any advances, they were from her side, for he was one of the most distinguished men of the day. In fact, the only reason that he could have had for abusing Rousseau was that he believed Rousseau deserved abuse. Whether he was right in believing so is a very different question. Most readers, at the present day, now that the whole noisy controversy has long taken its quiet place in the perspective of Time, would, I think, agree that Diderot and the rest of the Encyclopaedists were mistaken. As we see him now, in that long vista, Rousseau was not a wicked man; he was an unfortunate, a distracted, a deeply sensitive, a strangely complex, creature; and, above all else, he possessed one quality which cut him off from his contemporaries, which set an immense gulf betwixt him and them: he was modern. Among those quick, strong, fiery people of the eighteenth century, he belonged to another world—to the new world of self-consciousness, and doubt, and hesitation, of mysterious melancholy and quiet intimate delights, of long reflexions amid the solitudes of Nature, of infinite introspections amid the solitudes of the heart. Who can wonder that he was misunderstood, and buffeted, and driven mad? Who can wonder that, in his agitations, his perplexities, his writhings, he seemed, to the pupils of Voltaire, little less than a frenzied fiend? 'Cet homme est un forcené!' Diderot exclaims. 'Je tâche en vain de faire de la poésie, mais cet homme me revient tout à travers mon travail; il me trouble, et je suis comme si j'avais à côté de moi un damné: il est damné, cela est sûr. ... J'avoue que je n'ai jamais éprouvé un trouble d'âme si terrible que celui que j'ai ... Que je ne revoie plus cet homme-là, il me ferait croire au diable et à l'enfer. Si je suis jamais forcé de retourner chez lui, je suis sûr que je frémirai tout le long du chemin: j'avais la fièvre en revenant ... On entendait ses cris jusqu'au bout du jardin; et je le voyais!... Les poètes ont bien fait de mettre un intervalle immense entre le ciel et les enfers. En vérité, la main me tremble.' Every word of that is stamped with sincerity; Diderot was writing from his heart. But he was wrong; the 'intervalle immense,' across which, so strangely and so horribly, he had caught glimpses of what he had never seen before, was not the abyss between heaven and hell, but between the old world and the new.

1907.

NOTES:

[7] *Jean Jacques Rousseau: a New Criticism*, by Frederika Macdonald. In two volumes. Chapman and Hall. 1906.

THE POETRY OF BLAKE[8]

The new edition of Blake's poetical works, published by the Clarendon Press, will be welcomed by every lover of English poetry. The volume is worthy of the great university under whose auspices it has been produced, and of the great artist whose words it will help to perpetuate. Blake has been, hitherto, singularly unfortunate in his editors. With a single exception, every edition of his poems up to the present time has contained a multitude of textual errors which, in the case of any other writer of equal eminence, would have been well-nigh inconceivable. The great majority of these errors were not the result of accident: they were the result of deliberate falsification. Blake's text has been emended and corrected and 'improved,' so largely and so habitually, that there was a very real danger of its becoming permanently corrupted; and this danger was all the more serious, since the work of mutilation was carried on to an accompaniment of fervent admiration of the poet. 'It is not a little bewildering,' says Mr. Sampson, the present editor, 'to find one great poet and critic extolling Blake for the "glory of metre" and "the sonorous beauty of lyrical work" in the two opening lyrics of the *Songs of Experience*, while he introduces into the five short stanzas quoted no less than seven emendations of his own, involving additions of syllables and important changes of meaning.' This is Procrustes admiring the exquisite proportions of his victim. As one observes the countless instances accumulated in Mr. Sampson's notes, of the clippings and filings to which the free and spontaneous expression of Blake's genius has been subjected, one is reminded of a verse in one of his own lyrics, where he speaks of the beautiful garden in which—

> Priests in black gowns were walking their rounds,
> And binding with briers my joys and desires;

and one cannot help hazarding the conjecture, that Blake's prophetic vision recognised, in the lineaments of the 'priests in black gowns,' most of his future editors. Perhaps, though, if Blake's prescience had extended so far as this, he would have taken a more drastic measure; and we shudder to think of the sort of epigram with which the editorial efforts of his worshippers might have been rewarded. The present edition, however, amply compensates for the past. Mr. Sampson gives us, in the first place, the correct and entire text of the poems, so printed as to afford easy reading to those who desire access to the text and nothing more. At the same time, in a series of notes and prefaces, he has provided an elaborate commentary, containing, besides all the variorum readings, a great mass of bibliographical and critical matter; and, in addition, he has enabled the reader to obtain a clue through the labyrinth of Blake's mythology, by means of ample quotations from those passages in the *Prophetic Books*, which throw light upon the obscurities of the poems. The most important Blake document—the Rossetti MS.—has been freshly collated, with the generous aid of the owner, Mr. W.A. White, to whom the gratitude of the public is due in no common measure; and the long-lost Pickering MS.—the sole authority for some of the most mystical and absorbing of the poems—was, with deserved good fortune, discovered by Mr. Sampson in time for collation in the present edition. Thus there is hardly a line in the volume which has not been reproduced from an original, either written or engraved by the hand of Blake. Mr. Sampson's minute and ungrudging care, his high critical acumen, and the skill with which he has brought his wide knowledge of the subject to bear upon the difficulties of the text, combine to make his edition a noble and splendid monument of English scholarship. It will be long indeed before the poems of Blake cease to afford matter for fresh discussions and commentaries and interpretations; but it is safe to predict that, so far as their form is concerned, they will henceforward remain unchanged. There will be no room for further editing. The work has been done by Mr. Sampson, once and for all.

In the case of Blake, a minute exactitude of text is particularly important, for more than one reason. Many of his effects depend upon subtle differences of punctuation and of spelling, which are too easily lost in reproduction. 'Tiger, tiger, burning bright,' is the ordinary version of one of his most celebrated lines. But in Blake's original engraving the words appear thus— 'Tyger! Tyger! burning bright'; and who can fail to perceive the difference? Even more remarkable is the change which the omission of a single stop has produced in the last line of one of the succeeding stanzas of the same poem.

> And what shoulder, and what art,
> Could twist the sinews of thy heart?
> And when thy heart began to beat,
> What dread hand? and what dread feet?

So Blake engraved the verse; and, as Mr. Sampson points out,'the terrible, compressed force' of the final line vanishes to nothing in the 'languid punctuation' of subsequent editions:—'What dread hand and what dread feet?' It is hardly an exaggeration to say, that the re-discovery of this line alone would have justified the appearance of the present edition.

But these considerations of what may be called the mechanics of Blake's poetry are not—important as they are—the only justification for a scrupulous adherence to his autograph text. Blake's use of language was not guided by the ordinarily accepted rules of writing; he allowed himself to be trammelled neither by prosody nor by grammar; he wrote, with an extraordinary audacity, according to the mysterious dictates of his own strange and intimate conception of the beautiful and the just. Thus his compositions, amenable to no other laws than those of his own making, fill a unique place in the poetry of the world. They are the rebels and atheists of literature, or rather, they are the sanctuaries of an Unknown God; and to invoke that deity by means of orthodox incantations is to run the risk of hell fire. Editors may punctuate afresh the text of Shakespeare with impunity, and perhaps even with advantage; but add a comma to the text of Blake, and you put all Heaven in a rage. You have laid your hands upon the Ark of the Covenant. Nor is this all. When once, in the case of Blake, the slightest deviation has been made from the authoritative version, it is hardly possible to stop there. The emendator is on an inclined plane which leads him inevitably from readjustments of punctuation to corrections of grammar, and from corrections of grammar to alterations of rhythm; if he is in for a penny, he is in for a pound. The first poem in the Rossetti MS. may be adduced as one instance—out of the enormous number which fill Mr. Sampson's notes—of the dangers of editorial laxity.

> I told my love, I told my love,
> I told her all my heart;
> Trembling, cold, in ghastly fears,
> Ah! she doth depart.

This is the first half of the poem; and editors have been contented with an alteration of stops, and the change of 'doth' into 'did.' But their work was not over; they had, as it were, tasted blood; and their version of the last four lines of the poem is as follows:

> Soon after she was gone from me,
> A traveller came by,
> Silently, invisibly:
> He took her with a sigh.

Reference to the MS., however, shows that the last line had been struck out by Blake, and another substituted in its place—a line which is now printed for the first time by Mr. Sampson. So that the true reading of the verse is:

> Soon as she was gone from me,
> A traveller came by,

Silently, invisibly—
O! was no deny.

After these exertions, it must have seemed natural enough to Rossetti and his successors to print four other expunged lines as part of the poem, and to complete the business by clapping a title to their concoction—'Love's Secret'—a title which there is no reason to suppose had ever entered the poet's mind.

Besides illustrating the shortcomings of his editors, this little poem is an admirable instance of Blake's most persistent quality—his triumphant freedom from conventional restraints. His most characteristic passages are at once so unexpected and so complete in their effect, that the reader is moved by them, spontaneously, to some conjecture of 'inspiration.' Sir Walter Raleigh, indeed, in his interesting Introduction to a smaller edition of the poems, protests against such attributions of peculiar powers to Blake, or indeed to any other poet. 'No man,' he says, 'destitute of genius, could live for a day.' But even if we all agree to be inspired together, we must still admit that there are degrees of inspiration; if Mr. F's Aunt was a woman of genius, what are we to say of Hamlet? And Blake, in the hierarchy of the inspired, stands very high indeed. If one could strike an average among poets, it would probably be true to say that, so far as inspiration is concerned, Blake is to the average poet, as the average poet is to the man in the street. All poetry, to be poetry at all, must have the power of making one, now and then, involuntarily ejaculate: 'What made him think of that?' With Blake, one is asking the question all the time.

Blake's originality of manner was not, as has sometimes been the case, a cloak for platitude. What he has to say belongs no less distinctly to a mind of astonishing self-dependence than his way of saying it. In English literature, as Sir Walter Raleigh observes, he 'stands outside the regular line of succession.' All that he had in common with the great leaders of the Romantic Movement was an abhorrence of the conventionality and the rationalism of the eighteenth century; for the eighteenth century itself was hardly more alien to his spirit than that exaltation of Nature—the 'Vegetable Universe,' as he called it—from which sprang the pantheism of Wordsworth and the paganism of Keats. 'Nature is the work of the Devil,' he exclaimed one day; 'the Devil is in us as far as we are Nature.' There was no part of the sensible world which, in his philosophy, was not impregnated with vileness. Even the 'ancient heavens' were not, to his uncompromising vision, 'fresh and strong'; they were 'writ with Curses from Pole to Pole,' and destined to vanish into nothingness with the triumph of the Everlasting Gospel.

There are doubtless many to whom Blake is known simply as a charming and splendid lyrist, as the author of *Infant Joy*, and *The Tyger*, and the rest of the *Songs of Innocence and Experience*. These poems show but faint traces of any system of philosophy; but, to a reader of the Rossetti and Pickering MSS., the presence of a hidden and symbolic meaning in Blake's words becomes obvious enough—a meaning which receives its fullest expression in the *Prophetic Books*. It was only natural that the extraordinary nature of Blake's utterance in these latter works should have given rise to the belief that he was merely an inspired idiot—a madman who happened to be able to write good verses. That belief, made finally impossible by Mr. Swinburne's elaborate Essay, is now, happily, nothing more than a curiosity of literary history; and indeed signs are not wanting that the whirligig of Time, which left Blake for so long in the Paradise of Fools, is now about to place him among the Prophets. Anarchy is the most fashionable of creeds; and Blake's writings, according to Sir Walter Raleigh, contain a complete exposition of its doctrines. The same critic asserts that Blake was 'one of the most consistent of English poets and thinkers.' This is high praise indeed; but there seems to be some ambiguity in it. It is one thing to give Blake credit for that sort of consistency which lies in the repeated enunciation of the same body of beliefs throughout a large mass of compositions and over a long period of time, and which could never be possessed by a, madman or an incoherent charlatan. It is quite another thing to assert that his doctrines form in themselves a consistent whole, in the sense in which that quality would be ordinarily attributed to a system of philosophy. Does Sir Walter mean to assert that Blake is, in this sense too, 'consistent'? It is a little difficult to discover. Referring, in his Introduction, to Blake's abusive notes on Bacon's *Essays*, he speaks of—

> The sentimental enthusiast, who worships all great men indifferently, [and who] finds himself in a distressful position when his gods fall out among themselves. His case [Sir Walter wittily adds] is not much unlike that of Terah, the father of Abraham, who (if the legend be true) was a dealer in idols among the Chaldees, and, coming home to his shop one day, after a brief absence, found that the idols had quarrelled, and the biggest of them had smashed the rest to atoms. Blake is a dangerous idol for any man to keep in his shop.

We wonder very much whether he is kept in Sir Walter Raleigh's.

It seems clear, at any rate, that no claim for a 'consistency' which would imply freedom from self-contradiction can be validly made for Blake. His treatment of the problem of evil is enough to show how very far he was from that clarity of thought without which even prophets are liable, when the time comes, to fall into disrepute. 'Plato,' said Blake, 'knew of nothing but the virtues and vices, and good and evil. There is nothing in all that. Everything is good in God's eyes.' And this is the perpetual burden of his teaching. 'Satan's empire is the empire of nothing'; there is no such thing as evil—it is a mere 'negation.' And the 'moral virtues,' which attempt to discriminate between right and wrong, are the idlest of delusions; they are merely 'allegories and dissimulations,' they 'do not exist.' Such was one of the most fundamental of Blake's doctrines; but it requires only a superficial acquaintance with his writings to recognise that their whole tenour is an implicit contradiction of this very belief. Every page he wrote contains a moral exhortation; bad thoughts and bad feelings raised in him a fury of rage and indignation which the bitterest of satirists never surpassed. His epigrams on Reynolds are masterpieces of virulent abuse; the punishment which he devised for Klopstock—his impersonation of 'flaccid fluency and devout sentiment'—is unprintable; as for those who attempt to enforce moral laws, they shall be 'cast out,' for they 'crucify Christ with the head downwards.' The contradiction is indeed glaring. 'There is no such thing as wickedness,' Blake says in effect, 'and you are wicked if you think there is.' If it is true that evil does not exist, all Blake's denunciations are so much empty chatter; and, on the other hand, if there is a real distinction between good and bad, if everything, in fact, is *not* good in God's eyes—then why not say so? Really Blake, as politicians say, 'cannot have it both ways.'

But of course, his answer to all this is simple enough. To judge him according to the light of reason is to make an appeal to a tribunal whose jurisdiction he had always refused to recognise as binding. In fact, to Blake's mind, the laws of reason were nothing but a horrible phantasm deluding and perplexing mankind, from whose clutches it is the business of every human soul to free itself as speedily as possible. Reason is the 'Spectre' of Blake's mythology, that Spectre, which, he says,

> Around me night and day
> Like a wild beast guards my way.

It is a malignant spirit, for ever struggling with the 'Emanation,' or imaginative side of man, whose triumph is the supreme end of the universe. Ever since the day when, in his childhood, Blake had seen God's forehead at the window, he had found in imaginative vision the only reality and the only good. He beheld the things of this world 'not with, but through, the eye':

> With my inward Eye, 'tis an old Man grey,
> With my outward, a Thistle across my way.

It was to the imagination, and the imagination alone, that Blake yielded the allegiance of his spirit. His attitude towards reason was the attitude of the mystic; and it involved an inevitable dilemma. He never could, in truth, quite shake himself free of his 'Spectre'; struggle as he would, he could not escape altogether from the employment of the ordinary forms of thought and speech; he is constantly arguing, as if argument were really a means of approaching the truth; he was subdued to what he worked in. As in his own poem, he had, somehow or other, been locked into a crystal cabinet—the world of the senses and of reason—a gilded, artificial, gimcrack dwelling, after 'the wild' where he had danced so merrily before.

> I strove to seize the inmost Form
> With ardour fierce and hands of flame,
> But burst the Crystal Cabinet,
> And like a Weeping Babe became—
>
> A weeping Babe upon the wild....

To be able to lay hands upon 'the inmost form,' one must achieve the impossible; one must be inside and outside the crystal cabinet at the same time. But Blake was not to be turned aside by such considerations. He would have it both ways; and whoever demurred was crucifying Christ with the head downwards.

Besides its unreasonableness, there is an even more serious objection to Blake's mysticism—and indeed to all mysticism: its lack of humanity. The mystic's creed—even when arrayed in the wondrous and ecstatic beauty of Blake's verse—comes upon the ordinary man, in the rigidity of its uncompromising elevation, with a shock which is terrible, and almost cruel. The sacrifices which it demands are too vast, in spite of the divinity of what it has to offer. What shall it profit a man, one is tempted to exclaim, if he gain his own soul, and lose the whole world? The mystic ideal is the highest of all; but it has no breadth. The following lines express, with a simplicity and an intensity of inspiration which he never surpassed, Blake's conception of that ideal:

> And throughout all Eternity
> I forgive you, you forgive me.
> As our dear Redeemer said:
> 'This the Wine, & this the Bread.'

It is easy to imagine the sort of comments to which Voltaire, for instance, with his 'wracking wheel' of sarcasm and common-sense, would have subjected such lines as these. His criticism would have been irrelevant, because it would never have reached the heart of the matter at issue; it

would have been based upon no true understanding of Blake's words. But that they do admit of a real, an unanswerable criticism, it is difficult to doubt. Charles Lamb, perhaps, might have made it; incidentally, indeed, he has. 'Sun, and sky, and breeze, and solitary walks, and summer holidays, and the greenness of fields, and the delicious juices of meats and fishes, and society, and the cheerful glass, and candle-light, and fire-side conversations, and innocent vanities, and jests, and *irony itself*—do these things form no part of your Eternity?

The truth is plain: Blake was an intellectual drunkard. His words come down to us in a rapture of broken fluency from impossible intoxicated heights. His spirit soared above the empyrean; and, even as it soared, it stumbled in the gutter of Felpham. His lips brought forth, in the same breath, in the same inspired utterance, the *Auguries of Innocence* and the epigrams on Sir Joshua Reynolds. He was in no condition to chop logic, or to take heed of the existing forms of things. In the imaginary portrait of himself, prefixed to Sir Walter Raleigh's volume, we can see him, as he appeared to his own 'inward eye,' staggering between the abyss and the star of Heaven, his limbs cast abroad, his head thrown back in an ecstasy of intoxication, so that, to the frenzy of his rolling vision, the whole universe is upside down. We look, and, as we gaze at the strange image and listen to the marvellous melody, we are almost tempted to go and do likewise.

But it is not as a prophet, it is as an artist, that Blake deserves the highest honours and the most enduring fame. In spite of his hatred of the 'vegetable universe,' his poems possess the inexplicable and spontaneous quality of natural objects; they are more like the works of Heaven than the works of man. They have, besides, the two most obvious characteristics of Nature—loveliness and power. In some of his lyrics there is an exquisite simplicity, which seems, like a flower or a child, to be unconscious of itself. In his poem of *The Birds*—to mention, out of many, perhaps a less known instance—it is not the poet that one hears, it is the birds themselves.

> O thou summer's harmony,
> I have lived and mourned for thee;
> Each day I mourn along the wood,
> And night hath heard my sorrows loud.

In his other mood—the mood of elemental force—Blake produces effects which are unique in literature. His mastery of the mysterious suggestions which lie concealed in words is complete.

> He who torments the Chafer's Sprite
> Weaves a Bower in endless Night.

What dark and terrible visions the last line calls up! And, with the aid of this control over the secret springs of language, he is able to produce in poetry those vast and vague effects of gloom, of foreboding, and of terror, which seem to be proper to music alone. Sometimes his words are heavy with the doubtful horror of an approaching thunderstorm:

> The Guests are scattered thro' the land,
> For the Eye altering alters all;
> The Senses roll themselves in fear,
> And the flat Earth becomes a Ball;
> The Stars, Sun, Moon, all shrink away,
> A desert vast without a bound,
> And nothing left to eat or drink,
> And a dark desart all around.

And sometimes Blake invests his verses with a sense of nameless and infinite ruin, such as one feels when the drum and the violin mysteriously come together, in one of Beethoven's Symphonies, to predict the annihilation of worlds:

> On the shadows of the Moon,
> Climbing through Night's highest noon:
> In Time's Ocean falling, drowned:
> In Aged Ignorance profound,
> Holy and cold, I clipp'd the Wings
> Of all Sublunary Things:
> But when once I did descry
> The Immortal Man that cannot Die,
> Thro' evening shades I haste away
> To close the Labours of my Day.
> The Door of Death I open found,
> And the Worm Weaving in the Ground;
> Thou'rt my Mother, from the Womb;
> Wife, Sister, Daughter, to the Tomb:
> Weaving to Dreams the Sexual strife,
> And weeping over the Web of Life.

Such music is not to be lightly mouthed by mortals; for us, in our weakness, a few strains of it, now and then, amid the murmur of ordinary converse, are enough. For Blake's words will always be strangers on this earth; they could only fall with familiarity from the lips of his own Gods:

> above Time's troubled fountains,
> On the great Atlantic Mountains,
> In my Golden House on high.

They belong to the language of Los and Rahab and Enitharmon; and their mystery is revealed for ever in the land of the Sunflower's desire.

1906.

NOTES:

[8] *The Poetical Works of William Blake. A new and verbatim text from the manuscript, engraved, and letter-press originals, with variorum readings and bibliographical notes and prefaces.* By John Sampson, Librarian in the University of Liverpool. Oxford: At the Clarendon Press, 1905.

The Lyrical Poems of William Blake. Text by John Sampson, with an Introduction by Walter Raleigh. Oxford: At the Clarendon Press, 1905.

THE LAST ELIZABETHAN

The shrine of Poetry is a secret one; and it is fortunate that this should be the case; for it gives a sense of security. The cult is too mysterious and intimate to figure upon census papers; there are no turnstiles at the temple gates; and so, as all inquiries must be fruitless, the obvious plan is to take for granted a good attendance of worshippers, and to pass on. Yet, if Apollo were to come down (after the manner of deities) and put questions—must we suppose to the Laureate?—as to the number of the elect, would we be quite sure of escaping wrath and destruction? Let us hope for the best; and perhaps, if we were bent upon finding out the truth, the simplest way would be to watch the sales of the new edition of the poems of Beddoes, which Messrs. Routledge have lately added to the 'Muses' Library.' How many among Apollo's pew-renters, one wonders, have ever read Beddoes, or, indeed, have ever heard of him? For some reason or another, this extraordinary poet has not only never received the recognition which is his due, but has failed almost entirely to receive any recognition whatever. If his name is known at all, it is known in virtue of the one or two of his lyrics which have crept into some of the current anthologies. But Beddoes' highest claim to distinction does not rest upon his lyrical achievements, consummate as those achievements are; it rests upon his extraordinary eminence as a master of dramatic blank verse. Perhaps his greatest misfortune was that he was born at the beginning of the nineteenth century, and not at the end of the sixteenth. His proper place was among that noble band of Elizabethans, whose strong and splendid spirit gave to England, in one miraculous generation, the most glorious heritage of drama that the world has known. If Charles Lamb had discovered his tragedies among the folios of the British Museum, and had given extracts from them in the *Specimens of Dramatic Poets*, Beddoes' name would doubtless be as familiar to us now as those of Marlowe and Webster, Fletcher and Ford. As it happened, however, he came as a strange and isolated phenomenon, a star which had wandered from its constellation, and was lost among alien lights. It is to very little purpose that Mr. Ramsay Colles, his latest editor, assures us that 'Beddoes is interesting as marking the transition from Shelley to Browning'; it is to still less purpose that he points out to us a passage in *Death's Jest Book* which anticipates the doctrines of *The Descent of Man*. For Beddoes cannot be hoisted into line with his contemporaries by such methods as these; nor is it in the light of such after-considerations that the value of his work must be judged. We must take him on his own merits, 'unmixed with seconds'; we must discover and appraise his peculiar quality for its own sake.

> He hath skill in language;
> And knowledge is in him, root, flower, and fruit,
> A palm with winged imagination in it,Whose roots stretch
> even underneath the grave;
> And on them hangs a lamp of magic science
> In his soul's deepest mine, where folded thoughts
> Lie sleeping on the tombs of magi dead.

If the neglect suffered by Beddoes' poetry may be accounted for in more ways than one, it is not so easy to understand why more curiosity has never been aroused by the circumstances of his life. For one reader who cares to concern himself with the intrinsic merit of a piece of writing there are a thousand who are ready to explore with eager sympathy the history of the writer; and all that we know both of the life and the character of Beddoes possesses those very qualities of peculiarity, mystery, and adventure, which are so dear to the hearts of subscribers to circulating libraries. Yet only one account of his career has ever been given to the public; and that account, fragmentary and incorrect as it is, has long been out of print. It was supplemented some years ago by Mr. Gosse, who was able to throw additional light upon one important circumstance, and who has also published a small collection of Beddoes' letters. The main biographical facts, gathered from these sources, have been put together by Mr. Ramsay Colles, in his introduction to the new edition; but he has added nothing fresh; and we are still in almost complete ignorance as to the details of the last twenty years of Beddoes' existence—full as those years certainly were of interest and even excitement. Nor has the veil been altogether withdrawn from that strange tragedy which, for the strange tragedian, was the last of all.

Readers of Miss Edgeworth's letters may remember that her younger sister Anne, married a distinguished Clifton physician, Dr. Thomas Beddoes. Their eldest son, born in 1803, was named Thomas Lovell, after his father and grandfather, and grew up to be the author of *The Brides' Tragedy* and *Death's Jest Book*. Dr. Beddoes was a remarkable man, endowed with high and varied intellectual capacities and a rare independence of character. His scientific attainments were recognised by the University of Oxford, where he held the post of Lecturer in Chemistry, until the time of the French

Revolution, when he was obliged to resign it, owing to the scandal caused by the unconcealed intensity of his liberal opinions. He then settled at Clifton as a physician, established a flourishing practice, and devoted his leisure to politics and scientific research. Sir Humphry Davy, who was his pupil, and whose merit he was the first to bring to light, declared that 'he had talents which would have exalted him to the pinnacle of philosophical eminence, if they had been applied with discretion.' The words are curiously suggestive of the history of his son; and indeed the poet affords a striking instance of the hereditary transmission of mental qualities. Not only did Beddoes inherit his father's talents and his father's inability to make the best use of them; he possessed in a no less remarkable degree his father's independence of mind. In both cases, this quality was coupled with a corresponding eccentricity of conduct, which occasionally, to puzzled onlookers, wore the appearance of something very near insanity. Many stories are related of the queer behaviour of Dr. Beddoes. One day he astonished the ladies of Clifton by appearing at a tea-party with a packet of sugar in his hand; he explained that it was East Indian sugar, and that nothing would induce him to eat the usual kind, which came from Jamaica and was made by slaves. More extraordinary were his medical prescriptions; for he was in the habit of ordering cows to be conveyed into his patients' bedrooms, in order, as he said, that they might 'inhale the animals' breath.' It is easy to imagine the delight which the singular spectacle of a cow climbing upstairs into an invalid's bedroom must have given to the future author of *Harpagus* and *The Oviparous Tailor*. But 'little Tom,' as Miss Edgeworth calls him, was not destined to enjoy for long the benefit of parental example; for Dr. Beddoes died in the prime of life, when the child was not yet six years old.

The genius at school is usually a disappointing figure, for, as a rule, one must be commonplace to be a successful boy. In that preposterous world, to be remarkable is to be overlooked; and nothing less vivid than the white-hot blaze of a Shelley will bring with it even a distinguished martyrdom. But Beddoes was an exception, though he was not a martyr. On the contrary, he dominated his fellows as absolutely as if he had been a dullard and a dunce. He was at Charterhouse; and an entertaining account of his existence there has been preserved to us in a paper of school reminiscences, written by Mr. C.D. Bevan, who had been his fag. Though his place in the school was high, Beddoes' interests were devoted not so much to classical scholarship as to the literature of his own tongue. Cowley, he afterwards told a friend, had been the first poet he had understood; but no doubt he had begun to understand poetry many years before he went to Charterhouse; and, while he was there, the reading which he chiefly delighted in was the Elizabethan drama. 'He liked acting,' says Mr. Bevan, 'and was a good judge of it, and used to give apt though burlesque imitations of the popular actors, particularly Kean and Macready. Though his voice was harsh and his enunciation offensively conceited, he read with so much propriety of expression and manner, that I was always glad to listen: even when I was pressed into the service as his accomplice, his enemy, or his love, with a due accompaniment of curses, caresses, or kicks, as the course of his declamation required. One play in particular, Marlowe's *Tragedy of Dr. Faustus*, excited my admiration in this way; and a liking for the old English drama, which I still retain, was created and strengthened by such recitations.' But Beddoes' dramatic performances were not limited to the works of others; when the occasion arose he was able to supply the necessary material himself. A locksmith had incurred his displeasure by putting a bad lock on his bookcase; Beddoes vowed vengeance; and when next the man appeared he was received by a dramatic interlude, representing his last moments, his horror and remorse, his death, and the funeral procession, which was interrupted by fiends, who carried off body and soul to eternal torments. Such was the realistic vigour of the performance that the locksmith, according to Mr. Bevan, 'departed in a storm of wrath and execrations, and could not be persuaded, for some time, to resume his work.'

Besides the interlude of the wicked locksmith, Beddoes' school compositions included a novel in the style of Fielding (which has unfortunately disappeared), the beginnings of an Elizabethan tragedy, and much miscellaneous verse. In 1820 he left Charterhouse, and went to Pembroke College, Oxford, where, in the following year, while still a freshman, he published his first volume, *The Improvisatore*, a series of short narratives in verse. The book had been written in part while he was at school; and its immaturity is obvious. It contains no trace of the nervous vigour of his later style; the verse is weak, and the sentiment, to use his own expression, 'Moorish.' Indeed, the only interest of the little work lies in the evidence which it affords that the singular pre-occupation which eventually dominated Beddoes' mind had, even in these early days, made its appearance. The book is full of death. The poems begin on battle-fields and end in charnel-houses; old men are slaughtered in cold blood, and lovers are struck by lightning into mouldering heaps of corruption. The boy, with his elaborate exhibitions of physical horror, was doing his best to make his readers' flesh creep. But the attempt was far too crude; and in after years, when Beddoes had become a past-master of that difficult art, he was very much ashamed of his first publication. So eager was he to destroy every trace of its existence, that he did not spare even the finely bound copies of his friends. The story goes that he amused himself by visiting their libraries with a penknife, so that, when next they took out the precious volume, they found the pages gone.

Beddoes, however, had no reason to be ashamed of his next publication, *The Brides' Tragedy*, which appeared in 1822. In a single bound, he had reached the threshold of poetry, and was knocking at the door. The line which divides the best and most accomplished verse from poetry itself—that subtle and momentous line which every one can draw, and no one can explain—Beddoes had not yet crossed. But he had gone as far as it was possible to go by the aid of mere skill in the art of writing, and he was still in his twentieth year. Many passages in *The Brides' Tragedy* seem only to be waiting for the breath of inspiration which will bring them into life; and indeed, here and there, the breath has come, the warm, the true, the vital breath of Apollo. No one, surely, whose lips had not tasted of the waters of Helicon, could have uttered such words as these:

> Here's the blue violet, like Pandora's eye,
> When first it darkened with immortal life

or a line of such intense imaginative force as this:

> I've huddled her into the wormy earth;

or this splendid description of a stormy sunrise:

> The day is in its shroud while yet an infant;
> And Night with giant strides stalks o'er the world,
> Like a swart Cyclops, on its hideous front
> One round, red, thunder-swollen eye ablaze.

The play was written on the Elizabethan model, and, as a play, it is disfigured by Beddoes' most characteristic faults: the construction is weak, the interest fluctuates from character to character, and the motives and actions of the characters themselves are for the most part curiously remote from the realities of life. Yet, though the merit of the tragedy depends almost entirely upon the verse, there are signs in it that, while Beddoes lacked the gift of construction, he nevertheless possessed one important dramatic faculty—the power of creating detached scenes of interest and beauty. The scene in which the half-crazed Leonora imagines to herself, beside the couch on which her dead daughter lies, that the child is really living after all, is dramatic in the highest sense of the word; the situation, with all its capabilities of pathetic irony, is conceived and developed with consummate art and absolute restraint. Leonora's speech ends thus:

> ... Speak, I pray thee, Floribel,
> Speak to thy mother; do but whisper 'aye';
> Well, well, I will not press her; I am sure
> She has the welcome news of some good fortune,
> And hoards the telling till her father comes;
> ... Ah! She half laughed. I've guessed it then;
> Come tell me, I'll be secret. Nay, if you mock me,
> I must be very angry till you speak.
> Now this is silly; some of these young boys
> Have dressed the cushions with her clothes in sport.
> 'Tis very like her. I could make this imageAct all her
> greetings; she shall bow her head:
> 'Good-morrow, mother'; and her smiling face
> Falls on my neck.—Oh, heaven, 'tis she indeed!
> I know it all—don't tell me.

The last seven words are a summary of anguish, horror, and despair, such as Webster himself might have been proud to write.

The Brides' Tragedy was well received by critics; and a laudatory notice of Beddoes in the *Edinburgh*, written by Bryan Waller Procter—better known then than now under his pseudonym of Barry Cornwall—led to a lasting friendship between the two poets. The connection had an important result, for it was through Procter that Beddoes became acquainted with the most intimate of all his friends—Thomas Forbes Kelsall, then a young lawyer at Southampton. In the summer of 1823 Beddoes stayed at Southampton for several months, and, while ostensibly studying for his Oxford degree, gave up most of his time to conversations with Kelsall and to dramatic composition. It was a culminating point in his life: one of those moments which come, even to the most fortunate, once and once only—when youth, and hope, and the high exuberance of genius combine with circumstance and opportunity to crown the marvellous hour. The spade-work of *The Brides' Tragedy* had been accomplished; the seed had been sown; and now the harvest was beginning. Beddoes, 'with the delicious sense,' as Kelsall wrote long afterwards, 'of the laurel freshly twined around his head,' poured out, in these Southampton evenings, an eager stream of song. 'His poetic composition,' says his friend, 'was then exceedingly facile: more than once or twice has he taken home with him at night some unfinished act of a drama, in which the editor [Kelsall] had found much to admire, and, at the next meeting, has produced a new one, similar in design, but filled with other thoughts and fancies, which his teeming imagination had projected, in its sheer abundance, and not from any feeling, right or fastidious, of unworthiness in its predecessor. Of several of these very striking fragments, large and grand in their aspect as they each started into form,

> Like the red outline of beginning Adam,

... the only trace remaining is literally the impression thus deeply cut into their one observer's mind. The fine verse just quoted is the sole remnant, indelibly stamped on the editor's memory, of one of these extinct creations.' Fragments survive of at least four dramas, projected, and brought to various stages of completion, at about this time. Beddoes was impatient of the common restraints; he was dashing forward in the spirit of his own advice to another poet:

> Creep not nor climb,
> As they who place their topmost of sublime
> On some peak of this planet, pitifully.
> Dart eaglewise with open wings, and fly
> Until you meet the gods!

Eighteen months after his Southampton visit, Beddoes took his degree at Oxford, and, almost immediately, made up his mind to a course of action which had the profoundest effect upon his future life. He determined to take up the study of medicine; and with that end in view established himself, in 1825, at the University at Göttingen. It is very clear, however, that he had no intention of giving up his poetical work. He took with him to Germany the beginnings of a new play—'a very Gothic-styled tragedy,' he calls it, 'for which I have a jewel of a name—DEATH'S JEST-BOOK; of course,' he adds, 'no one will ever read it'; and, during his four years at Göttingen, he devoted most of his leisure to the completion of this work. He was young; he was rich; he was interested in medical science; and no doubt it seemed to him that he could well afford to amuse himself for half-a-dozen years, before he settled down to the poetical work which was to be the serious occupation of his life. But, as time passed, he became more and more engrossed in the study of medicine, for which he gradually discovered he had not only a taste but a gift; so that at last he came to doubt whether it might not be his true vocation to be a physician, and not a poet after all. Engulfed among the students of Göttingen, England and English ways of life, and even English poetry, became dim to him; 'dir, dem Anbeter der seligen Gottheiten der Musen, u.s.w.,' he wrote to Kelsall, 'was Unterhaltendes kann der Liebhaber von Knochen, der fleissige Botaniker und Phisiolog mittheilen?' In 1830 he was still hesitating between the two alternatives. 'I sometimes wish,' he told the same friend, 'to devote myself exclusively to the study of anatomy and physiology in science, of languages, and dramatic poetry'; his pen had run away with him; and his 'exclusive' devotion turned out to be a double one, directed towards widely different ends. While he was still in this state of mind, a new interest took possession of him—an interest which worked havoc with his dreams of dramatic authorship and scientific research: he became involved in the revolutionary movement which was at that time beginning to agitate Europe. The details of his adventures are unhappily lost to us, for we know nothing more of them than can be learnt from a few scanty references in his rare letters to English friends; but it is certain that the part he played was an active, and even a dangerous one. He was turned out of Würzburg by 'that ingenious Jackanapes,' the King of Bavaria; he was an intimate friend of Hegetschweiler, one of the leaders of liberalism in Switzerland; and he was present in Zurich when a body of six thousand peasants, 'half unarmed, and the other half armed with scythes, dungforks and poles, entered the town and overturned the liberal government.' In the tumult Hegetschweiler was killed, and Beddoes was soon afterwards forced to fly the canton. During the following years we catch glimpses of him, flitting mysteriously over Germany and Switzerland, at Berlin, at Baden, at Giessen, a strange solitary figure, with tangled hair and meerschaum pipe, scribbling lampoons upon the King of Prussia, translating Grainger's *Spinal Cord* into German, and Schoenlein's *Diseases of Europeans* into English, exploring Pilatus and the Titlis, evolving now and then some ghostly lyric or some rabelaisian tale, or brooding over the scenes of his 'Gothic-styled tragedy,' wondering if it were worthless or inspired, and giving it—as had been his wont for the last twenty years—just one more touch before he sent it to the press. He appeared in England once or twice, and in 1846 made a stay of several months, visiting the Procters in London, and going down to Southampton to be with Kelsall once again. Eccentricity had grown on him; he would shut himself for days in his bedroom, smoking furiously; he would fall into fits of long and deep depression. He shocked some of his relatives by arriving at their country house astride a donkey; and he amazed the Procters by starting out one evening to set fire to Drury Lane Theatre with a lighted five-pound note. After this last visit to England, his history becomes even more obscure than before. It is known that in 1847 he was in Frankfort, where he lived for six months in close companionship with a young baker called Degen—'a nice-looking young man, nineteen years of age,' we are told, 'dressed in a blue blouse, fine in expression, and of a natural dignity of manner'; and that, in the spring of the following year, the two friends went off to Zurich, where Beddoes hired the theatre for a night in order that Degen might appear on the stage in the part of Hotspur. At Basel, however, for some unexplained reason, the friends parted, and Beddoes fell immediately into the profoundest gloom. 'Il a été misérable,' said the waiter at the Cigogne Hotel, where he was staying, 'il a voulu se tuer.' It was true. He inflicted a deep wound in his leg with a razor, in the hope, apparently, of bleeding to death. He was taken to the hospital, where he constantly tore off the bandages, until at last it was necessary to amputate the leg below the knee. The operation was successful, Beddoes began to recover, and, in the autumn, Degen came back to Basel. It seemed as if all were going well; for the poet, with his books around him, and the blue-bloused Degen by his bedside, talked happily of politics and literature, and of an Italian journey in the spring. He walked out twice; was he still happy? Who can tell? Was it happiness, or misery, or what strange impulse, that drove him, on his third walk, to go to a chemist's shop in the town, and to obtain there a phial of deadly poison? On the evening of that day—the 26th of January, 1849—Dr. Ecklin, his physician, was hastily summoned, to find Beddoes lying insensible upon the bed. He never recovered consciousness, and died that night. Upon his breast was found a pencil note, addressed to one of his English friends. 'My dear Philips,' it began, 'I am food for what I am good for—worms.' A few testamentary wishes followed. Kelsall was to have the manuscripts; and—'W. Beddoes must have a case (50 bottles) of Champagne Moet, 1847 growth, to drink my death in ... I ought to have been, among other things,' the gruesome document concluded, 'a good poet. Life was too great a bore on one peg, and that a bad one. Buy for Dr. Ecklin one of Reade's best stomach-pumps.' It was the last of his additions to Death's Jest Book, and the most *macabre* of all.

Kelsall discharged his duties as literary executor with exemplary care. The manuscripts were fragmentary and confused. There were three distinct drafts of *Death's Jest Book*, each with variations of its own; and from these Kelsall compiled his first edition of the drama, which appeared in 1850. In the following year he brought out the two volumes of poetical works, which remained for forty years the only record of the full scope and power of Beddoes' genius. They contain reprints of *The Brides' Tragedy* and *Death's Jest Book*, together with two unfinished tragedies, and a great number of dramatic fragments and lyrics; and the poems are preceded by Kelsall's memoir of his friend. Of these rare and valuable volumes the Muses' Library edition is almost an exact reprint, except that it omits the memoir and revives *The Improvisatore*. Only one other edition of Beddoes exists—the limited one brought out by Mr. Gosse in 1890, and based upon a fresh examination of the manuscripts. Mr. Gosse was able to add ten lyrics and one dramatic fragment to those already published by Kelsall; he made public for the first time the true story of Beddoes' suicide, which Kelsall had concealed; and, in 1893, he followed up his edition of the poems by a volume of Beddoes' letters. It is clear, therefore, that there is no one living to whom lovers of Beddoes owe so much as to Mr. Gosse. He has supplied most important materials for the elucidation of the poet's history: and, among the lyrics which he has printed for the first time, are to be found one of the most perfect specimens of Beddoes' command of unearthly pathos—*The Old Ghost*—and one of the most singular examples of his vein of grotesque and ominous humour—*The Oviparous Tailor*. Yet it may be doubted whether even Mr. Gosse's edition is the final one. There are traces in Beddoes' letters of unpublished compositions which may still come to light. What has happened, one would like to know, to *The Ivory Gate*, that 'volume of prosaic poetry and poetical prose,' which Beddoes talked of publishing in 1837? Only a few fine stanzas from it have ever appeared. And, as Mr. Gosse himself tells us, the variations in *Death's Jest Book* alone would warrant the publication of a variorum edition of that work—'if,' he wisely adds, for the proviso contains the gist of the matter—'if the interest in Beddoes should continue to grow.'

'Say what you will, I am convinced the man who is to awaken the drama must be a bold, trampling fellow—no creeper into worm-holes—no reviver even—however good. These reanimations are vampire-cold.' The words occur in one of Beddoes' letters, and they are usually quoted by critics, on the rare occasions on which his poetry is discussed, as an instance of the curious incapacity of artists to practise what they preach. But the truth is that Beddoes was not a 'creeper into worm-holes,' he was not even a 'reviver'; he was a reincarnation. Everything that we know of him goes to show that the laborious and elaborate effort of literary reconstruction was quite alien to his spirit. We have Kelsall's evidence as to the ease and abundance of his composition; we have the character of the man, as it shines forth in his letters and in the history of his life—records of a 'bold, trampling fellow,' if ever there was one; and we have the evidence of his poetry itself. For the impress of a fresh and vital intelligence is stamped unmistakably upon all that is best in his work. His mature blank verse is perfect. It is not an artificial concoction galvanized into the semblance of life; it simply lives. And, with Beddoes, maturity was precocious, for he obtained complete mastery over the most difficult and dangerous of metres at a wonderfully early age. Blank verse is like the Djin in the Arabian Nights; it is either the most terrible of masters, or the most powerful of slaves. If you have not the magic secret, it will take your best thoughts, your bravest imaginations, and change them into toads and fishes; but, if the spell be yours, it will turn into a flying carpet and lift your simplest utterance into the highest heaven. Beddoes had mastered the 'Open, Sesame' at an age when most poets are still mouthing ineffectual wheats and barleys. In his twenty-second year, his thoughts filled and moved and animated his blank verse as easily and familiarly as a hand in a glove. He wishes to compare, for instance, the human mind, with its knowledge of the past, to a single eye receiving the light of the stars; and the object of the comparison is to lay stress upon the concentration on one point of a vast multiplicity of objects. There could be no better exercise for a young verse-writer than to attempt his own expression of this idea, and then to examine these lines by Beddoes—lines where simplicity and splendour have been woven together with the ease of accomplished art.

> How glorious to live! Even in one thought
> The wisdom of past times to fit together,
> And from the luminous minds of many men
> Catch a reflected truth; as, in one eye,
> Light, from unnumbered worlds and farthest planets
> Of the star-crowded universe, is gatheredInto one ray.

The effect is, of course, partly produced by the diction; but the diction, fine as it is, would be useless without the phrasing—that art by which the two forces of the metre and the sense are made at once to combat, to combine with, and to heighten each other. It is, however, impossible to do more than touch upon this side—the technical side—of Beddoes' genius. But it may be noticed that in his mastery of phrasing—as in so much besides—he was a true Elizabethan. The great artists of that age knew that without phrasing dramatic verse was a dead thing; and it is only necessary to turn from their pages to those of an eighteenth-century dramatist—Addison, for instance—to understand how right they were.

Beddoes' power of creating scenes of intense dramatic force, which had already begun to show itself in *The Brides' Tragedy*, reached its full development in his subsequent work. The opening act of *The Second Brother*—the most nearly complete of his unfinished tragedies—is a striking example of a powerful and original theme treated in such a way that, while the whole of it is steeped in imaginative poetry, yet not one ounce of its dramatic effectiveness is lost. The duke's next brother, the heir to the dukedom of Ferrara, returns to the city, after years of wandering, a miserable and sordid beggar—to find his younger brother, rich, beautiful, and reckless, leading a life of gay debauchery, with the assurance of succeeding to the dukedom when the duke dies. The situation presents possibilities for just those bold and extraordinary contrasts which were so dear to Beddoes' heart. While Marcello, the second brother, is meditating over his wretched fate, Orazio, the third, comes upon the stage, crowned and glorious, attended by a train of singing revellers, and with a courtesan upon either hand. 'Wine in a ruby!' he exclaims, gazing into his mistress's eyes:

> I'll solemnize their beauty in a draught
> Pressed from the summer of an hundred vines.

Meanwhile Marcello pushes himself forward, and attempts to salute his brother.

> *Orazio.* Insolent beggar!
>
> *Marcello.* Prince! But we must shake hands.
> Look you, the round earth's like a sleeping serpent,
> Who drops her dusky tail upon her crown
> Just here. Oh, we are like two mountain peaks
> Of two close planets, catching in the air:
> You, King Olympus, a great pile of summer,
> Wearing a crown of gods; I, the vast topOf the ghosts'
> deadly world, naked and dark,With nothing reigning on
> my desolate head
> But an old spirit of a murdered god,
> Palaced within the corpse of Saturn's father.

They begin to dispute, and at last Marcello exclaims—

> Aye, Prince, you have a brother—
>
> *Orazio.* The Duke—he'll scourge you.
>
> *Marcello.* Nay, *the second,* sir,
> Who, like an envious river, flows betweenYour footsteps and Ferrara's throne....
>
> *Orazio.* Stood he before me there,
> By you, in you, as like as you're unlike,
> Straight as you're bowed, young as you are old,
> And many years nearer than him to Death,
> The falling brilliancy of whose white sword
> Your ancient locks so silverly reflect,
> I would deny, outswear, and overreach,

And pass him with contempt, as I do you.
Jove! How we waste the stars: set on, my friends.

And so the revelling band pass onward, singing still, as they vanish down the darkened street:

> Strike, you myrtle-crownèd boys,
> Ivied maidens, strike together!...

and Marcello is left alone:

> I went forth
> Joyfully, as the soul of one who closes
> His pillowed eyes beside an unseen murderer,
> And like its horrible return was mine,
> To find the heart, wherein I breathed and beat,
> Cold, gashed, and dead. Let me forget to love,
> And take a heart of venom: let me make
> A staircase of the frightened breasts of men,
> And climb into a lonely happiness! And thou, who only art alone as I,
> Great solitary god of that one sun,
> I charge thee, by the likeness of our state,
> Undo these human veins that tie me close
> To other men, and let your servant griefs
> Unmilk me of my mother, and pour in
> Salt scorn and steaming hate!

A moment later he learnt that the duke has suddenly died, and that the dukedom is his. The rest of the play affords an instance of Beddoes' inability to trace out a story, clearly and forcibly, to an appointed end. The succeeding acts are crowded with beautiful passages, with vivid situations, with surprising developments, but the central plot vanishes away into nothing, like a great river dissipating itself among a thousand streams. It is, indeed, clear enough that Beddoes was embarrassed with his riches, that his fertile mind conceived too easily, and that he could never resist the temptation of giving life to his imaginations, even at the cost of killing his play. His conception of Orazio, for instance, began by being that of a young Bacchus, as he appears in the opening scene. But Beddoes could not leave him there; he must have a romantic wife, whom he has deserted; and the wife, once brought into being, must have an interview with her husband. The interview is an exquisitely beautiful one, but it shatters Orazio's character, for, in the course of it, he falls desperately in love with his wife; and meanwhile the wife herself has become so important and interesting a figure that she must be given a father, who in his turn becomes the central character in more than one exciting scene. But, by this time, what has happened to the second brother? It is easy to believe that Beddoes was always ready to begin a new play rather than finish an old one. But it is not so certain that his method was quite as inexcusable as his critics assert. To the reader, doubtless, his faulty construction is glaring enough; but Beddoes wrote his plays to be acted, as a passage in one of his letters very clearly shows. 'You are, I think,' he writes to Kelsall, 'disinclined to the stage: now I confess that I think this is the highest aim of the dramatist, and should be very desirous to get on it. To look down on it is a piece of impertinence, as long as one chooses to write in the form of a play, and is generally the result of one's own inability to produce anything striking and affecting in that way.' And it is precisely upon the stage that such faults of construction as those which disfigure Beddoes' tragedies matter least. An audience, whose attention is held and delighted by a succession of striking incidents clothed in splendid speech, neither cares nor knows whether the effect of the whole, as a whole, is worthy of the separate parts. It would be foolish, in the present melancholy condition of the art of dramatic declamation, to wish for the public performance of *Death's Jest Book*; but it is impossible not to hope that the time may come when an adequate representation of that strange and great work may be something more than 'a possibility more thin than air.' Then, and then only, shall we be able to take the true measure of Beddoes' genius.

Perhaps, however, the ordinary reader finds Beddoes' lack of construction a less distasteful quality than his disregard of the common realities of existence. Not only is the subject-matter of the greater part of his poetry remote and dubious; his very characters themselves seem to be infected by their creator's delight in the mysterious, the strange, and the unreal. They have no healthy activity; or, if they have, they invariably lose it in the second act; in the end, they are all hypochondriac philosophers, puzzling over eternity and dissecting the attributes of Death. The central idea of *Death's Jest Book*—the resurrection of a ghost—fails to be truly effective, because it is difficult to see any clear distinction between the phantom and the rest of the characters. The duke, saved from death by the timely arrival of Wolfram, exclaims 'Blest hour!' and then, in a moment, begins to ponder, and agonise, and dream:

> And yet how palely, with what faded lips
> Do we salute this unhoped change of fortune!
> Thou art so silent, lady; and I utterShadows of words, like
> to an ancient ghost,

> Arisen out of hoary centuries
> Where none can speak his language.

Orazio, in his brilliant palace, is overcome with the same feelings:

> Methinks, these fellows, with their ready jests,
> Are like to tedious bells, that ring alike Marriage or death.

And his description of his own revels applies no less to the whole atmosphere of Beddoes' tragedies:

> Voices were heard, most loud, which no man owned:
> There were more shadows too than there were men;
> And all the air more dark and thick than night
> Was heavy, as 'twere made of something more
> Than living breaths.

It would be vain to look, among such spectral imaginings as these, for guidance in practical affairs, or for illuminating views on men and things, or for a philosophy, or, in short, for anything which may be called a 'criticism of life.' If a poet must be a critic of life, Beddoes was certainly no poet. He belongs to the class of writers of which, in English literature, Spenser, Keats, and Milton are the dominant figures—the writers who are great merely because of their art. Sir James Stephen was only telling the truth when he remarked that Milton might have put all that he had to say in *Paradise Lost* into a prose pamphlet of two or three pages. But who cares about what Milton had to say? It is his way of saying it that matters; it is his expression. Take away the expression from the *Satires* of Pope, or from *The Excursion*, and, though you will destroy the poems, you will leave behind a great mass of thought. Take away the expression from *Hyperion*, and you will leave nothing at all. To ask which is the better of the two styles is like asking whether a peach is better than a rose, because, both being beautiful, you can eat the one and not the other. At any rate, Beddoes is among the roses: it is in his expression that his greatness lies. His verse is an instrument of many modulations, of exquisite delicacy, of strange suggestiveness, of amazing power. Playing on it, he can give utterance to the subtlest visions, such as this:

> Just now a beam of joy hung on his eyelash;
> But, as I looked, it sunk into his eye,
> Like a bruised worm writhing its form of rings Into a
> darkening hole.

Or to the most marvellous of vague and vast conceptions, such as this:

> I begin to hear
> Strange but sweet sounds, and the loud rocky dashing

> Of waves, where time into Eternity
> Falls over ruined worlds.

Or he can evoke sensations of pure loveliness, such as these:

> So fair a creature! of such charms compact
> As nature stints elsewhere: which you may find
> Under the tender eyelid of a serpent,
> Or in the gurge of a kiss-coloured rose,
> By drops and sparks: but when she moves, you see,
> Like water from a crystal overfilled,
> Fresh beauty tremble out of her and lave
> Her fair sides to the ground.

Or he can put into a single line all the long memories of adoration:

> My love was much;
> My life but an inhabitant of his.

Or he can pass in a moment from tiny sweetness to colossal turmoil:

> I should not say
> How thou art like the daisy in Noah's meadow,
> On which the foremost drop of rain fell warm
> And soft at evening: so the little flower
> Wrapped up its leaves, and shut the treacherous water
> Close to the golden welcome of its breast,
> Delighting in the touch of that which led
> The shower of oceans, in whose billowy drops
> Tritons and lions of the sea were warring,
> And sometimes ships on fire sunk in the blood,
> Of their own inmates; others were of ice,
> And some had islands rooted in their waves,
> Beasts on their rocks, and forest-powdering winds,
> And showers tumbling on their tumbling self,
> And every sea of every ruined star
> Was but a drop in the world-melting flood.

He can express alike the beautiful tenderness of love, and the hectic, dizzy, and appalling frenzy of extreme rage:—

> ... What shall I do? I speak all wrong,
> And lose a soul-full of delicious thought
> By talking. Hush! Let's drink each other upBy silent eyes.
> Who lives, but thou and I,
> My heavenly wife?
> ...I'll watch thee thus, till I can tell a second
> By thy cheek's change.

In that, one can almost feel the kisses; and, in this, one can almost hear the gnashing of the teeth. 'Never!' exclaims the duke to his son Torrismond:

> There lies no grain of sand between
> My loved and my detested! Wing thee hence,
> Or thou dost stand to-morrow on a cobweb
> Spun o'er the well of clotted Acheron,
> Whose hydrophobic entrails stream with fire!
> And may this intervening earth be snow,
> And my step burn like the mid coal of Aetna,
> Plunging me, through it all, into the core,
> Where in their graves the dead are shut like seeds,
> If I do not—O, but he is my son!

Is not that tremendous? But, to find Beddoes in his most characteristic mood, one must watch him weaving his mysterious imagination upon the woof of mortality. One must wander with him through the pages of *Death's Jest Book*, one must grow accustomed to the dissolution of reality, and the opening of the nettled lips of graves; one must learn that 'the dead are most and merriest,' one must ask—'Are the ghosts eaves-dropping?'—one must realise that 'murder is full of holes.' Among the ruins of his Gothic cathedral, on whose cloister walls the Dance of Death is painted, one may speculate at ease over the fragility of existence, and, within the sound of that dark ocean,

> Whose tumultuous waves
> Are heaped, contending ghosts,

one may understand how it is that

> Death is mightier, stronger, and more faithful
> To man than Life.

Lingering there, one may watch the Deaths come down from their cloister, and dance and sing amid the moonlight; one may laugh over the grotesque contortions of skeletons; one may crack jokes upon corruption; one may sit down with phantoms, and drink to the health of Death.

In private intercourse Beddoes was the least morbid of human beings. His mind was like one of those Gothic cathedrals of which he was so fond—mysterious within, and filled with a light at once richer and less real than the light of day; on the outside, firm, and towering, and immediately impressive; and embellished, both inside and out, with grinning gargoyles. His conversation, Kelsall tells us, was full of humour and vitality, and untouched by any trace of egoism or affectation. He loved discussion, plunging into it with fire, and carrying it onward with high dexterity and good-humoured force. His letters are excellent: simple, spirited, spicy, and as original as his verse; flavoured with that vein of rattling open-air humour which had produced his school-boy novel in the style of Fielding. He was a man whom it would have been a rare delight to know. His character, so eminently English, compact of courage, of originality, of imagination, and with something coarse in it as well, puts one in mind of Hamlet: not the melodramatic sentimentalist of the stage; but the real Hamlet, Horatio's Hamlet, who called his father's ghost old truepenny, who forged his uncle's signature, who fought Laertes, and ranted in a grave, and lugged the guts into the neighbour room. His tragedy, like Hamlet's, was the tragedy of an over-powerful will—a will so strong as to recoil upon itself, and fall into indecision. It is easy for a weak man to be decided—there is so much to make him so; but a strong man, who can do anything, sometimes leaves everything undone. Fortunately Beddoes, though he did far less than he might have done, possessed so rich a genius that what he did, though small in quantity, is in quality beyond price. 'I might have been, among other things, a good poet,' were his last words. 'Among other things'! Aye, there's the rub. But, in spite of his own 'might have been,' a good poet he was. Perhaps for him, after all, there was very little to regret; his life was full of high nobility; and what other way of death would have befitted the poet of death? There is a thought constantly recurring throughout his writings—in his childish as in his most mature work—the thought of the beauty and the supernal happiness of soft and quiet death. He had visions of 'rosily dying,' of 'turning to daisies gently in the grave,' of a 'pink reclining death,' of death coming like a summer cloud over the soul. 'Let her deathly life pass into death,' says one of his earliest characters, 'like music on the night wind.' And, in *Death's Jest Book*, Sibylla has the same thoughts:

> O Death! I am thy friend,
> I struggle not with thee, I love thy state:
> Thou canst be sweet and gentle, be so now;
> And let me pass praying away into thee,
> As twilight still does into starry night.

Did his mind, obsessed and overwhelmed by images of death, crave at last for the one thing stranger than all these—the experience of it? It is easy to believe so, and that, ill, wretched, and abandoned by Degen at the miserable Cigogne Hotel, he should seek relief in the gradual dissolution which attends upon loss of blood. And then, when he had recovered, when he was almost happy once again, the old thoughts, perhaps, came crowding back upon him—thoughts of the futility of life, and the supremacy of death and the mystical whirlpool of the unknown, and the long quietude of the grave. In the end, Death had grown to be something more than Death to him—it was, mysteriously and transcendentally, Love as well.

> Death's darts are sometimes Love's. So Nature tells,
> When laughing waters close o'er drowning men;
> When in flowers' honied corners poison dwells;
> When Beauty dies: and the unwearied ken
> Of those who seek a cure for long despairWill learn ...

What learning was it that rewarded him? What ghostly knowledge of eternal love?

> If there are ghosts to raise,
> What shall I call,
> Out of hell's murky haze,
> Heaven's blue pall?
> —Raise my loved long-lost boyTo lead me to his joy.—
> There are no ghosts to raise;
> Out of death lead no ways;
> Vain is the call.
>
> —Know'st thou not ghosts to sue?
> No love thou hast.
> Else lie, as I will do,
> And breathe thy last.
> So out of Life's fresh crown
> Fall like a rose-leaf down.
> Thus are the ghosts to woo;
> Thus are all dreams made true,
> Ever to last!

1907.

HENRI BEYLE

In the whole of French literature it would be difficult to point to a figure at once so important, so remarkable, and so little known to English readers as Henri Beyle. Most of us are, no doubt, fairly familiar with his pseudonym of 'Stendhal'; some of us have read *Le Rouge et Le Noir* and *La Chartreuse de Parme*; but how many of us have any further knowledge of a man whose works are at the present moment appearing in Paris in all the pomp of an elaborate and complete edition, every scrap of whose manuscripts is being collected and deciphered with enthusiastic care, and in honour of whose genius the literary periodicals of the hour are filling entire numbers with exegesis and appreciation? The eminent critic, M. André Gide, when asked lately to name the novel which stands in his opinion first among the novels of France, declared that since, without a doubt, the place belongs to one or other of the novels of Stendhal, his only difficulty was in making his choice among these; and he finally decided upon *La Chartreuse de Parme*. According to this high authority, Henri Beyle was indisputably the creator of the greatest work of fiction in the French language, yet on this side of the Channel we have hardly more than heard of him! Nor is it merely as a writer that Beyle is admired in France. As a man, he seems to have come in, sixty or seventy years after his death, for a singular devotion. There are 'Beylistes,' or 'Stendhaliens,' who dwell with rapture upon every detail of the master's private life, who extend with pious care the long catalogue of his amorous adventures, who discuss the shades of his character with the warmth of personal friendship, and register his opinions with a zeal which is hardly less than sectarian. But indeed it is precisely in these extremes of his French devotees that we shall find a clue to the explanation of our own indifference. Beyle's mind contained, in a highly exaggerated form, most of the peculiarly distinctive elements of the French character. This does not mean that he was a typical Frenchman; far from it. He did not, like Voltaire or Hugo, strike a note to which the whole national genius vibrated in response. He has never been, it is unlikely that he ever will be, a popular writer. His literary reputation in France has been confined, until perhaps quite lately, to a small distinguished circle. 'On me lira,' he was fond of saying, 'vers 1880'; and the 'Beylistes' point to the remark in triumph as one further proof of the almost divine prescience of the great man. But in truth Beyle was always read by the *élite* of French critics and writers—'the happy few,' as he used to call them; and among these he has never been without enthusiastic admirers. During his lifetime Balzac, in an enormous eulogy of *La Chartreuse de Parme*, paid him one of the most magnificent compliments ever received by a man of letters from a fellow craftsman. In the next generation Taine declared himself his disciple; a little later—'vers 1880,' in fact—we find Zola describing him as 'notre père à tous,' and M. Bourget followed with elaborate incense. To-day we have writers of such different tendencies as M. Barrès and M. Gide acclaiming him as a supreme master, and the fashionable idolatry of the 'Beylistes.' Yet, at the same time, running parallel to this stream of homage, it is easy to trace a line of opinion of a totally different kind. It is the opinion of the more solid, the more middle-class elements of French life. Thus Sainte-Beuve, in two characteristic 'Lundis,' poured a great deal of very tepid water upon Balzac's flaming panegyric. Then Flaubert—'vers 1880,' too—confessed that he could see very little in Stendhal. And, only a few years ago, M. Chuquet, of the Institute, took the trouble to compose a thick book in which he has collected with scrupulous detail all the known facts concerning the life and writings of a man whom he forthwith proceeds to damn through five hundred pages of faint praise. These discrepancies are curious: how can we account for such odd differences of taste? How are we to reconcile the admiration of Balzac with the dislike of Flaubert, the raptures of M. Bourget and M. Barrès with the sniffs of Sainte-Beuve and M. Chuquet of the Institute? The explanation seems to be that Beyle occupies a position in France analogous to that of Shelley in England. Shelley is not a national hero, not because he lacked the distinctive qualities of an Englishman, but for the opposite reason—because he possessed so many of them in an extreme degree. The idealism, the daring, the imagination, and the unconventionality which give Shakespeare, Nelson, and Dr. Johnson their place in our pantheon—all these were Shelley's, but they were his in too undiluted and intense a form, with the result that, while he will never fail of worshippers among us, there will also always be Englishmen unable to appreciate him at all. Such, *mutatis mutandis*—and in this case the proviso is a very large one—is the position of Beyle in France. After all, when Bunthorne asked for a not-too-French French bean he showed more commonsense than he intended. Beyle is a too-French French writer—too French even for the bulk of his own compatriots; and so for us it is only natural that he should be a little difficult. Yet this very fact is in itself no bad reason for giving him some attention. An understanding of this very Gallic individual might give us a new insight into the whole strange race. And besides, the curious creature is worth looking at for his own sake too.

But, when one tries to catch him and pin him down on the dissecting-table, he turns out to be exasperatingly elusive. Even his most fervent admirers cannot agree among themselves as to the true nature of his achievements. Balzac thought of him as an artist, Taine was captivated by his conception of history, M. Bourget adores him as a psychologist, M. Barrès lays stress upon his 'sentiment d'honneur,' and the 'Beylistes' see in him the embodiment of modernity. Certainly very few writers have had the good fortune to appeal at once so constantly and in so varied a manner to succeeding generations as Henri Beyle. The circumstances of his life no doubt in part account for the complexity of his genius. He was born in 1783, when the *ancien régime* was still in full swing; his early manhood was spent in the turmoil of the Napoleonic wars; he lived to see the Bourbon reaction, the Romantic revival, the revolution of 1830, and the establishment of Louis Philippe; and when he died, at the age of sixty, the nineteenth century was nearly half-way through. Thus his life exactly spans the interval between the old world and the new. His family, which belonged to the magistracy of Grenoble, preserved the living tradition of the eighteenth century. His grandfather was a polite, amiable, periwigged sceptic after the manner of Fontenelle, who always spoke of 'M. de Voltaire' with a smile 'mélangé de respect et d'affection'; and when the Terror came, two representatives of the people were sent down to Grenoble, with the result that Beyle's father was pronounced (with a hundred and fifty others) 'notoirement suspect' of disaffection to the Republic, and confined to his house. At the age of sixteen Beyle arrived in Paris, just after the *coup d'état* of the 18th Brumaire had made Bonaparte First Consul, and he immediately came under the influence of his cousin Daru, that extraordinary man to whose terrific energies was due the organisation of Napoleon's greatest armies, and whose leisure moments—for apparently he had leisure moments—were devoted to the composition of idylls in the style of Tibullus and to an enormous correspondence on literary topics with the poetasters of the day. It was as a subordinate to this remarkable personage that Beyle spent nearly the whole of the next fifteen years of his life—in Paris, in Italy, in Germany, in Russia—wherever the whirling tempest of the Napoleonic policy might happen to carry him. His actual military experience was considerably slighter than what, in after years, he liked to give his friends to understand it had been. For hardly more than a year, during the Italian campaign, he was in the army as a lieutenant of dragoons: the rest of his public service was spent in the commissariat department. The descriptions which he afterwards delighted to give of his adventures at Marengo, at Jéna, at Wagram, or at the crossing of the Niémen have been shown by M. Chuquet's unkind researches to have been imaginary. Beyle was present at only one great battle—Bautzen. 'Nous voyons fort bien,' he wrote in his journal on the following day, 'de midi à trois heures, tout ce qu'on peut voir d'une bataille, c'est à dire rien.' He was, however, at Moscow in 1812, and he accompanied the army through the horrors of the retreat. When the conflagration had broken out in the city he had abstracted from one of the deserted palaces a finely bound copy of the *Facéties* of Voltaire; the book helped to divert his mind as he lay crouched by the campfire through the terrible nights that followed; but, as his companions showed their disapproval of anyone who could smile over Akakia and Pompignan in such a situation, one day he left the red-morocco volume behind him in the snow.

The fall of Napoleon threw Beyle out of employment, and the period of his literary activity began. His books were not successful; his fortune gradually dwindled; and he drifted in Paris and Italy, and even in England, more and more disconsolately, with thoughts of suicide sometimes in his head. But in 1830 the tide of his fortunes turned. The revolution of July, by putting his friends into power, brought him a competence in the shape of an Italian consulate; and in the same year he gained for the first time some celebrity by the publication of *Le Rouge et Le Noir*. The rest of his life was spent in the easy discharge of his official duties at Civita Vecchia, alternating with periods of leave—one of them lasted for three years—spent in Paris among his friends, of whom the most distinguished was Prosper Mérimée. In 1839 appeared his last published work—*La Chartreuse de Parme*; and three years later he died suddenly in Paris. His epitaph, composed by himself with the utmost care, was as follows:

QUI GIACE
ARRIGO BEYLE MILANESE
VISSE, SCRISSE, AMO.

The words, read rightly, indicate many things—his adoration of Italy and Milan, his eccentricity, his scorn of the conventions of society and the limits of nationality, his adventurous life, his devotion to literature, and, lastly, the fact that, through all the varieties of his experience—in the earliest years of his childhood, in his agitated manhood, in his calm old age—there had never been a moment when he was not in love.

Beyle's work falls into two distinct groups—the first consisting of his novels, and the second of his miscellaneous writings, which include several biographies, a dissertation on Love, some books of criticism and travel, his letters and various autobiographical fragments. The bulk of the latter group is large; much of it has only lately seen the light; and more of it, at present in MS. at the library of Grenoble, is promised us by the indefatigable editors of the new complete edition which is now appearing in Paris. The interest of this portion of Beyle's writings is almost entirely personal: that of his novels is mainly artistic. It was as a novelist that Beyle first gained his celebrity, and it is still as a novelist—or rather as the author of *Le Rouge et Le Noir* and *La Chartreuse de Parme* (for an earlier work, *Armance*, some short stories, and some later posthumous fragments may be left out of account)—that he is most widely known to-day. These two remarkable works lose none of their significance if we consider the time at which they were composed. It was in the full flood of the Romantic revival, that marvellous hour in the history of French literature when the tyranny of two centuries was shattered for ever, and a boundless wealth of inspirations, possibilities, and beauties before undreamt-of suddenly burst upon the view. It was the hour of Hugo, Vigny, Musset, Gautier, Balzac, with their new sonorities and golden cadences, their new lyric passion and dramatic stress, their new virtuosities, their new impulse towards the strange and the magnificent, their new desire for diversity and the manifold comprehension of life. But, if we turn to the contemporaneous pages of Stendhal, what do we find? We find a succession of colourless, unemphatic sentences; we find cold reasoning and exact narrative; we find polite irony and dry wit. The spirit of the eighteenth century is everywhere; and if the old gentleman with the perruque and the 'M. de Voltaire' could have taken a glance at his grandson's novels, he would have rapped his snuff-box and approved. It is true that Beyle joined the ranks of the Romantics for a moment with a *brochure* attacking Racine at the expense of Shakespeare; but this was merely one of those contradictory changes of front which were inherent in his nature; and in reality the whole Romantic movement meant nothing to him. There is a story of a meeting in the house of a common friend between him and Hugo, in which the two men faced each other like a couple of cats with their backs up and their whiskers bristling. No wonder! But Beyle's true attitude towards his great contemporaries was hardly even one of hostility: he simply could not open their books. As for Chateaubriand, the god of their idolatry, he loathed him like poison. He used to describe how, in his youth, he had been on the point of fighting a duel with an officer who had ventured to maintain that a phrase in *Atala*—'la cime indéterminée des forêts'—was not intolerable. Probably he was romancing (M. Chuquet says so); but at any rate the story sums up symbolically Beyle's attitude towards his art. To him the whole apparatus of 'fine writing'—the emphatic phrase, the picturesque epithet, the rounded rhythm—was anathema. The charm that such ornaments might bring was in reality only a cloak for loose thinking and feeble observation. Even the style of the eighteenth century was not quite his ideal; it was too elegant; there was an artificial neatness about the form which imposed itself upon the substance, and degraded it. No, there was only one example of the perfect style, and that was the *Code Napoléon*; for there alone everything was subordinated to the exact and complete expression of what was to be said. A statement of law can have no place for irrelevant beauties, or the vagueness of personal feeling; by its very nature, it must resemble a sheet of plate glass through which every object may be seen with absolute distinctness, in its true shape. Beyle declared that he was in the habit of reading several paragraphs of the Code every morning after breakfast 'pour prendre le ton.' This again was for long supposed to be one of his little jokes; but quite lately the searchers among the MSS. at Grenoble have discovered page after page copied out from the Code in Beyle's handwriting. No doubt, for that wayward lover of paradoxes, the real joke lay in everybody taking for a joke what *he* took quite seriously.

This attempt to reach the exactitude and the detachment of an official document was not limited to Beyle's style; it runs through the whole tissue of his work. He wished to present life dispassionately and intellectually, and if he could have reduced his novels to a series of mathematical symbols, he would have been charmed. The contrast between his method and that of Balzac is remarkable. That wonderful art of materialisation, of the sensuous evocation of the forms, the qualities, the very stuff and substance of things, which was perhaps Balzac's greatest discovery, Beyle neither possessed nor wished to possess. Such matters were to him of the most subordinate importance, which it was no small part of the novelist's duty to keep very severely in their place. In the earlier chapters of *Le Rouge et Le Noir*, for instance, he is concerned with almost the same subject as Balzac in the opening of *Les Illusions Perdues*—the position of a young man in a provincial town, brought suddenly from the humblest surroundings into the midst of the leading society of the place through his intimate relations with a woman of refinement. But while in Balzac's pages what emerges is the concrete vision of provincial life down to the last pimple on the nose of the lowest footman, Beyle concentrates his whole attention on the personal problem, hints in a few rapid strokes at what Balzac has spent all his genius in describing, and reveals to us instead, with the precision of a surgeon at an operation, the inmost fibres of his hero's mind. In fact, Beyle's method is the classical method—the method of selection, of omission, of unification, with the object of creating a central impression of supreme reality. Zola criticises him for disregarding 'le milieu.'

> Il y a [he says] un épisode célèbre dans 'Le Rouge et Le Noir,' la scène où Julien, assis un soir à côté de Mme. de Rénal, sous les branches noires d'un arbre, se fait un devoir de lui prendre la main, pendant qu'elle cause avec Mme. Derville. C'est un petit drame muet d'une grande puissance, et Stendhal y a analysé merveilleusement les états d'âme

de ses deux personnages. Or, le milieu n'apparaît pas une seule fois. Nous pourrions être n'importe où dans n'importe quelles conditions, la scène resterait la même pourvu qu'il fît noir ... Donnez l'épisode à un écrivain pour qui les milieux existent, et dans la défaite de cette femme, il fera entrer la nuit, avec ses odeurs, avec ses voix, avec ses voluptés molles. Et cet écrivain sera dans la vérité, son tableau sera plus complet.

More complete, perhaps; but would it be more convincing? Zola, with his statistical conception of art, could not understand that you could tell a story properly unless you described in detail every contingent fact. He could not see that Beyle was able, by simply using the symbol 'nuit,' to suggest the 'milieu' at once to the reader's imagination. Everybody knows all about the night's accessories—'ses odeurs, ses voix, ses voluptés molles'; and what a relief it is to be spared, for once in a way, an elaborate expatiation upon them! And Beyle is perpetually evoking the gratitude of his readers in this way. 'Comme il insiste peu!' as M. Gide exclaims. Perhaps the best test of a man's intelligence is his capacity for making a summary. Beyle knew this, and his novels are full of passages which read like nothing so much as extraordinarily able summaries of some enormous original narrative which has been lost.

It was not that he was lacking in observation, that he had no eye for detail, or no power of expressing it; on the contrary, his vision was of the sharpest, and his pen could call up pictorial images of startling vividness, when he wished. But he very rarely did wish: it was apt to involve a tiresome insistence. In his narratives he is like a brilliant talker in a sympathetic circle, skimming swiftly from point to point, taking for granted the intelligence of his audience, not afraid here and there to throw out a vague 'etc.' when the rest of the sentence is too obvious to state; always plain of speech, never self-assertive, and taking care above all things never to force the note. His famous description of the Battle of Waterloo in *La Chartreuse de Parme* is certainly the finest example of this side of his art. Here he produces an indelible impression by a series of light touches applied with unerring skill. Unlike Zola, unlike Tolstoi, he shows us neither the loathsomeness nor the devastation of a battlefield, but its insignificance, its irrelevant detail, its unmeaning grotesquenesses and indignities, its incoherence, and its empty weariness. Remembering his own experience at Bautzen, he has made his hero—a young Italian impelled by Napoleonic enthusiasm to join the French army as a volunteer on the eve of the battle—go through the great day in such a state of vague perplexity that in the end he can never feel quite certain that he really *was* at Waterloo. He experiences a succession of trivial and unpleasant incidents, culminating in his being hoisted off his horse by two of his comrades, in order that a general, who has had his own shot from under him, might be supplied with a mount; for the rest, he crosses and recrosses some fields, comes upon a dead body in a ditch, drinks brandy with a *vivandière*, gallops over a field covered with dying men, has an indefinite skirmish in a wood—and it is over. At one moment, having joined the escort of some generals, the young man allows his horse to splash into a stream, thereby covering one of the generals with muddy water from head to foot. The passage that follows is a good specimen of Beyle's narrative style:

> En arrivant sur l'autre rive, Fabrice y avait trouvé les généraux tout seuls; le bruit du canon lui sembla redoubler; ce fut à peine s'il entendit le général, par lui si bien mouillé, qui criait à son oreille:
>
> Où as-tu pris ce cheval?
>
> Fabrice était tellement troublé, qu'il répondit en Italien: *l'ho comprato poco fa*. (Je viens de l'acheter à l'instant.)
>
> Que dis-tu? lui cria le général.
>
> Mais le tapage devint tellement fort en ce moment, que Fabrice ne put lui répondre. Nous avouerons que notre héros était fort peu héros en ce moment. Toutefois, la peur ne venait chez lui qu'en seconde ligne; il était surtout scandalisé de ce bruit qui lui faisait mal aux oreilles. L'escorte prit le galop; on traversait une grande pièce de terre labourée, située au delà du canal, et ce champ était jonché de cadavres.

How unemphatic it all is! What a paucity of epithet, what a reticence in explanation! How a Romantic would have lingered over the facial expression of the general, and how a Naturalist would have analysed that 'tapage'! And yet, with all their efforts, would they have succeeded in conveying that singular impression of disturbance, of cross-purposes, of hurry, and of ill-defined fear, which Beyle with his quiet terseness has produced?

It is, however, in his psychological studies that the detached and intellectual nature of Beyle's method is most clearly seen. When he is describing, for instance, the development of Julien Sorel's mind in *Le Rouge et Le Noir*, when he shows us the soul of the young peasant with its ignorance, its ambition, its pride, going step by step into the whirling vortex of life—then we seem to be witnessing not so much the presentment of a fiction as the unfolding of some scientific fact. The procedure is almost mathematical: a proposition is established, the inference is drawn, the next proposition follows, and so on until the demonstration is complete. Here the influence of the eighteenth century is very strongly marked. Beyle had drunk deeply of that fountain of syllogism and analysis that flows through the now forgotten pages of Helvétius and Condillac; he was an ardent votary of logic in its austerest form—'la lo-gique' he used to call it, dividing the syllables in a kind of awe-inspired emphasis; and he considered the ratiocinative style of Montesquieu almost as good as that of the *Code Civil*.

If this had been all, if we could sum him up simply as an acute and brilliant writer who displays the scientific and prosaic sides of the French genius in an extreme degree, Beyle's position in literature would present very little difficulty. He would take his place at once as a late— an abnormally late—product of the eighteenth century. But he was not that. In his blood there was a virus which had never tingled in the veins of Voltaire. It was the virus of modern life—that new sensibility, that new passionateness, which Rousseau had first made known to the world, and which had won its way over Europe behind the thunder of Napoleon's artillery. Beyle had passed his youth within earshot of that mighty roar, and his inmost spirit could never lose the echo of it. It was in vain that he studied Condillac and modelled his style on the Code; in vain that he sang the praises of *la lo-gique*, shrugged his shoulders at the Romantics, and turned the cold eye of a scientific investigator upon the phenomena of life; he remained essentially a man of feeling. His unending series of *grandes passions* was one unmistakable sign of this; another was his intense devotion to the Fine Arts. Though his taste in music and painting was the taste of his time—the literary and sentimental taste of the age of Rossini and Canova—he nevertheless brought to the appreciation of works of art a kind of intimate gusto which reveals the genuineness of his emotion. The 'jouissances d'ange,' with which at his first entrance into Italy he heard at Novara the *Matrimonio Segreto* of Cimarosa, marked an epoch in his life. He adored Mozart: 'I can imagine nothing more distasteful to me,' he said, 'than a thirty-mile walk through the mud; but I would take one at this moment if I knew that I should hear a good performance of *Don Giovanni* at the end of it.' The Virgins of Guido Reni sent him into ecstasies and the Goddesses of Correggio into raptures. In short, as he himself admitted, he never could resist 'le Beau' in whatever form he found it. *Le Beau!* The phrase is characteristic of the peculiar species of ingenuous sensibility which so oddly agitated this sceptical man of the world. His whole vision of life was coloured by it. His sense of values was impregnated with what he called his 'espagnolisme'—his immense admiration for the noble and the high-sounding in speech or act or character—an admiration which landed him often enough in hysterics and absurdity. Yet this was the soil in which a temperament of caustic reasonableness had somehow implanted itself.

The contrast is surprising, because it is so extreme. Other men have been by turns sensible and enthusiastic: but who before or since has combined the emotionalism of a schoolgirl with the cold penetration of a judge on the bench? Beyle, for instance, was capable of writing, in one of those queer epitaphs of himself which he was constantly composing, the high-falutin' words 'Il respecta un seul homme: Napoléon'; and yet, as he wrote them, he must have remembered well enough that when he met Napoleon face to face his unabashed scrutiny had detected swiftly that the man was a play-actor, and a vulgar one at that. Such were the contradictions of his double nature, in which the elements, instead of being mixed, came together, as it were, in layers, like superimposed strata of chalk and flint.

In his novels this cohabitation of opposites is responsible both for what is best and what is worst. When the two forces work in unison the result is sometimes of extraordinary value—a product of a kind which it would be difficult to parallel in any other author. An eye of icy gaze is turned upon the tumultuous secrets of passion, and the pangs of love are recorded in the language of Euclid. The image of the surgeon inevitably suggests itself—the hand with the iron nerve and the swift knife laying bare the trembling mysteries within. It is the intensity of Beyle's observation, joined with such an exactitude of exposition, that makes his dry pages sometimes more thrilling than the wildest tale of adventure or all the marvels of high romance. The passage in *La Chartreuse de Parme* describing Count Mosca's jealousy has this quality, which appears even more clearly in the chapters of *Le Rouge et Le Noir* concerning Julien Sorel and Mathilde de la Mole. Here Beyle has a subject after his own heart. The loves of the peasant youth and the aristocratic girl, traversed and agitated by their overweening pride, and triumphing at last rather over themselves than over each other—these things make up a gladiatorial combat of 'espagnolismes,' which is displayed to the reader with a supreme incisiveness. The climax is reached when Mathilde at last gives way to her passion, and throws herself into the arms of Julien, who forces himself to make no response:

> Ses bras se roidirent, tant l'effort imposé par la politique était pénible. Je ne dois pas même me permettre de presser contre mon coeur ce corps souple et charmant; ou elle me méprise, ou elle me maltraite. Quel affreux caractère!
>
> Et en maudissant le caractère de Mathilde, il l'en aimait cent fois plus; il lui semblait avoir dans ses bras une reine.
>
> L'impassible froideur de Julien redoubla le malheur de Mademoiselle de la Mole. Elle était loin d'avoir le sang-froid nécessaire pour chercher à deviner dans ses yeux ce qu'il

sentait pour elle en cet instant. Elle ne put se résoudre à le regarder; elle tremblait de rencontrer l'expression du mépris.

Assise sur le divan de la bibliothèque, immobile et la tête tournée du côté opposé à Julien, elle était en proie aux plus vives douleurs que l'orgueil et l'amour puissent faire éprouver à une âme humaine. Dans quelle atroce démarche elle venait de tomber!

Il m'était réservé, malheureuse que je suis! de voir repoussées les avances les plus indécentes! Et repoussées par qui? ajoutait l'orgueil fou de douleur, repoussées par un domestique de mon père.

C'est ce que je ne souffrirai pas, dit-elle à haute voix.

At that moment she suddenly sees some unopened letters addressed to Julien by another woman.

—Ainsi, s'écria-t-elle hors d'elle-même, non seulement vous êtes bien avec elle, mais encore vous la méprisez. Vous, un homme de rien, mépriser Madame la Maréchale de Fervaques!

—Ah! pardon, mon ami, ajouta-t-elle en se jetant à ses genoux, méprise-moi si tu veux, mais aime-moi, je ne puis plus vivre privée de ton amour. Et elle tomba tout à fait évanouie.

—La voilà donc, cette orgueilleuse, à mes pieds! se dit Julien.

Such is the opening of this wonderful scene, which contains the concentrated essence of Beyle's genius, and which, in its combination of high passion, intellectual intensity, and dramatic force, may claim comparison with the great dialogues of Corneille.

'Je fais tous les efforts possibles pour être *sec*,' he says of himself. 'Je veux imposer silence à mon coeur, qui croit avoir beaucoup à dire. Je tremble toujours de n'avoir écrit qu'un soupir, quand je crois avoir noté une vérité.' Often he succeeds, but not always. At times his desire for dryness becomes a mannerism and fills whole pages with tedious and obscure argumentation. And, at other times, his sensibility gets the upper hand, throws off all control, and revels in an orgy of melodrama and 'espagnolisme.' Do what he will, he cannot keep up a consistently critical attitude towards the creatures of his imagination: he depreciates his heroes with extreme care, but in the end they get the better of him and sweep him off his feet. When, in *La Chartreuse de Parme*, Fabrice kills a man in a duel, his first action is to rush to a looking-glass to see whether his beauty has been injured by a cut in the face; and Beyle does not laugh at this; he is impressed by it. In the same book he lavishes all his art on the creation of the brilliant, worldly, sceptical Duchesse de Sanseverina, and then, not quite satisfied, he makes her concoct and carry out the murder of the reigning Prince in order to satisfy a desire for amorous revenge. This really makes her perfect. But the most striking example of Beyle's inability to resist the temptation of sacrificing his head to his heart is in the conclusion of Le Rouge et Le Noir, where Julien, to be revenged on a former mistress who defames him, deliberately goes down into the country, buys a pistol, and shoots the lady in church. Not only is Beyle entranced by the *bravura* of this senseless piece of brutality, but he destroys at a blow the whole atmosphere of impartial observation which fills the rest of the book, lavishes upon his hero the blindest admiration, and at last, at the moment of Julien's execution, even forgets himself so far as to write a sentence in the romantic style: 'Jamais cette tête n'avait été aussi poétique qu'au moment où elle allait tomber.' Just as Beyle, in his contrary mood, carries to an extreme the French love of logical precision, so in these rhapsodies he expresses in an exaggerated form a very different but an equally characteristic quality of his compatriots—their instinctive responsiveness to fine poses. It is a quality that Englishmen in particular find it hard to sympathise with. They remain stolidily unmoved when their neighbours are in ecstasies. They are repelled by the 'noble' rhetoric of the French Classical Drama; they find the tirades of Napoleon, which animated the armies of France to victory, pieces of nauseous clap-trap. And just now it is this side—to us the obviously weak side—of Beyle's genius that seems to be most in favour with French critics. To judge from M. Barrès, writing dithyrambically of Beyle's 'sentiment d'honneur,' that is his true claim to greatness. The sentiment of honour is all very well, one is inclined to mutter on this side of the Channel; but oh, for a little sentiment of humour too!

The view of Beyle's personality which his novels give us may be seen with far greater detail in his miscellaneous writings. It is to these that his most modern admirers devote their main attention—particularly to his letters and his autobiographies; but they are all of them highly characteristic of their author, and—whatever the subject may be, from a guide to Rome to a life of Napoleon—one gathers in them, scattered up and down through their pages, a curious, dimly adumbrated philosophy—an ill-defined and yet intensely personal point of view—*le Beylisme*. It is in fact almost entirely in this secondary quality that their interest lies; their ostensible subject-matter is unimportant. An apparent exception is the book in which Beyle has embodied his reflections upon Love. The volume, with its meticulous apparatus of analysis, definition, and classification, which gives it the air of being a parody of *L'Esprit des Lois*, is yet full of originality, of lively anecdote and keen observation. Nobody but Beyle could have written it; nobody but Beyle could have managed to be at once so stimulating and so jejune, so clear-sighted and so exasperating. But here again, in reality, it is not the question at issue that is interesting—one learns more of the true nature of Love in one or two of La Bruyère's short sentences than in all Beyle's three hundred pages of disquisition; but what is absorbing is the sense that comes to one, as one reads it, of the presence, running through it all, of a restless and problematical spirit. 'Le Beylisme' is certainly not susceptible of any exact definition; its author was too capricious, too unmethodical, in spite of his *lo-gique*, ever to have framed a coherent philosophy; it is essentially a thing of shreds and patches, of hints, suggestions, and quick visions of flying thoughts. M. Barrès says that what lies at the bottom of it is a 'passion de collectionner les belles énergies.' But there are many kinds of 'belles énergies,' and some of them certainly do not fit into the framework of 'le Beylisme.' 'Quand je suis arrêté par des voleurs, ou qu'on me tire des coups de fusil, je me sens une grande colère contre le gouvernement et le curé de l'endroit. Quand au voleur, il me plaît, s'il est énergique, car il m'amuse.' It was the energy of self-assertiveness that pleased Beyle; that of self-restraint did not interest him. The immorality of the point of view is patent, and at times it appears to be simply based upon the common selfishness of an egotist. But in reality it was something more significant than that. The 'chasse au bonheur' which Beyle was always advocating was no respectable epicureanism; it had about it a touch of the fanatical. There was anarchy in it—a hatred of authority, an impatience with custom, above all a scorn for the commonplace dictates of ordinary morality. Writing his memoirs at the age of fifty-two, Beyle looked back with pride on the joy that he had felt, as a child of ten, amid his royalist family at Grenoble, when the news came of the execution of Louis XVI. His father announced it:

—C'en est fait, dit-il avec un gros soupir, ils l'ont assassiné.

Je fus saisi d'un des plus vifs mouvements de joie que j'ai éprouvé en ma vie. Le lecteur pensera peut-être que je suis cruel, mais tel j'étais à 5 X 2, tel je suis à 10 X 5 + 2 ... Je puis dire que l'approbation des êtres, que je regarde comme faibles, m'est absolument indifférente.

These are the words of a born rebel, and such sentiments are constantly recurring in his books. He is always discharging his shafts against some established authority; and, of course, he reserved his bitterest hatred for the proudest and most insidious of all authorities—the Roman Catholic Church. It is odd to find some of the 'Beylistes' solemnly hailing the man whom the power of the Jesuits haunted like a nightmare, and whose account of the seminary in *Le Rouge et Le Noir* is one of the most scathing pictures of religious tyranny ever drawn, as a prophet of the present Catholic movement in France. For in truth, if Beyle was a prophet of anything he was a prophet of that spirit of revolt in modern thought which first reached a complete expression in the pages of Nietzsche. His love of power and self-will, his aristocratic outlook, his scorn of the Christian virtues, his admiration of the Italians of the Renaissance, his repudiation of the herd and the morality of the herd—these qualities, flashing strangely among his observations on Rossini and the Coliseum, his reflections on the memories of the past and his musings on the ladies of the present, certainly give a surprising foretaste of the fiery potion of Zarathustra. The creator of the Duchesse de Sanseverina had caught more than a glimpse of the transvaluation of all values. Characteristically enough, the appearance of this new potentiality was only observed by two contemporary forces in European society— Goethe and the Austrian police. It is clear that Goethe alone among the critics of the time understood that Beyle was something more than a novelist, and discerned an uncanny significance in his pages. 'I do not like reading M. de Stendhal,' he observed to Winckelmann, 'but I cannot help doing so. He is extremely free and extremely impertinent, and ... I recommend you to buy all his books.' As for the Austrian police, they had no doubt about the matter. Beyle's book of travel, *Rome, Naples et Florence*, was, they decided, pernicious and dangerous in the highest degree; and the poor man was hunted out of Milan in consequence.

It would be a mistake to suppose that Beyle displayed in his private life the qualities of the superman. Neither his virtues nor his vices were on the grand scale. In his own person he never seems to have committed an 'espagnolisme.' Perhaps his worst sin was that of plagiarism: his earliest book, a life of Haydn, was almost entirely 'lifted' from the work of a learned German; and in his next he embodied several choice extracts culled from the *Edinburgh Review*. On this occasion he was particularly delighted, since the *Edinburgh*, in reviewing the book, innocently selected for special approbation the very passages which he had stolen. It is singular that so original a writer should have descended to pilfering. But Beyle was nothing if not inconsistent. With all his Classicism he detested Racine; with all his love of music he could see nothing in Beethoven; he adored Italy, and, so soon as he was given his Italian consulate, he was usually to be found in Paris. As his life advanced he grew more and more wayward, capricious, and eccentric. He indulged in queer mystifications, covering his papers with false names and anagrams—for the police, he said, were on his track, and he must be careful. His love-affairs became less and less fortunate; but he was still sometimes successful, and when he was he registered the fact—upon his braces. He dreamed and drifted a great deal. He went up to San Pietro in

Montorio, and looking over Rome, wrote the initials of his past mistresses in the dust. He tried to make up his mind whether Napoleon after all *was* the only being he respected; no—there was also Mademoiselle de Lespinasse. He went to the opera at Naples and noted that 'la musique parfaite, comme la pantomime parfaite, me fait songer à ce qui forme actuellement l'objet de mes rêveries et me fait venir des idées excellentes: ... or, ce soir, je ne puis me dissimuler que j'ai le malheur *of being too great an admirer of Lady L*....' He abandoned himself to 'les charmantes visions du Beau qui souvent encore remplissent ma tête à l'âge de *fifty-two*.' He wondered whether Montesquieu would have thought his writings worthless. He sat scribbling his reminiscences by the fire till the night drew on and the fire went out, and still he scribbled, more and more illegibly, until at last the paper was covered with hieroglyphics undecipherable even by M. Chuquet himself. He wandered among the ruins of ancient Rome, playing to perfection the part of cicerone to such travellers as were lucky enough to fall in with him; and often his stout and jovial form, with the satyric look in the sharp eyes and the compressed lips, might be seen by the wayside in the Campagna, as he stood and jested with the reapers or the vine-dressers or with the girls coming out, as they had come since the days of Horace, to draw water from the fountains of Tivoli. In more cultivated society he was apt to be nervous; for his philosophy was never proof against the terror of being laughed at. But sometimes, late at night, when the surroundings were really sympathetic, he could be very happy among his friends. 'Un salon de huit ou dix personnes,' he said, 'dont toutes les femmes ont eu des amants, où la conversation est gaie, anecdotique, et où l'on prend du punch léger à minuit et demie, est l'endroit du monde où je me trouve le mieux.'

And in such a Paradise of Frenchmen we may leave Henri Beyle.

1914

LADY HESTER STANHOPE

The Pitt nose has a curious history. One can watch its transmigrations through three lives. The tremendous hook of old Lord Chatham, under whose curve Empires came to birth, was succeeded by the bleak upward-pointing nose of William Pitt the younger—the rigid symbol of an indomitable *hauteur*. With Lady Hester Stanhope came the final stage. The nose, still with an upward tilt in it, had lost its masculinity; the hard bones of the uncle and the grandfather had disappeared. Lady Hester's was a nose of wild ambitions, of pride grown fantastical, a nose that scorned the earth, shooting off, one fancies, towards some eternally eccentric heaven. It was a nose, in fact, altogether in the air.

Noses, of course, are aristocratic things; and Lady Hester was the child of a great aristocracy. But, in her case, the aristocratic impulse, which had carried her predecessors to glory, had less fortunate results. There has always been a strong strain of extravagance in the governing families of England; from time to time they throw off some peculiarly ill-balanced member, who performs a strange meteoric course. A century earlier, Lady Mary Wortley Montagu was an illustrious example of this tendency: that splendid comet, after filling half the heavens, vanished suddenly into desolation and darkness. Lady Hester Stanhope's spirit was still more uncommon; and she met with a most uncommon fate.

She was born in 1776, the eldest daughter of that extraordinary Earl Stanhope, Jacobin and inventor, who made the first steamboat and the first calculating machine, who defended the French Revolution in the House of Lords and erased the armorial bearings—'damned aristocratical nonsense'— from his carriages and his plate. Her mother, Chatham's daughter and the favourite sister of Pitt, died when she was four years old. The second Lady Stanhope, a frigid woman of fashion, left her stepdaughters to the care of futile governesses, while 'Citizen Stanhope' ruled the household from his laboratory with the violence of a tyrant. It was not until Lady Hester was twenty-four that she escaped from the slavery of her father's house, by going to live with her grandmother, Lady Chatham. On Lady Chatham's death, three years later, Pitt offered her his protection, and she remained with him until his death in 1806.

Her three years with Pitt, passed in the very centre of splendid power, were brilliant and exciting. She flung herself impetuously into the movement and the passion of that vigorous society; she ruled her uncle's household with high vivacity; she was liked and courted; if not beautiful, she was fascinating—very tall, with a very fair and clear complexion, and dark-blue eyes, and a countenance of wonderful expressiveness. Her talk, full of the trenchant nonchalance of those days, was both amusing and alarming: 'My dear Hester, what are you saying?' Pitt would call out to her from across the room. She was devoted to her uncle, who warmly returned her affection. She was devoted, too—but in a more dangerous fashion—to the intoxicating Antinous, Lord Granville Leveson Gower. The reckless manner in which she carried on this love-affair was the first indication of something overstrained, something wild and unaccountable, in her temperament. Lord Granville, after flirting with her outrageously, declared that he could never marry her, and went off on an embassy to St. Petersburg. Her distraction was extreme: she hinted that she would follow him to Russia; she threatened, and perhaps attempted, suicide; she went about telling everybody that he had jilted her. She was taken ill, and then there were rumours of an accouchement, which, it was said, she took care to *afficher*, by appearing without rouge and fainting on the slightest provocation. In the midst of these excursions and alarums there was a terrible and unexpected catastrophe. Pitt died. And Lady Hester suddenly found herself a dethroned princess, living in a small house in Montague Square on a pension of £1200 a year.

She did not abandon society, however, and the tongue of gossip continued to wag. Her immediate marriage with a former lover, Mr. Hill, was announced: 'il est bien bon,' said Lady Bessborough. Then it was whispered that Canning was 'le régnant'—that he was with her 'not only all day, but almost all night.' She quarrelled with Canning and became attached to Sir John Moore. Whether she was actually engaged to marry him—as she seems to have asserted many years later—is doubtful; his letters to her, full as they are of respectful tenderness, hardly warrant the conclusion; but it is certain that he died with her name on his lips. Her favourite brother, Charles, was killed beside him; and it was natural that under this double blow she should have retired from London. She buried herself in Wales; but not for long. In 1810 she set sail for Gibraltar with her brother James, who was rejoining his regiment in the Peninsula. She never returned to England.

There can be no doubt that at the time of her departure the thought of a lifelong exile was far from her mind. It was only gradually, as she moved further and further eastward, that the prospect of life in England— at last even in Europe—grew distasteful to her; as late as 1816 she was talking of a visit to Provence. Accompanied by two or three English fellow travellers, her English maid, Mrs. Fry, her private physician, Dr. Meryon, and a host of servants, she progressed, slowly and in great state, through Malta and Athens, to Constantinople. She was conveyed in battleships, and lodged with governors and ambassadors. After spending many months in Constantinople, Lady Hester discovered that she was 'dying to see Napoleon with her own eyes,' and attempted accordingly to obtain passports to France. The project was stopped by Stratford Canning, the English Minister, upon which she decided to visit Egypt, and, chartering a Greek vessel, sailed for Alexandria in the winter of 1811. Off the island of Rhodes a violent storm sprang up; the whole party were forced to abandon the ship, and to take refuge upon a bare rock, where they remained without food or shelter for thirty hours. Eventually, after many severe privations, Alexandria was reached in safety; but this disastrous voyage was a turning-point in Lady Hester's career. At Rhodes she was forced to exchange her torn and dripping raiment for the attire of a Turkish gentleman—a dress which she never afterwards abandoned. It was the first step in her orientalization.

She passed the next two years in a triumphal progress. Her appearance in Cairo caused the greatest sensation, and she was received in state by the Pasha, Mehemet Ali. Her costume on this occasion was gorgeous: she wore a turban of cashmere, a brocaded waistcoat, a priceless pelisse, and a vast pair of purple velvet pantaloons embroidered all over in gold. She was ushered by chamberlains with silver wands through the inner courts of the palace to a pavilion in the harem, where the Pasha, rising to receive her, conversed with her for an hour. From Cairo she turned northwards, visiting Jaffa, Jerusalem, Acre, and Damascus. Her travelling dress was of scarlet cloth trimmed with gold, and, when on horseback, she wore over the whole a white-hooded and tasselled burnous. Her maid, too, was forced, protesting, into trousers, though she absolutely refused to ride astride. Poor Mrs. Fry had gone through various and dreadful sufferings—shipwreck and starvation, rats and black-beetles unspeakable—but she retained her equanimity. Whatever her Ladyship might think fit to be, *she* was an Englishwoman to the last, and Philippaki was Philip Parker and Mustapha Mr. Farr.

Outside Damascus, Lady Hester was warned that the town was the most fanatical in Turkey, and that the scandal of a woman entering it in man's clothes, unveiled, would be so great as to be dangerous. She was begged to veil herself, and to make her entry under cover of darkness. 'I must take the bull by the horns,' she replied, and rode into the city unveiled at midday. The population were thunderstruck; but at last their amazement gave way to enthusiasm, and the incredible lady was hailed everywhere as Queen, crowds followed her, coffee was poured out before her, and the whole bazaar rose as she passed. Yet she was not satisfied with her triumphs; she would do something still more glorious and astonishing; she would plunge into the desert and visit the ruins of Palmyra, which only half-a-dozen of the boldest travellers had ever seen. The Pasha of Damascus offered her a military escort, but she preferred to throw herself upon the hospitality of the Bedouin Arabs, who, overcome by her horsemanship, her powers of sight, and her courage, enrolled her a member of their tribe. After a week's journey in their company, she reached Palmyra, where the inhabitants met her with wild enthusiasm, and under the Corinthian columns of Zenobia's temple crowned her head with flowers. This happened in March 1813; it was the apogee of Lady Hester's life. Henceforward her fortunes gradually but steadily declined.

The rumour of her exploits had spread through Syria, and from the year 1813 onwards, her reputation was enormous. She was received everywhere as a royal, almost as a supernatural, personage: she progressed from town to town amid official prostrations and popular rejoicings. But she herself was in a state of hesitation and discontent. Her future was uncertain; she had grown scornful of the West—must she return to it? The East alone was sympathetic, the East alone was tolerable—but could she cut herself off for ever from the past? At Laodicea she was suddenly struck down by the plague, and, after months of illness, it was borne in upon her that all was vanity. She rented an empty monastery on the slopes of Mount Lebanon, not far from Sayda (the ancient Sidon), and took up her abode there. Then her mind took a new surprising turn; she dashed to Ascalon, and, with the permission of the Sultan, began excavations in a ruined temple with the object of discovering a hidden treasure of three million pieces of gold. Having unearthed nothing but an antique statue, which, in order to prove her disinterestedness, she ordered her appalled doctor to break into little bits, she returned to her monastery. Finally, in 1816, she moved to another house, further up Mount Lebanon, and near the village of Djoun; and at Djoun she remained until her death, more than twenty years later.

Thus, almost accidentally as it seems, she came to the end of her wanderings, and the last, long, strange, mythical period of her existence began. Certainly the situation that she had chosen was sublime. Her house, on the top of a high bare hill among great mountains, was a one-storied group of buildings, with many ramifying courts and out-houses, and a garden of several acres surrounded by a rampart wall. The garden, which she herself had planted and tended with the utmost care, commanded a glorious prospect. On every side but one the vast mountains towered, but to the west there was an opening, through which, in the far distance, the deep blue Mediterranean was revealed. From this romantic hermitage, her singular renown spread over the world. European travellers who had been admitted to her presence brought back stories full of Eastern mystery; they told of a peculiar grandeur, a marvellous prestige, an imperial power. The precise nature of Lady Hester's empire was, indeed, dubious; she was in fact merely the tenant of her Djoun establishment, for which she paid a rent of £20 a year. But her dominion was not subject to such limitations. She ruled imaginatively, transcendentally; the solid glory of Chatham had been transmuted into the phantasy of an Arabian Night. No doubt she herself believed that she was something more than a chimerical Empress. When a French traveller was murdered in the desert, she issued orders for the punishment of the offenders; punished they were, and Lady Hester actually received the solemn thanks of the French Chamber. It seems probable, however, that it was the Sultan's orders rather than Lady Hester's which produced the desired effect. In her feud with her terrible neighbour, the Emir Beshyr, she maintained an undaunted front. She kept the tyrant at bay; but perhaps the Emir, who, so far as physical force was concerned, held her in the hollow of his hand, might have proceeded to extremities if he had not received a severe admonishment from Stratford Canning at Constantinople. What is certain is that the ignorant and superstitious populations around her feared and loved her, and that she, reacting to her own mysterious prestige, became at last even as they. She plunged into astrology and divination; she awaited the moment when, in accordance with prophecy, she should enter Jerusalem side by side with the Mahdi, the Messiah; she kept two sacred horses, destined, by sure signs, to carry her and him to their last triumph. The Orient had mastered her utterly. She was no longer an Englishwoman, she declared; she loathed England; she would never go there again; and if she went anywhere, it would be to Arabia, to 'her own people.'

Her expenses were immense—not only for herself but for others, for she poured out her hospitality with a noble hand. She ran into debt, and was swindled by the moneylenders; her steward cheated her, her servants pilfered her; her distress was at last acute. She fell into fits of terrible depression, bursting into dreadful tears and savage cries. Her habits grew more and more eccentric. She lay in bed all day, and sat up all night, talking unceasingly for hour upon hour to Dr. Meryon, who alone of her English attendants remained with her, Mrs. Fry having withdrawn to more congenial scenes long since. The doctor was a poor-spirited and muddle-headed man, but he was a good listener; and there he sat while that extraordinary talk flowed on—talk that scaled the heavens and ransacked the earth, talk in which memories of an abolished past—stories of Mr. Pitt and of George III., vituperations against Mr. Canning, mimicries of the Duchess of Devonshire—mingled phantasmagorically with doctrines of

Fate and planetary influence, and speculations on the Arabian origin of the Scottish clans, and lamentations over the wickedness of servants; till the unaccountable figure, with its robes and its long pipe, loomed through the tobacco-smoke like some vision of a Sibyl in a dream. She might be robbed and ruined, her house might crumble over her head; but she talked on. She grew ill and desperate; yet still she talked. Did she feel that the time was coming when she should talk no more?

Her melancholy deepened into a settled gloom when the news came of her brother James's death. She had quarrelled with all her English friends, except Lord Hardwicke—with her eldest brother, with her sister, whose kind letters she left unanswered; she was at daggers drawn with the English consul at Alexandria, who worried her about her debts. Ill and harassed, she hardly moved from her bedroom, while her servants rifled her belongings and reduced the house to a condition of indescribable disorder and filth. Three dozen hungry cats ranged through the rooms, filling the courts with frightful noises. Dr. Meryon, in the midst of it all, knew not whether to cry or laugh. At moments the great lady regained her ancient fire; her bells pealed tumultuously for hours together; or she leapt up, and arraigned the whole trembling household before her, with her Arab war-mace in her hand. Her finances grew more and more involved—grew at length irremediable. It was in vain that the faithful Lord Hardwicke pressed her to return to England to settle her affairs. Return to England, indeed! To England, that ungrateful, miserable country, where, so far as she could see, they had forgotten the very name of Mr. Pitt! The final blow fell when a letter came from the English authorities threatening to cut off her pension for the payment of her debts. Upon that, after dispatching a series of furious missives to Lord Palmerston, to Queen Victoria, to the Duke of Wellington, she renounced the world. She commanded Dr. Meryon to return to Europe, and he—how could he have done it?—obeyed her. Her health was broken, she was over sixty, and, save for her vile servants, absolutely alone. She lived for nearly a year after he left her—we know no more. She had vowed never again to pass through the gate of her house; but did she sometimes totter to her garden—that beautiful garden which she had created, with its roses and its fountains, its alleys and its bowers—and look westward at the sea? The end came in June 1839. Her servants immediately possessed themselves of every moveable object in the house. But Lady Hester cared no longer: she was lying back in her bed—inexplicable, grand, preposterous, with her nose in the air.

1919.

MR. CREEVEY

Clio is one of the most glorious of the Muses; but, as everyone knows, she (like her sister Melpomene) suffers from a sad defect: she is apt to be pompous. With her buskins, her robes, and her airs of importance she is at times, indeed, almost intolerable. But fortunately the Fates have provided a corrective. They have decreed that in her stately advances she should be accompanied by certain apish, impish creatures, who run round her tittering, pulling long noses, threatening to trip the good lady up, and even sometimes whisking to one side the corner of her drapery, and revealing her undergarments in a most indecorous manner. They are the diarists and letter-writers, the gossips and journalists of the past, the Pepyses and Horace Walpoles and Saint-Simons, whose function it is to reveal to us the littleness underlying great events and to remind us that history itself was once real life. Among them is Mr. Creevey. The Fates decided that Mr. Creevey should accompany Clio, with appropriate gestures, during that part of her progress which is measured by the thirty years preceding the accession of Victoria; and the little wretch did his job very well.

It might almost be said that Thomas Creevey was 'born about three of the clock in the afternoon, with a white head and something a round belly.' At any rate, we know nothing of his youth, save that he was educated at Cambridge, and he presents himself to us in the early years of the nineteenth century as a middle-aged man, with a character and a habit of mind already fixed and an established position in the world. In 1803 we find him what he was to be for the rest of his life—a member of Parliament, a familiar figure in high society, an insatiable gossip with a rattling tongue. That he should have reached and held the place he did is a proof of his talents, for he was a very poor man; for the greater part of his life his income was less than £200 a year. But those were the days of patrons and jobs, pocket-boroughs and sinecures; they were the days, too, of vigorous, bold living, torrential talk, and splendid hospitality; and it was only natural that Mr. Creevey, penniless and immensely entertaining, should have been put into Parliament by a Duke, and welcomed in every great Whig House in the country with open arms. It was only natural that, spending his whole political life as an advanced Whig, bent upon the destruction of abuses, he should have begun that life as a member for a pocket-borough and ended it as the holder of a sinecure. For a time his poverty was relieved by his marriage with a widow who had means of her own; but Mrs. Creevey died, her money went to her daughters by her previous husband, and Mr. Creevey reverted to a possessionless existence—without a house, without servants, without property of any sort—wandering from country mansion to country mansion, from dinner-party to dinner-party, until at last in his old age, on the triumph of the Whigs, he was rewarded with a pleasant little post which brought him in about £600 a year. Apart from these small ups and downs of fortune, Mr. Creevey's life was static—static spiritually, that is to say; for physically he was always on the move. His adventures were those of an observer, not of an actor; but he was an observer so very near the centre of things that he was by no means dispassionate; the rush of great events would whirl him round into the vortex, like a leaf in an eddy of wind; he would rave, he would gesticulate, with the fury of a complete partisan; and then, when the wind dropped, he would be found, like the leaf, very much where he was before. Luckily, too, he was not merely an agitated observer, but an observer who delighted in passing on his agitations, first with his tongue, and then—for so the Fates had decided—with his pen. He wrote easily, spicily, and persistently; he had a favourite stepdaughter, with whom he corresponded for years; and so it happens that we have preserved to us, side by side with the majestic march of Clio (who, of course, paid not the slightest attention to him), Mr. Creevey's exhilarating *pas de chat*.

Certainly he was not over-given to the praise of famous men. There are no great names in his vocabulary—only nicknames: George III. is 'Old Nobs,' the Regent 'Prinney,' Wellington 'the Beau,' Lord John Russell 'Pie and Thimble,' Brougham, with whom he was on friendly terms, is sometimes 'Bruffam,' sometimes 'Beelzebub,' and sometimes 'Old Wickedshifts'; and Lord Durham, who once remarked that one could 'jog along on £40,000 a year,' is 'King Jog.' The latter was one of the great Whig potentates, and it was characteristic of Creevey that his scurrility should have been poured out with a special gusto over his own leaders. The Tories were villains, of course—Canning was all perfidy and 'infinite meanness,' Huskisson a mass of 'intellectual confusion and mental dirt,' Castlereagh ... But all that was obvious and hardly worth mentioning; what was really too exacerbating to be borne was the folly and vileness of the Whigs. 'King Jog,' the 'Bogey,' 'Mother Cole,' and the rest of them—they were either knaves or imbeciles. Lord Grey was an exception; but then Lord Grey, besides passing the Reform Bill, presented Mr. Creevey with the Treasurership of the Ordnance, and in fact was altogether a most worthy man.

Another exception was the Duke of Wellington, whom, somehow or other, it was impossible not to admire. Creevey, throughout his life, had a trick of being 'in at the death' on every important occasion; in the House, at Brooks's, at the Pavilion, he invariably popped up at the critical moment; and so one is not surprised to find him at Brussels during Waterloo. More than that, he was the first English civilian to see the Duke after the battle, and his report of the conversation is admirable; one can almost hear the 'It has been a damned serious business. Blücher and I have lost 30,000 men. It has been a damned nice thing—the nearest run thing you ever saw in your life,' and the 'By God! I don't think it would have done if I had not been there.' On this occasion the Beau spoke, as was fitting, 'with the greatest gravity all the time, and without the least approach to anything like triumph or joy.' But at other times he was jocular, especially when 'Prinney' was the subject. 'By God! you never saw such a figure in your life as he is. Then he speaks and swears so like old Falstaff, that damn me if I was not ashamed to walk into the room with him.'

When, a few years later, the trial of Queen Caroline came on, it was inevitable that Creevey should be there. He had an excellent seat in the front row, and his descriptions of 'Mrs. P.,' as he preferred to call her Majesty, are characteristic:

> Two folding doors within a few feet of me were suddenly thrown open, and in entered her Majesty. To describe to you her appearance and manner is far beyond my powers. I had been taught to believe she was as much improved in looks as in dignity of manners; it is therefore with much pain I am obliged to observe that the nearest resemblance I can recollect to this much injured Princess is a toy which you used to call Fanny Royds (a Dutch doll). There is another toy of a rabbit or a cat, whose tail you squeeze under its body, and then out it jumps in half a minute off the ground into the air. The first of these toys you must suppose to represent the person of the Queen; the latter the manner by which she popped all at once into the House, made a *duck* at the throne, another to the Peers, and a concluding jump into the chair which was placed for her. Her dress was black figured gauze, with a good deal of trimming, lace, &c., her sleeves white, and perfectly episcopal; a handsome white veil, so thick as to make it very difficult to me, who was as near to her as anyone, to see her face; such a back for variety and inequality of ground as you never beheld; with a few straggling ringlets on her neck, which I flatter myself from their appearance were not her Majesty's own property.

Mr. Creevey, it is obvious, was not the man to be abashed by the presence of Royalty.

But such public episodes were necessarily rare, and the main stream of his life flowed rapidly, gaily, and unobtrusively through the fat pastures of high society. Everywhere and always he enjoyed himself extremely, but his spirits and his happiness were at their highest during his long summer sojourns at those splendid country houses whose hospitality he chronicles with indefatigable *verve*. 'This house,' he says at Raby, 'is itself *by far* the most magnificent and unique in several ways that I have ever seen.... As long as I have heard of anything, I have heard of being driven into the hall of this house in one's carriage, and being set down by the fire. You can have no idea of the magnificent perfection with which this is accomplished.' At Knowsley 'the new dining-room is opened; it is 53 feet by 37, and such a height that it destroys the effect of all the other apartments.... There are two fireplaces; and the day we dined there, there were 36 wax candles over the table, 14 on it, and ten great lamps on tall pedestals about the room.' At Thorp Perrow 'all the living rooms are on the ground floor, one a very handsome one about 50 feet long, with a great bow furnished with rose-coloured satin, and the whole furniture of which cost £4000.' At Goodwood the rooms were done up in 'brightest yellow satin,' and at Holkham the walls were covered with Genoa velvet, and there was gilding worth a fortune on 'the roofs of all the rooms and the doors.' The fare was as sumptuous as the furniture. Life passed amid a succession of juicy chops, gigantic sirloins, plump fowls, pheasants stuffed with pâté de foie gras, gorgeous Madeiras, ancient Ports. Wine had a double advantage: it made you drunk; it also made you sober: it was its own cure. On one occasion, when Sheridan, after days of riotous living, showed signs of exhaustion, Mr. and Mrs. Creevey pressed upon him 'five or six glasses of light French wine' with excellent effect. Then, at midnight, when the talk began to flag and the spirits grew a little weary, what could be more rejuvenating than to ring the bell for a broiled bone? And one never rang in vain—except, to be sure, at King Jog's. There, while the host was guzzling, the guests starved. This was too much for Mr. Creevey, who, finding he could get nothing for breakfast, while King Jog was 'eating his own fish as comfortably as could be,' fairly lost his temper.

> My blood beginning to boil, I said: 'Lambton, I wish you could tell me what quarter I am to apply to for some fish.' To which he replied in the most impertinent manner: 'The servant, I suppose.' I turned to Mills and said pretty loud: 'Now, if it was not for the fuss and jaw of the thing, I would leave the room and the house this instant'; and dwelt on the

damned outrage. Mills said: 'He hears every word you say': to which I said: 'I hope he does.' It was a regular scene.

A few days later, however, Mr. Creevey was consoled by finding himself in a very different establishment, where 'everything is of a piece—excellent and plentiful dinners, a fat service of plate, a fat butler, a table with a barrel of oysters and a hot pheasant, &c., wheeled into the drawing-room every night at half-past ten.'

It is difficult to remember that this was the England of the Six Acts, of Peterloo, and of the Industrial Revolution. Mr. Creevey, indeed, could hardly be expected to remember it, for he was utterly unconscious of the existence—of the possibility—of any mode of living other than his own. For him, dining-rooms 50 feet long, bottles of Madeira, broiled bones, and the brightest yellow satin were as necessary and obvious a part of the constitution of the universe as the light of the sun and the law of gravity. Only once in his life was he seriously ruffled; only once did a public question present itself to him as something alarming, something portentous, something more than a personal affair. The occasion is significant. On March 16, 1825, he writes:

> I have come to the conclusion that our Ferguson is *insane*. He quite foamed at the mouth with rage in our Railway Committee in support of this infernal nuisance—the locomotive Monster, carrying *eighty tons* of goods, and navigated by a tail of smoke and sulphur, coming thro' every man's grounds between Manchester and Liverpool.

His perturbation grew. He attended the committee assiduously, but in spite of his efforts it seemed that the railway Bill would pass. The locomotive was more than a joke. He sat every day from 12 to 4; he led the opposition with long speeches. 'This railway,' he exclaims on May 31, 'is the devil's own.' Next day, he is in triumph: he had killed the Monster.

> Well—this devil of a railway is strangled at last.... To-day we had a clear majority in committee in our favour, and the promoters of the Bill withdrew it, and took their leave of us.

With a sigh of relief he whisked off to Ascot, for the festivities of which he was delighted to note that 'Prinney' had prepared 'by having 12 oz. of blood taken from him by cupping.'

Old age hardly troubled Mr. Creevey. He grew a trifle deaf, and he discovered that it was possible to wear woollen stockings under his silk ones; but his activity, his high spirits, his popularity, only seemed to increase. At the end of a party ladies would crowd round him. 'Oh, Mr. Creevey, how agreeable you have been!' 'Oh, thank you, Mr. Creevey! how useful you have been!' 'Dear Mr. Creevey, I laughed out loud last night in bed at one of your stories.' One would like to add (rather late in the day, perhaps) one's own praises. One feels almost affectionate; a certain sincerity, a certain immediacy in his response to stimuli, are endearing qualities; one quite understands that it was natural, on the pretext of changing house, to send him a dozen of wine. Above all, one wants him to go on. Why should he stop? Why should he not continue indefinitely telling us about 'Old Salisbury' and 'Old Madagascar'? But it could not be.

> Le temps s'en va, le temps s'en va, Madame;
> Las! Le temps non, mais nous, nous en allons.

It was fitting that, after fulfilling his seventy years, he should catch a glimpse of 'little Vic' as Queen of England, laughing, eating, and showing her gums too much at the Pavilion. But that was enough: the piece was over; the curtain had gone down; and on the new stage that was preparing for very different characters, and with a very different style of decoration, there would be no place for Mr. Creevey.

1919.

INDEX

Algarotti

Anne, Queen

Arnold, Matthew

Arouet.

See

'Voltaire'

Bailey, Mr. John

Balzac

Barrès, M.

Beddoes, Dr. Thomas

Beddoes, Thos. Lovell

Beethoven

Berkeley

Bernhardt

Bernières, Madame de

Bernstorff

Berry, Miss

Beshyr, Emir

Bessborough, Lady

Bevan, Mr. C.D.

Beyle, Henri

Blake

Blücher

Boileau

Bolingbroke

Bonaparte

Boswell
Boufflers, Comtesse de
Boufflers, Marquise de
Bourget, M.
Brandes Dr.
Brink, Mr. Ten
Broome, Major
Brougham
Browne, Sir Thomas
Buffon
Burke
Butler, Bishop
Canning, George
Canning, Stratford
Caraccioli
Carlyle
Caroline Queen
Carteret
Castlereagh
Cellini
Chasot
Chateaubriand
Châtelet, Madame du
Chatham, Lady
Chatham, Lord
Chesterfield, Lord
Choiseul, Duc de
Choiseul, Duchesse de
Chuquet, M.
Cicero
Cimarosa

Claude
Coleridge
Colles, Mr. Ramsay
Collins, Anthony
Collins, Churton
Condillac
Congreve
Conti, Prince de
Corneille
Correggio
Cowley
Creevey, Mr.
D'Alembert
Dante
d'Argens
d'Argental
Darget
Daru
Davy, Sir Humphry
Deffand, Madame du
Degen
d'Egmont, Madame
Denham
Denis, Madame
d'Epinay, Madame
Descartes
Desnoiresterres
Devonshire, Duchess of
d'Houdetot, Madame
Diderot
Diogenes

Boswell

Boufflers, Comtesse de

Boufflers, Marquise de

Bourget, M.

Brandes Dr.

Brink, Mr. Ten

Broome, Major

Brougham

Browne, Sir Thomas

Buffon

Burke

Butler, Bishop

Canning, George

Canning, Stratford

Caraccioli

Carlyle

Caroline Queen

Carteret

Castlereagh

Cellini

Chasot

Chateaubriand

Châtelet, Madame du

Chatham, Lady

Chatham, Lord

Chesterfield, Lord

Choiseul, Duc de

Choiseul, Duchesse de

Chuquet, M.

Cicero

Cimarosa

Claude
Coleridge
Colles, Mr. Ramsay
Collins, Anthony
Collins, Churton
Condillac
Congreve
Conti, Prince de
Corneille
Correggio
Cowley
Creevey, Mr.
D'Alembert
Dante
d'Argens
d'Argental
Darget
Daru
Davy, Sir Humphry
Deffand, Madame du
Degen
d'Egmont, Madame
Denham
Denis, Madame
d'Epinay, Madame
Descartes
Desnoiresterres
Devonshire, Duchess of
d'Houdetot, Madame
Diderot
Diogenes

Donne
Dowden, Prof.
Dryden
Durham, Lord
Ecklin, Dr.
Edgeworth, Miss
Euler
Falkener, Everard
Fielding
Flaubert
Fleury, Cardinal
Fontenelle
Foulet, M. Lucien
Fox, Charles James
Frederick the Great
Fry, Mrs.
Furnivall, Dr.
Gautier
Gay
George III
Gibbon
Gide, M. André
Goethe
Gollancz, Sir I.
Goncourts, De
Gosse, Mr.
Gramont, Madame de
Granville, Lord
Gray
Grey, Lord
Grimm

Hardwicke, Lord
Hegetschweiler
Helvétius
Hénault
Herrick
Higginson, Edward
Hill, Dr. George Birkbeck
Hill, Mr.
Hugo, Victor
Hume
Huskisson
Ingres
Johnson, Dr.
Jordan
Jourdain, Mr.
Keats
Kelsall, Thomas Forbes
Klopstock
Koenig
La Beaumelle
Lamb, Charles
Lambton
La Mettrie
Lanson, M.
Latimer
Lecouvreur, Adrienne
Lee, Sir Sidney
Leibnitz
Lemaître, M.
Lemaur
Lespinasse, Mlle. de

Leveson Gower, Lord Granville
Locke
Louis Philippe
Louis XIV.
Lulli
Luxembourg, Maréchale de
Macaulay
Macdonald, Mrs. Frederika
Maine, Duchesse du
Malherbe
Marlborough, Duke of
Marlborough, Duchess of
Marlowe
Massillon
Matignon, Marquis de
Maupertuis
Mehemet Ali
Mérimée, Prosper
Meryon, Dr.
Middleton
Milton
Mirepoix, Bishop of
Mirepoix, Maréchale de
Molière
Moncrif
Montagu, Lady Mary Wortley
Montespan, Madame de
Montesquieu
Moore, Sir John
Morley, Lord
Moses

Mozart
Musset
Napoleon
Necker
Nelson
Newton, Sir Isaac
Pascal
Pater
Peterborough, Lord
Pitt, William, the younger
Plato
Pöllnitz
Pompadour, Madame de
PontdeVeyle
Pope
Prie, Madame de
Prior
Proctor, Bryan Waller
Puffendorf
Quinault
Racine
Raleigh, Sir Walter
Regent, the Prince
Reni, Guido
Reynolds, Sir Joshua
Richardson
Richelieu
RohanChabot, Chevalier de
Rossetti
Rousseau
Rubens

Russell, Lord John
SainteBeuve
SaintLambert
SaintSimon
Sampson, Mr. John
Sanadon, Mlle.
Shaftesbury
Shakespeare
Shelley
Sheridan
Sophocles
Spenser
Stanhope, Lady Hester
'Stendhal.'
Beyle, Henri
Stephen, Sir James
Sully, Duc de
Swift
Swinburne
Taine
Thévenart
Thomson
Tindal
Toland
Tolstoi
Toynbee, Mrs. Paget
Turgot
Velasquez
Vigny
Virgil
Voltaire

Walpole, Horace
Webster
Wellington, Duke of
White, W.A.
Winckelmann
Wolf
Wollaston
Woolston
Wordsworth
Würtemberg, Duke of
Yonge, Miss
Young, Dr.
Zola